EUROPEAN TRADE UNION IN FIGURES

European Trade Unions in Figures

by

Jelle Visser

KLUWER LAW AND TAXATION PUBLISHERS
Deventer - Boston

Kluwer Law and Taxations Publishers
P.O. Box 23
7400 GA Deventer
The Netherlands

Tel.: 31-5700-47261
Telex: 49295
Fax: 31-5700-22244

Library of Congress Cataloging in Publications Data
Visser, Jelle.
  European trade unions in figures / by Jelle Visser.
    p.   cm.
  Bibliography: p.
  ISBN 9065444092
  1. Trade-unions--Europe--Statistics. I. Title.
HD6657.V57 1989
331.88'094'021--dc19

89-2249
CIP

Cover design: Rinde

ISBN 90 6544 409 2

ACKNOWLEDGEMENTS

The research for this book was conducted at several places. The main and most important part was completed between 1982 and 1984 at the European University Institute, in Florence (Italy), where I started to collect data on trade unions in the margin of a comparative project on employers' associations. I am most grateful to the directors of that project, Philippe Schmitter and Wolfgang Streeck, to have encouraged me all along.

Another context for comparative research was offered at the Institut für Sozialwissenschaften of the University of Mannheim, where I stayed little less than a year between 1986-1987 while working on another international research enterprise: the DUES-project on 'The Development of Trade Unions in European Societies After 1945'. I would like to express thanks to my colleagues in Mannheim, Peter Flora for his many lessons about the hardship and pitfalls of cross-national empirical research, Margaret Herden for her help with my English, Klaus Armingeon, Franz Kraus and Winfried Pfenning for their support with sources and data. In particular, I am indebted to Bernard Ebbinghaus for his critical and supporting intellectual company.

Most of the finalization of the research, as well as the actual writing, was done at the Sociological Institute of the University of Amsterdam. Ad Teulings encouraged me to complete this lengthy and rather solitary research project.

I dedicate this book to Monika Fermé who is such a good friend, and ensured that despite all travels there was always a home in Amsterdam.

1

TABLE OF CONTENTS

INTRODUCTION

The main purpose of *European Trade Unions in Figures* is to present a comparative set of data and sources on union membership in ten European countries. The study covers the development in unionization during the largest part of the Twentieth Century, from the First World War until the mid-1980s. The countries included are Austria, Denmark, France, (West-) Germany, Italy, the Netherlands, Norway, Sweden, Switzerland, and the United Kingdom.

The lack of data - data that is truly comparative across time and between nations - on trade union organization and membership at various levels of aggregation is a major obstacle for systematic research. If one wishes to study union growth and development, the impact of employment shifts and business cycles, the importance of union organization and membership composition for policies they conduct or support[1], two major lacunae in empirical data become apparent. First, comparative and preferably continuous time-series data on the development of union membership and organization over a long range of years are lacking in most countries. Second, almost no data exist which allow us to compare unions and unionization in particular industries or occupations. This monograph is an attempt to provide some comparative data in both directions. It is best seen as a follow-up of the invaluable study of George Sayers Bain and Robert Price, *Profiles of Union Growth. A Comparative Statistical Portrait of Eight Countries* (Bain & Price, 1980), which is the major comparative data-book and has set landmarks in the field. However, *Profiles* covers only five European countries - Great Britain, Germany, Denmark, Sweden and Norway -, takes only developments until the mid-1970s into account, and in all countries except Britain its emphasis is on aggregate annual statistics.

1. Comparability

Emphasis has been given to comparable definitions of union membership and unions density, i.e. the ratio of actual to potential membership. As much as is possible in a cross-national study, I have applied the same definitions of (1) what constitutes a trade union, (2) who is counted as a trade union member, and (3) who are part of the dependent labour force or the potential recruitment area of trade unions. In all three areas I have followed, as closely as possible, the definitions used in *Profiles* (Bain & Price, 1980, in particular pp.1-12).

As to (1) the most serious problem relates to the status of

---

[1] These are the major themes of my *In Search of Inclusive Unionism* which is the twin monograph to this one, and will be published as special issue of the <u>Bulletin of Comparative Industrial Relations</u> (General Editor: Roger Blanpain), no. 18, Deventer (Kluwer) 1989

professional associations (of teachers, artists, doctors, architects, etc.) and of the 'unions' of managerial staffs which have emerged in recent years (ETUI, 1982; Bamber, 1985). If such associations *de facto* perform a bargaining function *vis à vis* employers, governments or state agencies, on behalf of their members-employees and independent of their interlocutors, I have included them under the definition of trade unions. As most definitions, this does leave us with ambiguous cases. It also follows that in making historical comparisons we must be aware that trade unionism - and henceforth trade union membership - has become more inclusive over the years. Many of the professional associations which have assumed a trade union function in recent years have been founded long ago. Again the transition from professional association to trade union will not always be clear-cut. I should also mention, that there are differences across nations as to how professional or managerial associations are treated in national statistical yearbooks, registrars and the like. In Britain, France, the Scandinavian countries and also in the Netherlands and West-Germany they are counted as unions and included in the statistics if their membership is at all known. In the Austria, Switzerland, and Italy definitions and statistics appear to be rather more restrictive.

With regard to (2) the most problematic area is that of the 'labour market status' of the membership in trade unions. Most trade unions in Europe include to a various degree the membership of pensioners or retired workers, students, conscripts, in some cases also self-employed people or tenant farmers. Together these groups may make up 20-30 percent of the total membership in some of the major confederations in Europe, but actual practices differ a great deal between union organizations. The inclusion of these members, who have no equivalent status as wage or salary earners, may cause a considerable overstatement of union density rates. It readily distorts the comparison of unionization levels between years and, especially, across nations. In addition to the 'raw' data as reported by the trade unions or statistical bureaux, I have therefore compiled a series for the 'active' union membership - corresponding with the dependent labour force or the total number of employed and unemployed wage and salary earners. Union members out of employment have of course been counted as 'active' in this sense. However, not in all countries was it possible to identify the self-employed and retired workers in the reported membership (see *infra* the chapters on Austria, Denmark, Norway and Britain).

Other differences in the 'member count' relate to the differences between 'reported' and 'paying' members, different administrative treatment of members who are in arrear with the payment of dues, and indeed different requirements on members. Using administrative rater than survey data, we must be aware that the structure and quality of the data 'mirror the internal characteristics of organizations collecting them' (Jacobs, 1984: 41). Union membership statistics are not kept or collected for the purpose of scientific analysis, but as part of administrating the collection of dues or the distribution of benefits, seats, influence, funds, rights, entitlements, etc. In administrative data there may be a bias towards overstating the organization's membership. Actually, in a number of studies it is found that reported membership exceeds paying membership by some 10-15% (see: Bain & Price, 1980; Streeck, 1981). I have nevertheless followed these authors in using membership rather than financial data, unless there was clear evidence of exaggeration or desinformation. The use of financial data would restrict the possibilities of disaggregation to a very considerable extent. The only case where I have used financial data in order to check, and correct, membership claims is France.

Of course, these standardizations do not guarantee that trade union membership has the same meaning across countries. It probably does not - the degree of 'compulsion' in union membership differs with the existence of 'closed shops', 'works' councils' 'check-off agreements', union-related unemployment or pension funds, and so on. All these institutions enter the equation of what makes workers join or not join a trade union. Institutional differences tell us a great deal about the differences in the opportunities and rewards of union membership, between, say, France on the one hand and Britain or Sweden on the other. But it does not invalidate the cross-national comparison of union membership statistics as has been argued by Mouriaux (1983: 70). Measuring the absolute and relative membership in trade unions - its level and development - still is a short-hand way of comparing the degree of representation and power of unions across industries and nations. Next, we might add to such comparisons the differences in dues and benefits, in participation in elections or strikes, and in member involvement in the union (Regaglia, 1987)

As to (3) the main problems arise from the different treatment in labour force statistics, between years and countries, of the part-time labour force, the unemployed (first-job seekers, part-time unemployed), and the armed forces. In using data from the national Bureaus of Statistics, I have tried to apply as much as possible the same (OECD and ILO) standards and definitions (see: ILO, *Yearbook of Labour Statistics*, Geneva, annual; OECD, *Labour Force Statistics*, Paris, annual). I should like to add that I have greatly benefitted from, an made extensive use of, the handbooks, compiled by Peter Flora and his collaborators, *State, Economy, and Society in Western Europe 1815-1975* (Vol.1: Flora, 1983; Vol.2: Flora, Kraus & Pfenning 1987). In particular their reclassification of census data relating to the labour force (Vol.2, Chapter 7.: 443-609) was indispensable for my enterprise.

2. Outline

In presenting data and sources I have followed a standardized outline which is followed through with few variations in each of the ten country chapters. Each chapter begins with a summary description of the major union confederations, their date of birth and, if it applies, data on merger patterns. This is followed by a description of the state of the statistics on trade unions and their members, and the principle data sources or files. Separate entries deal with retired workers, pensioners and self-employed members, female members, membership by industry and occupational status, and public sector unionism. Finally, the principal sources of labour force statistics are listed, and the main issues in compiling comparative and continuous labour force series briefly discussed.

The second part of each chapter contains three groups of standardized tables. The tables in the first group present annual data - from 1913 to 1985 - on union membership and union density. Table 1 presents the aggregate membership by confederation, table 2 the membership shares of each confederation expressed as a percentage of the aggregate membership. In table 3 information is presented on the number and share of retired and self-employed members in the reported 'raw' membership of confederations. Table 4 presents continuous time-series data and indicators on unionization: the total membership in trade unions (with and without pensioners and self-employed members), the total number of wage & salary earners (with and without the unemployed), and three density rates: (a) 'gross density' (calculated over the 'raw membership'), (b) 'net density' (exclusive self-employed and retired members), and (c) union density calculated for the employed only (excluding unemployed workers).

The next group of tables presents disaggregated data for selected years. As a rule, a table (5/1-8) is presented for each first year of a decade: 1920, 1930, 1940, 1950, 1960, 1970, 1980, and in addition 1985 - or the nearest census year. Within each table the following information is presented for each major union confederation:

a. membership by gender
b. membership by private or public employment
c. membership by status
d. membership by status, and private or public employment
e. membership by industry
f. membership by industry, and private or public employment
g. membership by industry, and status
h. membership by industry, status, and private or public employment

As a rule, the membership figures presented exclude pensioners and self-employed workers, although distortions are caused in the case of Austria and Norway, and to a minor degree also in Denmark and Great Britain.

The corresponding labour force statistics, for each census year and 1985, are presented in a final set of tables (6/1-7).

3.   Classifications and distinctions

The four major distinctions in this study of union membership relate to gender, industry, occupational status, and employment in the public sector.
In most countries and for most years it has been possible to disaggregate union membership accordingly, although in most cases only the marginal distributions can be produced.

With regard to industry, I have used the 1958 International Standard Industrial Classification of all economic activities (ISIC-1958) in stead of newer (1968, 1980) classifications. This did best allow comparability over time, and was also the classification used by Flora, Kraus & Pfenning (1987) while re-arranging census data over a range of hundred years.[2] The major differences compared with later

---

[2] See for details the introduction to Chapter 7 in their book, Flora, Kraus & Pfenning 1987, pp.446-447. Further details on the important 1968 revision of the ISIC can be found in a United Nations publications: U.N., Statistical Papers, Series M., no.4, revision 2, New York 1968

regard a) repair activities (in the relevant industries - ISIC 3 - in stead of 'commerce and retail trade' -ISIC 6), b) hotel, restaurants and catering services (in 'community, social and personal services' or 'other or miscellaneous services' - ISIC 9 - in stead of 'commerce and retail trade' - ISIC 6), and real estate and business services in 'other or miscellaneous services' (ISIC 9) in stead of 'finance and insurance' (ISIC 8).

As a rule, I have made a division in six industrial sectors. I have taken together industry and mining, and also between commerce and finance. In some countries further precision in disaggregating membership figures would have been possible, but at the cost of reliability. Already, the breakdowns presented do involve estimations. So, the industrial classification used in this handbook is as follows:

ISIC 1   : Agriculture, Hunting, Forestry and Fishing
ISIC 2-4 : Mining an Quarrying, Manufacturing, Electricity, Gas
            and Water
ISIC 5   : Construction
ISIC 6+8 : Wholesale and Retail Trade, Banking and Insurance
ISIC 7   : Transport, Storage and Communication
ISIC 9   : Other Services: Community, Social and Personal
            Services, Restaurants and Hotels, Real Estate and
            Business Services
ISIC 0   : Unknown, and activities not adequately defined

Although a different classification might have been desirable from the point of view of economic or sociological theory, especially for a better understanding of the structure and dynamics of the service sector (see: Siegelman, 1978; also Scharpf, 1986), in comparing countries over almost a century I had little choice but to adhere to existing classifications.

With regard to occupational status, a distinction is made between blue- and white-collar workers, or between manual and non-manual occupations. I have followed Bain who in *The Growth of White-Collar Unions*, categorized the following groups under non-manual occupations: 'foremen, overlookers, and supervisors; scientists, technologists, and technicians; clerical and administrative workers; security personnel; professionals; salesmen, commercial travellers, and shop assistants; government administrators and executive officials; and special "creative" occupations such as artists, musicians, and entertainers' (Bain, 1970: 4). In terms of the International Standard Classification of Occupations (ISCO) of the United Nations[3], our non-manual category includes the following major groups: professional, technical, and related workers (ISCO 0/1); administrative and managerial workers (ISCO 2); clerical and related workers (ISCO 3); sales workers (ISCO 4, except ISCO 4-1 or working proprietors); service managers and supervisors (ISCO 5-0 and 5-2); agricultural managers and supervisors (ISCO 6-0); and production supervisors and general foremen (ISCO 7-0).

---

[3] For full details see International labour Organization (ILO), *International Standard Classification of Occupations*, revised edition 1968, Geneva 1969

distinction manual versus non-manual is bound to be unsatisfactorily (see: Goldthorpe, 1980, 1986). Unfortunately no further distinction, within each of the two groups, could be made on the basis of administrative data. It is in this area that survey research would be essential - variables such as skill, education and age (except, perhaps, the very young or old) are rarely present in union membership files. The broad distinction manual/non-manual remains relevant - it is still reflected in many practices governing collective bargaining (ILO, 1978), in legal rules (Blanpain 1978-), in insurance and pension funds (Ebbinghaus, 1988), and in the organization of interests (Visser, 1989). Of course, how it is recognized and where the 'collarline' (Kocka, 1980) is exactly drawn, differs between countries.

Finally, I have tried to differentiate between trade unionism, and union membership, in the private and in the public sector. This distinction has become more important in recent decades, as industrial relation practices often vary a great deal (Cordóva, 1985; Keller, 1983). In this study the public sector includes public transport (railways, ferries, tram and bus), the Post Office, public administration (including social insurance, police and professional military), education, health, welfare and related community services, in some countries also public utilities (gas, water and electricity production or distribution), sheltered workshops and public gardening. Not included in the public sector are nationalized industries (mining, steel) or firms, as this would complicate cross-national and intertemporal comparisons very much given the large differences across countries and the fact that industries and firms have sometimes been shifted back and forth between the market and government sector. Of course, the same problems will appear in the future in the case of the Post Office and public transport after the privatization which is now taking place in a number of countries.

4. Range of Years and Choice of Countries

A few observations need to be made about the range of years and the choice of countries in this study. The decision to commence the time-series in the year before the outbreak of the First World War is of course to some extent arbitrary. The major rationales were my interest in a comparison of 'war effects' on membership growth (see: Dunlop, 1949), and the comparative study of 'business cycle' effects in the 1920s and 1930s as well as in our days (see: Davis, 1941; Bain & Esheikh, 1976; Fiorito & Greer, 1982). Going back to the years before 1913 would be possible in some countries (see: Bain & Price, 1980), but in most countries the difficulties of collecting reliable data on unions and membership increase to a very considerable degree. 1985 is the last year; often there is a considerable delay in the publication or availability of union statistics, or later revisions are made, and the data-base was completed in the Summer of 1987. Starting in 1913 and ending in 1985 yields 73 observations which should permit the use of sophisticated techniques of econometric analysis. Of course, in a number of countries (Italy, Germany, Austria) we have major interruptions or gaps due to the repression of the democratic labour movement, while in France, the Netherlands and Norway the series is discontinued during the war-time occupation.

I have limited this study to one region of the World. The focus on

Western Europe, rather than all advanced industrial nations, offers the possibility of relating this particular piece of historical-empirical research in the area of trade unions and industrial relations to the development of theories on the causes, development stages and structure of historical socio-political and cultural cleavages among European populations (Rokkan & Lipset, 1967; Rokkan, 1970; Flora, 1981). An additional reason is that outside Europe a number of quantitative studies and data handbooks exist. Such is the case for unionism in Australia (Sutcliffe, 1967; Rawson, 1977), Canada (Eaton & Ashagrie, 1967; Eaton, 1976), Japan (JIL, 1983) or the United States (Wolman, 1936; Troy, 1965; Troy & Sheflin, 1983). All these countries, except Japan, are included in Bain & Price (1980).

A comparison of trade unions in countries that are otherwise highly similar in economic, political and cultural development has important advantages. 'The gross differences between economically developed and underdeveloped nations or between democratic and authoritarian nations are so pervasive that it is relatively simple to show how differences in the character of national substructures (such as national labor movements) are intimately linked to these gross differences. Yet focussing on these large differences may unwittingly inhibit more detailed specifications of explanatory variables. Such detailed specifications are more feasible when one examens the differences in the character of substructures among nations which are relatively similar in important characteristics' (Lipset, 1961: 76).
For the same reason I have not sought to include Greece, Spain and Portugal in my study. The many long years of suppression of democracy and independent union organization makes a comparison with the other countries in my sample extremely difficult. Unfortunately, comparative data on union organization in the last ten years, after the return to democracy, is very difficult to come by. A widening of our comparison, within Western Europe, to these new democracies would of course be most desirable. At present, I only can refer the reader to the useful overviews and studies of Fakiolas (1978) and Katsanevas (1984) on trade unions in Greece, of Estivill (1984), Ludevid (1987) and Estivill and Hoz (1989) on Spanish, and of Pinto (1989) on Portuguese unionism.

The reasons why I did not include Finland, Ireland and Belgium are of a different order. In these three countries it proved very difficult to find, and ascertain, a comparable set of data. Limits to travel money and, in the Finish case, language difficulties added to the obstacles. In the meantime, some very valuable statistics on Irish unions and union membership in the Irish Repubic since the 1940s have been collected by Bill Roche and Joe Larragy (Roche & Larragy, 1987). With respect to Belgium it still is difficult to find reliable and comparable data on trade unions, but in addition to the older study of Spitaels (1967), information on union membership and density in recent years has been collected by Armand Spineux (1981; 1984), and Albert Martin (1985).

5.   Data-collection

The sources used for compiling these statistics are national, such as published by national statistical offices, confederations, trade union research centra, in statistical yearbooks, monographs, trade union yearbooks, journals and surveys. In all countries I have paid several visits to the national Bureaux of Statistics, union headquarters and libraries, and research institutes. In one case - the United Kingdom - I have entirely relied upon data published by Bain & Price (1980: 13-78), except for some additional data on the TUC, a somewhat different aggregation of data, and information on recent years. Another exception is France, where I have encountered the usual difficulties in ascertaining the membership claims of unions or otherwise reported membership figures. It is the only country where I had to work with only secondary sources. Elsewhere access to union membership files, mainly through confederations and statistical bureaux, has been possible. The collection of reliable membership statistics in Denmark, Norway, Sweden, in Austria, Switzerland and West-Germany, in the Netherlands and Italy is a task which is most often tedious, but not impossible to accomplish. In most cases I have had much support and help from confederal officials and librarians, and from students and researchers in each country. Most difficult and time-consuming has been the compilation of reliable statistics on the membership in unions which are not affiliated with the main confederations, on retired and self-employed workers within the reported membership, and the disaggregation, by industry and status, of the membership in the larger general unions. Both craft or occupation unions and industrial unions present in this respect difficulties of their own. Especially in the latter case, I have had to make use of more or less informed estimates. In order to direct the readers attention to the less than exact nature of the resulting figures, I have rounded off these figures to the nearest thousand.[4]

After some years of collecting and scrutinizing data on trade unions, I clearly understand what Bain & Price meant when they wrote that collecting more data 'would merely contribute to description at the expense of explanation' (Bain & Price, 1980: 10). Where one stops depends on which theories one wants to address, and on how much one underestimates the time and effort it costs to add a further country, year, or distinction. I believe that the present data does allow us to address, and test, a number of theories on trade union development, membership growth, organizational politics - as I have tried to show in *In Search of Inclusive Unionism*. I hope that the data and sources in this handbook will find other users as well.

---

[4] In the tables all absolute figures (membership, labour force) are expressed in thousands (000's) with the nearest hundred expressed after the final comma (000,0).

12

Chapter 1: AUSTRIA

LIST OF UNION CONFEDERATIONS: name, abbreviation and foundation year

1 *Bund Freier Gewerkschaften* (BFG), 1894-1934
   Free Trade Union Confederation

2 *Zentralkommission der Christlichen Gewerkschaften* (ZKCG),
   1900-1934, Central Organization of Christian Trade Unions

3 *Völkisch Deutsche Gewerkschaften* (NATION), 1923
   Nationalist Federation of Trade Unions; the continuation of
   Reichsverband deutscher Arbeitnehmervereinigungen, ...

4 *Österreichische Gewerkschaftsbund* (ÖGB), 1945-
   Austrian Confederation of Trade Unions

1.   AGGREGATE MEMBERSHIP STATISTICS

1.1   General Series

Austrian trade union history can be divided in two periods. The first
ends in 1934 when a clerical-authoritarian regime was installed and
independent trade unions were placed outside the law. The second period
begins with the defeat of the nazi-regime and the end of World War Two.
Between 1938 and 1945 Austria was part of the German Reich.
     Three main currents existed in the Austrian trade union movement
before 1934, sharply divided between them by religious, political and
ideological cleavages in a Free or Socialist, a Christian and a
(German) Nationalist camp. The membership of the unions belonging to
the three peak associations - the socialist *Bund Freier Gewerkschaften*,
the catholic *Zentralkommission der Christlichen Gewerkschaften*, and the
(German) nationalist *Völkisch Deutsche Gewerkschaften* - was published,
with certain intervals, by the Austrian Bureau of Statistics. I have
relied upon the series which was published in the Statistische Nachrichten, vol.10, 1932: 170. The latest year for which membership was
reported is 1931. The 1932 data are taken from the 1933 and 1934 Annual
Reports of the *International Federation of Trade Unions* (IFTU).
     Membership figures of unions which had not affiliated with one of
the three aforementioned peak associations are reported, for some of
the years, in Gülick (1948: 343-) and Traxler (1982: 153,table 19).
Such 'independent' or non-affiliated unions include both Communist, and
Conservative, 'employer-friendly' or 'yellow' unions. It appears that
the combined membership of these independent unions declined from about
150,000 members in the early 1920s to about half that number in 1931.

13

As the status of these unions is not clear and no annual time series can be constructed, I have decided not to include the (estimated) membership of these unions in the overall series on Austrian union membership before 1934.

After 1945 the Austrian trade union movement was united in one organization, the *Österreichische Gewerkschaftsbund* (ÖGB). ÖGB-membership equals total membership. Independent unions, outside the ÖGB, do not exist or are not recognized as trade unions. As a matter of fact, union membership in Austria may be defined along a more narrow line than, for instance, in Sweden or Britain, excluding professional associations. The postwar membership series is based on the Annual Reports of the ÖGB (ÖGB, Tätigkeitsbericht, Vienna, annual). Both the pre- and postwar membership figures refer to 31 December of each year.

1.2 Retired Members

Unfortunately the ÖGB does not report separate figures for pensioners or retired members. From the figures presented by Traxler (1982: 250), who calculates union density rates in railways and the Post Office of 120-170%, it would appear that (some) ÖGB unions do include a considerable number of retired members. On the basis of the membership figures for 1966 of the *Gewerkschaft der Privatangestellten* (GPA), the union of salaried employees which became Austria's largest single union, it can be calculated that 13.5% did not belong to the labour force (Lakerbacher 1967: 411, table A). From a comparison of sectoral and occupational membership on the one hand and labour force data on the other, it follows that there must be a large proportion of retired members hidden in the reported membership of the ÖGB. Particularly large is the disparity in the public sector, and in some manual worker unions in industry. It is also quite likely that the proportion of retired workers has increased following the widening of pre-retirement schemes in recent years. My cautious estimate is that 10-15% of the ÖGB's membership has retired from the active labour force. Although it is impossible to readjust the annual membership or union density series for Austria, it is safe to say to that the density figures for Austria suffer from a conspicuous overstatement (5-10 points) comparative to other countries.

1.3 Female Membership

Before 1934 male and female membership can be distinguished for the socialist *Bund Freier Gewerkschaften (BFG) only*. The source is the BFG Gewerkschaftsbericht (Annual Report), Vienna. The ÖGB Tätigkeitsberichte (Annual Reports) also report annual membership by gender.

2.   MEMBERSHIP BY INDUSTRY AND STATUS

The table for the socialist unions, presented on the next page, has been pieced together from the Statistische Nachrichten of the Austrian Bureau of Statistics, the BFG Annual Reports, and the additional data presented by Botz, 1981. All these sources present disagggregated data

Members in Free Unions (BFG) by industry and status, 1919-1932								
	1919	1921	1923	1928	1929	1930	1931	1932
Workers	*537*	*756*	*611*	*499*	*482*	*421*	*371*	*332*
agriculture	32	71	59	34	33	32	30	.
industry	411	554	461	387	374	321	280	.
private services	91	127	78	74	70	64	56	.
domestic servants	3	4	3	5	5	4	4	.
Employees	*236*	*324*	*286*	*267*	*256*	*235*	*212*	*188*
private sector	115	138	132	97	93	87	82	75
railways	82	107	92	89	87	77	63	55
post office	26	30	24	28	25	23	22	17
public sector	13	49	38	54	50	48	46	42

Source: 1919-1931: Statistische Nachrichten, Austrian Bureau of Statistics, Vienna (1923: 102; 1928: 73-74; 1930: 144; 1932: 163); and BFG, Gewerkschaftsbericht BFG, Vienna, several years; 1932: Botz (1981: 219, table 3).

Members in Christian Unions (ZKCG) by industry and status 1919-1931					
	1921	1923	1928	1929	1931
Workers	*47*	*46*	*48*	*46*	*46*
agriculture	6	.	.	11	.
industry	23	.	.	.	.
private services	11	.	.	.	.
domestic servants	6	.	12	.	.
Employees	*32*	*33*	*52*	*61*	*62*
private services	6	6	7	7	8
rail & post	14	13	16	17	18
public services	13	14	30	37	37

Members in Nation. Unions (NATION) by industry and status 1919-1932					
	1921	1923	1928	1929	1931
Workers	*1*	*1*	*4*	*4*	*4*
Employees	*40*	*44*	*48*	*46*	*47*
private services	11	11	13	12	12
rail & post	26	29	30	29	30
public services	3	4	5	5	5

Source: Statistische Nachrichten, Austrian Bureau of Statistics, Vienna, 1924: 183; Palla 1931: 1198; Botz 1981: 218, table 2. According to Botz (ibid.) the independent white-collar unions organized 2,900 members in 1923 and about 10,000 in 1931. The autonomous civil servant organizations, the Beamtenverbände, claimed 90,000 members in 1923 and 55,000 in 1931.

for some years. What becomes clear from this data, is that during the 1920s and early 1930s there was a steady decline in union membership among manual workers, whereas white-collar and public sector unions maintained membership support until at least the early 1930s.

From the same sources we learn that the German nationalist unions organized mainly white-collar employees, and that manual workers were soon outnumbered in the Christian unions.

2.1 Classification by Industry

2.1.1 Classification by Industry before 1934

1 Agriculture: *Landarbeiter; Gärtner*

2-5 Mining, industry & construction: *Bauarbeiter; Bergarbeiter; Buch-drucker; Buchbinder; Buchdruckereihilfsarbeiter; Chemische Arbeiter; Glasarbeiter; Holzarbeiter; Hutarbeiter; Juweliere; Kartonnagarbeiter; Kurschner; Lebensmittelarbeiter; Lederarbeiter; Ledergalanteriearbeiter; Lithographen; Photographen; Maschinisten; Metallarbeiter; Sattler; Schneider; Schuhmacher; Textilarbeiter; Industrieangestellten; Faktorenverband; Technische Union*

6+8 Commerce, Banking & Insurances: *Bankbeamte; Bankgehilfen; Buchhan-delsangestellten; Bürogehilfen; Guterbeamte; Handelsagenten; Kauf-männische Angestellten; Versicherungsangestellten*

7 Transport and Communication: *Handels- und Transportarbeiter* (later to become the *Freier Gewerkschaftsverband)*, its members are partly in commerce; *Eisenbahner; Postangestellten*

9 Other Services: *Blumenarbeiter; Buhnenpersonale; Friseurgehilfen; Hausgehilfinnen; Heimarbeiter; Hotel und Kaffeehaus angestellten; Portiere und Hausbesorger; Kanalraümer Wien; Rauchfangkehrer; Advokatursangestellten; Artisten; Bühnenverein; Musiker; Sozial-versicherungsangestellten; Zahntechnische Angestellten; Zeitungs-beamte; Gemeindebedienstete Graz; Krankenpflegepersonal; Militär-verband; Öffentliche Angestellten; Stadtschützwache Wien*

It should be observed that the (legal) distinction between *Arbeiter and Angestellte/Beamte* made by the Austrian Bureau of Statistics and the Austrian trade unions is not congruent with the common division between manual/non-manual labour. Particularly in the public sector, manual workers are included in the category of *Beamte*, for example railway workers or municipal workers. Hence, compared with the Anlosaxon or Scandinavian countries, the total number of manual workers is underestimated in Austria. However, the distinction reflects real status distinctions in Austria (as it does in Germany): it refers to special legal rights involving job tenure, pensions etc. bestowed upon *Angestellte* or *Beamte* (Kocka, 1980; Ebbinghaus, 1986). Similar status distinctions are made with respect to the labour force and it would be quite hard to calculate union densities for manual or non-manual employees in the Anglosaxon definition.

On the basis of the öGB Tätigkeitsberichte it has been possible to disaggregate union membership by industry and status in a similar way

as was done for the period before 1933. As I have not been able, with
the exception of 1966 (Lakenbacher, 1967), to find data on the membership composition of the large catch-all union of salaried employees in
the private sector - the *Gewerkschaft der Privatangestellten* (GPA) - ,
I had to make some rather heroic assumptions about the sectoral distribution of this union's membership (50% in industry and 50% in commerce,
banking and insurances).

2.1.2 Classification by Industry after 1945

1 Agriculture & Forestry: *Gewerkschaft in der Land und Forst
wirstchaft*

2-5 Mining, Industry, Gas, Water & Electricity, and Construction:
*Gewerkschaft der Bau- und Holzarbeiter; Gewerkschaft der Chemie-
arbeiter; Gewerkschaft Druck und Papier; Gewerkschaft der Lebens-
und Genussmittelarbeiter; Gewerkschaft Metall-Bergbau-Energie;
Gewerkschaft Textil, Bekleidung und Leder*

6+8 Commerce, Banking & Insurances: *Gewerkschaft der Privatangestellten* (50% in industry)

7 Transport & Communications: *Gewerkschaft Handel, Transport und
Verkehr* (25% in commerce); *Gewerkschaft der Eisenbahner; Gewerkschaft der Post- und Fernmeldebediensteten*

9 Other Services: *Gewerkschaft der gastgewerblicher Arbeitnehmer;
Gewerkschaft der persönlicher Dienst*; in 1978 merged into *Gewerk-
schaft Hotel, Gastgewerbe und Persönlicher Dienst; Gewerkschaft
Kunst, Medien und Freie Berufe; Gewerkschaft der Öffentliche
Dienst; Gewerkschaft der Gemeindebediensteten*

2.2 Classification by Status

White-collar employees in the private economy are organized in the
Gewerkschaft der Privatangestellten and in the small *Gewerkschaft
Medien, Kunst und Freie Berufe*. Civil servants constitute a part of the
membership of the four public sector unions: the two unions in railways
and in the Post Office, and the two unions in central and local government.

2.3 Public Sector Unionism

The four public sector unions - the *Gewerkschaft der Öffentliche
Dienst, Gewerkschaft der Gemeindebediensteten, Gewerkschaft der Eisenbahner*, and *Gewerkschaft der Post- und Fernmeldebediensteten* - recruit
members in central and local government, including educational, health
and welfare services, police and social insurances, public transport
and communication services. Not included are: nationalized industries,
banking and public utilities (energy production and distribution).

3. LABOUR FORCE STATISTICS

The pre-war series of employees in employment is taken from the Statistische Nachrichten (1923-). The number of unemployed is added on the basis of the figures reported by Stiefel (1979: 29). The post-war labour force data haven been taken from the Statistische Handbuch für die Republik Österreich (Austrian Statistical Yearbook), published annually by the Austrian Bureau of Statistics in Vienna. Before the introduction of bi-annual labour force sample survey, in 1968, the labour force statistics are derived from social insurance registration data. Given the very extensive coverage of social insurance in Austria (ILO, 1978), the change in method is of little consequence. With respect to the unemployed, I have used the figures of Rothschild (1977: 81), who adjusts for the changes in registration and method which took place in 1962 and 1973.

The breakdown of the labour force statistics, by occupational status and industrial sector, has been made on the basis of the 1934, 1951, 1961 and 1971 censuses, as reported in Flora, Kraus & Pfenning (1987: 456-8). The 1980- and 1985-figures are calculated from the July 1980 and July 1985 Micro-census (see: Statistische Handbuch für die Republik Österreich 1980: 318; 1985: 125).

Employment in the public sector in 1951 and 1971 has been calculated from the data published by the Austrian Institute for Economic Research in Vienna (WIFO, Monatsberichte, 1976: 64-75) as well as from the census data for these years. The figures given include central and local government, gas, water and electricity, Post Office and railways, health, social security and education, and includes a wider group than only civil servants and related employees. Hence, the figures given are higher than would be the case had I used the man-year data which the Bureau of Statistics publishes at 1 October of each year ('Ist-stände der Beamten und Bundesbedienstete'). Employment in the public sector in 1985 has been estimated on the basis of the latter source and the micro-census figures.

Apprentices and unemployed persons are included in the census data. The micro-censuses do refer to the employees in employment only. Unfortunately, it was impossible to classify the unemployed by industry and status in 1980 and 1985. In order to restore comparability, I have deemed all unemployed in the manual category.

4. TABLES

table: AU 1/1		Membership by Confederations						AUSTRIA
year	BFG (1)		ZKCG (2)		NATION (3)		other	total
	abs	%	abs	%	abs	%	abs	abs
1913	.		.		.		.	.
1914	240,7		22,7		.		.	263,4
1915	177,1	92.8	13,7	7.2	.		.	190,8
1916	166,9		13,8		.		.	180,7
1917	311,1		18,6		.		.	329,7
1918	412,9		20,6		.		.	433,5
1919	712,1		30,7		35,1		.	777,9
1920	900,8	89.7	64,5	6.4	38,6	3.8	.	1,003,9
1921	1,079,8		78,7		40,2		.	1,198,7
1922	1,049,9		78,1		43,1		.	1,171,1
1923	896,8		79,4		45,4		.	1,021,6
1924	828,1		80,1		46,9		.	955,1
1925	807,5	86.7	77,2	8.3	47,0	5.0	.	931,7
1926	756,4		76,1		50,9		.	883,4
1927	772,8		78,9		47,9		.	899,6
1928	766,2		101,0		51,2		.	918,4
1929	737,3		107,7		47,3		.	892,3
1930	655,2	80.2	111,9	13.7	49,6	6.1	.	816,7
1931	582,7		108,4		49,6		.	740,7
1932	520,2		100,6		49,6		.	670,4
1933	500,0	76.7	102,0	15.6	50,0	7.7	.	652,0
1934	.		.		.		.	.

table: AU 1/2	Membership by Confederations		non-affiliated	AUSTRIA
year	ÖGB (4)		non-affiliated	total
	abs	%	abs	abs
1945	298,4	100.0	0	298,4
1946	924,3		0	924,3
1947	1,238,1		0	1,238,1
1948	1,278,7		0	1,278,7
1949	1,279,5		0	1,279,5
1950	1,290,6	100.0	0	1,290,6
1951	1,310,2		0	1,310,2
1952	1,319,3		0	1,310,3
1953	1,320,3		0	1,320,3
1954	1,347,6		0	1,347,6
1955	1,398,4	100.0	0	1,398,4
1956	1,427,3		0	1,427,3
1957	1,438,8		0	1,438,8
1958	1,458,3		0	1,458,3
1959	1,474,9		0	1,474,9
1960	1,501,0	100.0	0	1,501,0
1961	1,518,0		0	1,518,0
1962	1,518,1		0	1,518,1
1963	1,531,7		0	1,531,7
1964	1,539,6		0	1,539,6
1965	1,542,8	100.0	0	1,542,8
1966	1,543,0		0	1,543,0
1967	1,512,4		0	1,512,4
1968	1,514,0		0	1,514,0
1969	1,517,1		0	1,517,1
1970	1,520,3	100.0	0	1,520,3
1971	1,526,4		0	1,526,4
1972	1,542,0		0	1,542,0
1973	1,559,5		0	1,559,5
1974	1,580,4		0	1,580,4
1975	1,587,5	100.0	0	1,587,5
1976	1,604,7		0	1,604,7
1977	1,619,1		0	1,619,1
1978	1,628,1		0	1,628,1
1979	1,641,5		0	1,641,5
1980	1,661,0	100.0	0	1,661,0
1981	1,677,3		0	1,677,3
1982	1,672,5		0	1,672,5
1983	1,660,5		0	1,660,5
1984	1,672,8		0	1,672,8
1985	1,671,4	100.0	0	1,671,4

table: AU.4/1			density rates				AUSTRIA
year	membership		dep.labour force		density rates		
	total	less pens.	total	employed only	gross	employed only	net
	1	2	3	4	1:3	1:4	2:3
1914	263,4	.	.	.	.	.	.
1915	190,8	.	.	.	.	.	.
1916	180,7	.	.	.	.	.	.
1917	329,7	.	.	.	.	.	.
1918	433,5	.	.	.	.	.	.
1919	777,9	.	1,885	.	41.3	.	.
1920	1,003,9	.	1,970	.	51.0	.	.
1921	1,198,7	.	2,050	2,030	58.5	59.0	.
1922	1,171,1	.	2,146	2,043	54.6	57.3	.
1923	1,021,6	.	2,206	1,994	46.3	51.2	.
1924	955,1	.	2,238	2,050	42.7	46.6	.
1925	931,7	.	2,222	2,002	41.9	46.5	.
1926	883,4	.	2,218	1,974	39.8	44.8	.
1927	899,6	.	2,214	1,993	40.6	45.1	.
1928	918,4	.	2,205	2,022	41.7	45.4	.
1929	892,3	.	2,182	1,990	40.9	44.8	.
1930	816,7	.	2,170	1,927	37.6	42.4	.
1931	740,7	.	2,169	1,835	34.2	40.4	.
1932	670,4	.	2,157	1,689	31.1	39.7	.
1933	652,0	.	2,142	1,585	30.4	41.1	.
1934	.	.	2,137	1,581	.	.	.
1935	.	.	2,137	1,592	.	.	.
1945	298,4	.	.	.	.	.	.
1946	924,3	.	1,825	1,716	50.6	53.9	.
1947	1,238,1	.	1,918	1,849	64.6	67.0	.
1948	1,278,7	.	1,972	1,918	64.8	66.7	.
1949	1,279,5	.	2,023	1,932	63.2	66.2	.

table: AU 4/2			density rates				AUSTRIA
year	membership		dep.labour force		density rates		
	total	less pens.	total	employed only	gross	employed only	net
	1	2	3	4	1:3	1:4	2:3
1950	1,290,6	.	2,071	1,942	62.3	66.5	.
1951	1,310,2	.	2,102	1,984	62.3	66.0	.
1952	1,318,3	.	2,097	1,939	62.9	68.0	.
1953	1,320,3	.	2,104	1,919	62.8	68.8	.
1954	1,347,6	.	2,140	1,975	63.0	68.2	.
1955	1,398,4	.	2,196	2,074	63.7	67.4	.
1956	1,427,3	.	2,257	2,137	63.2	66.8	.
1957	1,438,8	.	2,298	2,185	62.6	65.8	.
1958	1,458,3	.	2,327	2,203	62.7	66.2	.
1959	1,474,9	.	2,349	2,236	62.8	66.0	.
1960	1,501,0	.	2,369	2,282	63.4	65.8	.
1961	1,518,0	.	2,391	2,322	63.5	65.4	.
1962	1,518,1	.	2,406	2,340	63.1	64.9	.
1963	1,531,7	.	2,414	2,342	63.5	65.4	.
1964	1,539,6	.	2,431	2,364	63.3	65.1	.
1965	1,542,8	.	2,448	2,382	63.0	64.8	.
1966	1,543,0	.	2,450	2,387	63.0	64.7	.
1967	1,512,4	.	2,426	2,360	62.4	64.1	.
1968	1,514,0	.	2,412	2,339	62.8	64.7	.
1969	1,517,1	.	2,426	2,358	62.5	64.3	.
1970	1,520,3	.	2,448	2,389	62.1	63.6	.
1971	1,526,4	.	2,507	2,455	60.9	62.2	.
1972	1,542,0	.	2,562	2,513	60.2	61.4	.
1973	1,559,5	.	2,649	2,608	58.9	59.8	.
1974	1,580,4	.	2,698	2,657	58.6	59.5	.
1975	1,587,5	.	2,712	2,656	58.5	59.8	.
1976	1,604,7	.	2,741	2,686	58.5	59.7	.
1977	1,619,1	.	2,788	2,737	58.1	59.2	.
1978	1,628,1	.	2,813	2,758	57.9	59.0	.
1979	1,641,5	.	2,830	2,774	58.0	59.2	.
1980	1,661,0	.	2,842	2,789	58.4	59.6	.
1981	1,677,3	.	2,868	2,799	58.5	59.9	.
1982	1,672,5	.	2,872	2,766	58.2	60.5	.
1983	1,660,5	.	2,862	2,735	58.0	60.7	.
1984	1,672,8	.	2,875	2,745	58.2	61.0	.
1985	1,671,4	.	2,889	2,760	57.9	60.6	.

year:1923		total		market			public			status	
isic	conf.	all	female	b-c	w-c	total	b-c	w-c	total	b-c	w-c
1	BFG	60	.	60		60				60	
1	ZKCG	6	.	6		6				6	
		66	.	*66*		*66*				*66*	
2-5	BFG	535	.	457	78	535				457	78
2-5	ZKCG	26	.	23	3	26				23	3
2-5	NATION	1	.	1		1				1	
		562	.	*480*	*81*	*561*				*481*	*81*
6+8	BFG	63	.	9	54	63				9	54
6+8	ZKCG	3	.		3	3					3
6+8	NATION	6	.		6	6					6
		72	.	*9*	*57*	*66*				*9*	*63*
7	BFG	110	.	9		9	92	10	101	100	10
7	ZKCG	14	.	1		1	8	4	13	10	4
7	NATION	29	.					29	29		29
		153	.	*10*		*10*	*100*	*43*	*143*	*110*	*43*
9	BFG	128	.	32	9	42	2	85	87	34	95
9	ZKCG	30	.	15		15		14	14	15	14
9	NATION	9	.		5	5		4	4		9
		167	.	*47*	*14*	*62*	*2*	*103*	*105*	*49*	*118*
	BFG	897	204	567	142	709	93	95	188	660	237
	ZKCG	79	.	46	6	52	8	19	27	54	25
		45	.	1	11	12		33	33	1	44
		1,021	.	*614*	*159*	*773*	*101*	*147*	*248*	*715*	*306*

23

		total		market			public			status	
isic	conf.	all	female	b-c	w-c	total	b-c	w-c	total	b-c	w-c
1	BFG	32	.	32		32				32	
1	ZKCG	12	.	12		12				12	
		43	.	*43*		*43*				*43*	
2-5	BFG	379	.	321	58	379				321	58
2-5	ZKCG	26	.	23	3	26				23	3
2-5	NATION	3	.	3		3					3
		408	.	*347*	*61*	*408*				*344*	*64*
6+8	BFG	29	.		29	29					29
6+8	ZKCG	5	.		5	5					5
6+8	NATION	6	.		6	6					6
		39	.		*39*	*39*					*39*
7	BFG	89	.				77	12	89	77	12
7	ZKCG	18	.				9	9	18	9	9
7	NATION	30	.					30	30		30
		107	.				*86*	*51*	*137*	*86*	*51*
9	BFG	127	.	25	6	32	1	95	96	26	101
9	ZKCG	50	.	12		12		38	38	12	38
9	NATION	11	.		6	6		5	5		11
		188	.	*37*	*12*	*50*		*138*	*138*	*38*	*150*
	BFG	655	142	378	92	471	78	107	185	456	199
	ZKCG	112	.	46	8	54	10	48	58	56	56
	NATION	50	.	3	12	15		35	35	3	47
		817	.	*427*	*112*	*540*	*88*	*190*	*278*	*515*	*302*

Table AU 5/2 Union Membership by Sex, Industry and Status   AUSTRIA

year:1930

24

Table AU 5/3 Union Membership by Sex, Industry and Status — AUSTRIA

year:1951	total		market			public			status	
isic conf.	all	female	b-c	w-c	total	b-c	w-c	total	b-c	w-c
1 ÖGB	68	.	68		68				68	
	68	.	*68*		*68*				*68*	
2-5 ÖGB	697	.	628	69	697				628	69
	697	.	*628*	*69*	*697*				*628*	*69*
6+8 ÖGB	82	.	12	69	82				12	69
	82	.	*12*	*69*	*82*				*12*	*69*
7 ÖGB	171	.	12		12	119	40	159	131	40
	171	.	*12*		*12*	*119*	*40*	*159*	*131*	*40*
9 ÖGB	284	.	49	16	65	55	164	219	104	179
	284	.	*49*	*16*	*65*	*55*	*164*	*219*	*104*	*179*
ÖGB	1,310	341	770	154	924	174	204	378	944	357
	1,310	*341*	*770*	*154*	*924*	*174*	*204*	*378*	*944*	*357*

Table AU 5/4 Union Membership by Sex, Industry and Status — AUSTRIA

year:1961	total		market			public			status	
isic conf.	all	female	b-c	w-c	total	b-c	w-c	total	b-c	w-c
1 ÖGB	63	.	63		63				63	
	63	.	*63*		*63*				*63*	
2-5 ÖGB	846	.	728	118	846				728	118
	846	.	*728*	*118*	*846*				*728*	*118*
6+8 ÖGB	131	.	13	118	131				13	118
	131	.	*13*	*118*	*131*				*13*	*118*
7 ÖGB	188	.	13		13	124	51	175	137	51
	188	.	*13*		*13*	*124*	*51*	*175*	*137*	*51*
9 ÖGB	291	.	38	16	54	60	177	237	97	194
	291	.	*38*	*16*	*54*	*60*	*177*	*237*	*97*	*194*
ÖGB	1,518	433	855	251	1,106	184	228	412	1,039	479
	1,518	*433*	*855*	*251*	*1,106*	*184*	*228*	*412*	*1,039*	*479*

Table AU 5/5 Union Membership by Sex, Industry and Status   AUSTRIA

year:1971	total		market			public			status	
isic|conf.	all	female	b-c	w-c	total	b-c	w-c	total	b-c	w-c
1 ÖGB	35	.	35		35				35	
	35	*.*	*35*		*35*				*35*	
2-5 ÖGB	828	.	695	133	828				695	133
	828	*.*	*695*	*133*	*828*				*695*	*133*
6+8 ÖGB	147	.	14	133	147				14	133
	147	*.*	*14*	*133*	*147*				*14*	*133*
7 ÖGB	192	.	14		14	117	62	178	131	62
	192	*.*	*14*		*14*	*117*	*62*	*178*	*131*	*62*
9 ÖGB	324	.	38	15	53	69	201	270	107	216
	324	*.*	*38*	*15*	*53*	*69*	*201*	*270*	*107*	*216*
ÖGB	1,526	422	796	282	1,078	186	263	449	982	544
	1,526	*422*	*796*	*282*	*1,078*	*186*	*263*	*449*	*982*	*544*

Table AU 5/6 Union Membership by Sex, Industry and Status   AUSTRIA

year:1980	total		market			public			status	
isic|conf.	all	female	b-c	w-c	total	b-c	w-c	total	b-c	w-c
1 ÖGB	21	.	21		21				21	
	21	*.*	*21*		*21*				*21*	
2-5 ÖGB	836	.	667	169	836				667	169
	836	*.*	*667*	*169*	*836*				*667*	*169*
6+8 ÖGB	187	.	18	169	187				18	169
	187	*.*	*18*	*169*	*187*				*18*	*169*
7 ÖGB	205	.	18		18	118	70	188	135	70
	205	*.*	*18*		*18*	*118*	*70*	*188*	*135*	*70*
9 ÖGB	412	.	43	17	60	79	273	352	123	290
	412	*.*	*43*	*17*	*60*	*79*	*273*	*352*	*123*	*290*
ÖGB	1,661	499	766	355	1,121	197	343	540	963	698
	1,661	*499*	*766*	*355*	*1,121*	*197*	*343*	*540*	*963*	*698*

Table AU 5/7 Union Membership by Sex, Industry and Status										AUSTRIA
year:1985		total		market			public			status
isic	conf.	all	female	b-c	w-c	total	b-c	w-c	total	b-c	w-c
1	ÖGB	20	.	20		20				20	
		20	.	20		20				20	
2-5	ÖGB	784	.	610	174	784				610	174
		784	.	610	174	784				610	174
6+8	ÖGB	193	.	19	174	193				19	174
		193	.	19	174	193				19	174
7	ÖGB	212	.	19		19	117	75	193	136	75
		212	.	19		19	117	75	193	136	75
9	ÖGB	464	.	52	18	70	84	309	394	137	327
		464	.	52	18	70	84	309	394	137	327
	ÖGB	1,671	515	720	365	1,085	202	385	586	922	750
		1,671	515	720	365	1,085	202	385	586	922	750

Table AU 6/1 Dependent Labour Force by Sex, Industry and Status   AUSTRIA

1923	total		market			public			status	
isic	all	female	b-c	w-c	total	b-c	w-c	total	b-c	w-c
1	482	.	.	.	.	.	.	.	.	.

Table AU 6/2 Dependent Labour Force by Sex, Industry and Status   AUSTRIA

1934	total		market			public			status	
isic	all	female	b-c	w-c	total	b-c	w-c	total	b-c	w-c
1	360	.	.	.	.	.	.	.	348	12
2-5	880	.	.	.	.	.	.	.	777	103
6+8	165	.	.	.	.	.	.	.	32	133
7	134	.	.	.	.	.	.	.	91	43
9	489	.	.	.	.	.	.	.	318	170
0	94	.	.	.	.	.	.	.	82	12
	2,121	715	.	.	.	.	.	.	1,649	474

Table AU 6/3 Dependent Labour Force by Sex, Industry and Status   AUSTRIA

1951	total		market			public			status	
isic	all	female	b-c	w-c	total	b-c	w-c	total	b-c	w-c
1	229	.	219	10	229	.	.	.	219	10
2-5	1,093	.	949	144	1093	.	.	.	949	144
6+8	165	.	40	125	165	.	.	.	40	125
7	164	.	.	.	28	.	.	137	48	116
9	476	.	.	.	170	.	.	307	204	273
0	39	.	.	.	39	.	.	.	26	13
	2,166	2	.	.	1,723	.	.	443	1,487	679

28

Table AU 6/4 Dependent Labour Force by Sex, Industry and Status   AUSTRIA

1961	total		market			public			status	
isic	all	female	b-c	w-c	total	b-c	w-c	total	b-c	w-c
1	121	.	.	.	.	.	.	.	111	10
2-5	1,239	.	.	.	.	.	.	.	1,035	205
6+8	256	.	.	.	.	.	.	.	53	203
7	186	.	.	.	.	.	.	.	48	138
9	547	.	.	.	.	.	.	.	196	351
0	38	.	.	.	.	.	.	.	31	8
	2,387	867	.	.	.	.	.	.	1,473	914

Table AU 6/5 Dependent Labour Force by Sex, Industry and Status   AUSTRIA

1971	total		market			public			status	
isic	all	female	b-c	w-c	total	b-c	w-c	total	b-c	w-c
1	61	.	52	9	61	.	.	.	52	9
2-5	1,198	.	929	269	1,198	.	.	.	929	269
6+8	336	.	73	263	336	.	.	.	73	263
7	184	.	.	.	52	.	.	132	50	134
9	620	.	.	.	215	.	.	405	207	413
0	44	.	.	.	44	.	.	.	31	13
	2,442	900	.	.	1,905	.	.	537	1,342	1,100

Table AU 6/6 Dependent Labour Force by Sex, Industry and Status AUSTRIA										
1980	total		market			public			status	
isic	all	female	b-c	w-c	total	b-c	w-c	total	b-c	w-c
1	41	.	.	.	.	.	.	.	.	.
2-5	1,247	.	.	.	.	.	.	.	.	.
6+8	470	.	.	.	.	.	.	.	.	.
7	207	.	.	.	.	.	.	.	.	.
9	876	.	.	.	.	.	.	.	.	.
0	1	.	.	.	.	.	.	.	.	.
	2,842	1,143	.	.	.	.	.	.	1,476	1,365

Table AU 6/7 Dependent Labour Force by Sex, Industry and Status AUSTRIA										
1985	total		market			public			status	
isic	all	female	b-c	w-c	total	b-c	w-c	total	b-c	w-c
1	40	.	.	.	40	.	.	.	.	.
2-4	1,228	.	.	.	1.228	.	.	.	.	.
6+8	482	.	.	.	482	.	.	.	.	.
7	211	.	.	.	62	.	.	149	.	.
9	902	.	.	.	227	.	.	676	.	.
0	35	.	.	.	35	.	.	.	.	.
	2,899	1,183	.	.	2,075	.	.	825	1,424	1,475

30

Chapter 2: DENMARK

LIST OF UNION CONFEDERATIONS: name, abbreviation and foundation year

1   *Landsorganisationen i Danmark* (LO): 1898–
    Danish Confederation of Trade Unions

2   *Fællesrådet for danske Tjenestemands- og Funktionærorganisationer*
    (FTF): 1952–
    Joint Council of Public Servants & Salaried Employees Associations

3   *Hovedorganisationen for Arbejdsleder- og Tekniske*
    Funktionærforeninger i Danmark (FR): 1953–
    Federation of Supervisory and Technical Staff Associations

4   *Statstjenestemændenes Centralorganisation I* (CO-1): 1953–
    Association of Unions of Lower Grade Public Servants

5   *Akademikernes Centralorganisation* (AC): 1972–
    Central Organization of Professional Employees

---

1.   AGGREGATE MEMBERSHIP STATISTICS

1.1   General Series

From the beginning of the century union membership figures have been
published annually by the Danish Bureau of Statistics in the Statistisk
Årbog (Danish Statistical Yearbook), Copenhagen. This series included
only the membership of unions affiliated with the LO, or *De samvirkende
Fagforbund i Danmark* as it was then called, and a group of independent
unions of mainly manual workers. As a matter of fact, the Yearbook's
statistics were entirely based upon, and limited to, the figures
disclosed by the LO (see: De samvirkende fagforbund i Danmark 1898-
1923, Copenhagen 1924: 214-228; and LO, Beretning (Annual Reports),
Copenhagen.
      Only from 1953, following the formation of the federations of
employee unions, the Statistical Yearbook includes figures on white-
collar union membership outside the LO as well. This series has become
more inclusive over the years. The Statistical Yearbook included the
membership of the *Akademikernes Centralorganisation* (AC) only from
1972, after its reconstitution from a loose coordinating body (the
Akademikernes Samarbejdsudvalg or AS). In 1975 coverage was once more
widened as a number of independent unions and federations, mainly
representing professional and white-collar employees, began to report
membership. Among these organizations are also two Christian Federations, the *Kristelig Fagforening* (workers) and the *Kristelig Funktio-*

nær-Organisation (employees), which together report some 13,000 members in 1984. According to Von Bülow a Christian Trade Union Federation had been founded in 1899, but membership and influence were as negligible as it is today (Von Bülow 1931: 329).

On the basis of internal reports of a number of white-collar unions, in particular the *Foreningen af Arbejdsledere i Danmark*, the *Danske Formanforening*, the *Teknisk Landsforbund*, the *Danske Farmaceutforening* and the *Dansk Sygeplejerråd*, organizations which later joined the FTF or FR, I have been able to include the membership in white-collar unions also before 1952 (as was also done by Plovsing, 1973 and Pedersen, 1979). The same procedure was followed with respect to the unions which later joined the CO-1. As a cartel the CO-1 combines a number of LO- and, from 1953, FTF-unions together with a number of independent unions. The CO-1 membership is calculated so as to exclude double counting, and the membership of LO and FTF affiliates has been reported under LO and FTF respectively. In addition to the CO-1, which combines the unions of lower-grade public servants (the so-called 'silvercords'), there exists a second body for higher grade civil servants or 'goldcords' (the CO-II). All CO-II unions are also affiliated with the FTF. The same is true for the unions co-operating in the *Laerernes Centralorganisation*, a federation of teachers' unions which recently has been reorganized into a single union. The AC/AS-membership before 1972 is, partly, reported by Plovsing (1973: 11 and 37-). Additional information comes from Floryan & Lindholm, 1982. In 1975 the Danish Bureau of Statistics reported the membership in the unions for commercial travellers, journalists, managerial staffs, electronic data operators for the first time, together with the membership in two unions for supervisory and technical staff which had left the FR a few years earlier. On the basis of the organizational and membership data reported in Plovsing (1971: 60-61), Buksti & Johansen (1977) and Buksti (1982), I have been able to include the membership in these unions from 1968 onwards.

In conclusion, my series is more inclusive than the series reported by Kjellberg (1983: 280-281) who omitted the non-manual membership of the unions before their affiliation to FTF, FR or AC. My series has also a wider coverage than the one presented by Bain & Price (1980: 149-152) who did not include the membership of non-reporting white--collar unions before 1975. It has been observer by many authors that time series of union membership in Denmark are distorted by the statistics becoming more inclusive over time. By tracing back the membership of unions before they first reported or before they first federated (which is often the same thing) - provided these unions fulfilled our definition of what constitutes a trade union -, the series presented in this chapter corrects for some of the discontinuity arising from changes in statistical coverage.

With a brief interruption, from 1925 to 1927, the LO and the independent unions reported their membership on 31 December of each year. White-Collar federations used to report on 31 March. After 1972, all organizations reported on January 1st. I have followed the example of Bain & Price (1980: 152) and equated 1 January to 31 December of the previous year. Thus, the 1972 membership is the membership reported at 1 January 1973, and so on.

1.2 Retired Members

Reported membership of FTF, AC, FR, CO-1 and independent unions does not include pensioners. Retired members are however not separable in the reported membership of the main union confederation, the LO. Until recent their number was probably not very large, perhaps only some 3-4% of the total LO-membership in the early 1970s (Kjellberg, 1983: 238). However, the institutional reforms in 1976 which made pre-retirement from the labour market more attractive and made pre-retirement benefits payable through funds which are closely associated with the unions (Scheuer, 1986), may have boosted the number of retired members as the new scheme did incentive membership retention. Union membership figures and density rates in recent years may therefore be inflated in comparison with the past, and with other countries.

The AC- and FR-affiliates also recruit self-employed professionals. The self-employed account for 30-35% of the AC's membership according to Lund (1983), but only its membership among salary earners is reported in the Statistical Yearbook and here.

1.3 Female Membership

A full series of membership by sex is only available for the LO and some independent unions of manual workers (Statistisk Årbog; and the LO Beretning, both annually). The 1986-Statistical Yearbook, reporting on the 1984 membership, gave for the first time female and male membership outside the LO, although the FTF- and CO-1 returns were less than complete. The 1984 female membership of the FTF- and CO-1 affiliates has been estimated for the non-reporting affiliates - together representing about one-fifth of the FTF and CO-1 membership - by taking the average for the reporting affiliates.

2. MEMBERSHIP BY INDUSTRY AND STATUS

2.1 Classification by Industry

1 Agriculture, Forestry & Fishing: *Agronomforening; Gartnerforbund; Jordbruksteknikere; Jordbrugsvidenskappelige Kandidatforbund; Landarbejderforbund; Landmejeristers Forbund; Undermejerist Forbund*

2-5 Mining, Industry, Construction & Utilities: *Arbejdsmandsforbund; Arbejdsmandsforbund for Lolland og Falster; Arbejdsmands- og Specialarbejderforbundet; Bageri- og Konditoriarbejdernes Forbund; Beklædingsarbejderforbund; Beklædings- og Tekstilarbejder Forbundet; Billedskærer- og Dekorationsbilldhuggerforbund; Blikkenslagerforbundet; Blikkenslager-, Sanitets- og Rørarbejderforbundet; Bogbinderforbundet; Bogbinder- og Kartonnagearbejder Forbund; Brolæggerforbund; Bryggeriarbejdernes Forbund; Bryggeri-, Brænderi- og Mineralvandsarbejder Forbund; Bygningskontruktørforening; Bødkerforbundet; Børsteindustriarbejderforbundet; Drejerforbundet; Dykkerfornening; EL-Forbundet; Farmaceutforening; Forening af Arbejdsledere; Forgylderforbundet; Formandsforening;*

33

Formerforbund; Former- og Støberiarbejderforbund; Fotografisk Landsforbund; Funktionær-Forbund; Garverforbund; Glarmestersvendenes Forbund; Glasarbejderforbund;   Grafiske Funkt. Landsforening; Guld- og Solvarbejderernes Forbund; Guld-, Sølv- og Elektroarbejdernes Forbund; Gørtler- og Metalarbejderforbundet; Handskemagerforbundet; Hatte- og Bundtmagerforbundet; Ingeniørforening; Ingeniør-Sammenslutningen; Jern- og Metalsliber Forbund; Karretmagerforbund; Karretmager- og Karosseribyggerforbund; Kedel- og Maskinpasser Forbund; Keramisk Forbund; Kobbersmedenes Forbund; Korskærernes og Sortererskernes Forbund; Kristelig Fagforbund; Kristelig Funktionær-Organisation; Kurvemagerforbundet; Kvindeligt Arbejderforbund; Litografsk Forbund; Lædder- og Skindarbejderforbund; Malerforbund; Mejeristforbund; Metalarbejder-Forbund; Metaltrykkerforbund; Murerforbund; Mælkeriindustriarbejdernes Forbund; Nærings- og Nyderlsesmiddelarbejderforbund; Papirindustriarbejder Forbund; Prosa; Rebslageriarbejderforbund; Riggernes og Sejlmagernes Forbund; Sadelmager- og Tapetserforbundet; Sammenslutning af Firma-Funktionærer; Skibstømrerforbund; Skotøjsarbejderforbundet; Skraatobaksarbejdernesforbund; Skrædderforbund; Slagteriarbejderforbund; Smede- og Maskinarbejderforbund; Snedkerforbund; Snedker- og Tømrerforbundet; Specialarbejderforbundet; Stenindustriarbejderforbund; Stukkatørernes Fagforening af 1920; Sukkervare- og Chokoladearbejdernes Forbund; Sukkervare-, Chokolade- og Bisquitarbejdernes Forbund; Tandteknikerforbund; Tekstilarbejderforbund; Tobaksarbejderforbundet; Tobaksindustriens Funktionærforening; Træindustriarbejderforbundet; Teknisk Landsforbund; Typografforbund; Tømrerforbund; Urmager Fagforbund; Urmager- og Optiker-Forbundet; økonomaforeningen; and all FR--affiliates.

6+8   Commerce, Banking & Insurances: *Apoteksteknikeres Forening; Bankfunkt. Landsforening; Centralforening for Danske Assurandører; Danmarks Aktive Handelsrejsende; Forsikringsfunkt. Landsforening; Handels- og Kontorfunkt. Forbund; Kredit- og Hypotekforeningsfunktionærers Fællesrad; Realkreditfunkt. Landsforening; Sparkassefunkt. Landsforening*

7   Transport & Communication: *Centralorg. for Telefonstanden; Chaufførnernes Forbund; Fællesorg. DSB; Foreningen af Funkt. SAS; Funktionære i FDB; Jernbane Forbund; Jernbaneforeningen; Kabinepersonaleforening; Lokomotivmands Forening; Luftfartsvæsenets Personaleforening; Nævigatørernes Fællesforening; Postforbund; Post- og Telegrafforening; Privatbanefunkt. Forbund; Radiotelegrafistforeningen af 1917; Sammensl. af Overord. Funkt. SAS; Skibsførerforening; Styrmandsforening; Søfyrbodernes Forbund; Sømændenes Forbund; Sø-Restaurations Forening; Teleforbundet*

9   Other Services: *Alg. Danske Lægeforening; Artist Forbund; Arkitekters Landsforbund; Centralforening for kontraktansat Stampersonel; Dyrlægeforening; Erhvervssprogligt Forbund; Faglært Køkkenpersonales Forbund; Fængselforbund; Foreningen af Danske Civiløkonomer; Foreningen af Kommunale Embedsmænd; Forvarsgruppen i AC; Frisørforbund; Gastronomisk Landsforbund; Gymnasieskolernes Lærerforening; Hospitalsforbund pa Statshospitalerne; Hotel- og Restaurationspers. Forbund; Hospitalsforbund; Husassistenternes*

Forbund; Husligt Arbejder Forbund; Hærens Konstabel og Korporal-forening; Journalistforbund; Jurist- og økonomforening; Kellner-forbund; Kokkeforening af 1913; Kommunalarbejderforbund; Magister-forening; Musiker Forbund; Mølleriarbejder Forbund; Pædagogisk Medhjælper Forbund; Plejerforbund; Præsteforening; Psykolog-forening; Skolebetjentenes Organisation; Skorstensfejersvendenes Forbund; Soignerings-, Toilet- og Sanitetsarbejderforbund; Stam-personel i Søværnet; Sygeplejerrad; Tandlægeforening; Tjener-forbundet and all affiliates of FTF or CO-1 not listed above.

It should be noted that this breakdown of union membership by industry is far from perfect, given the existence of large general unions - in particular the *Specialarbejderforbundet i Denmark* (General Workers' Union), which is Denmark's by far largest union (representing almost a quarter of LO's combined membership in 1984), and the *Kvinde-ligt Arbejderforbundet* (Women Workers' Union) which is LO's fifth largest affiliate. It is impossible to distinguish between manu-facturing and construction, and also the distinction between industry and transport (that is, road traffic, storage and ports) is only a approximation. As a consequence union membership in industry is over-, and union membership in transport understated. Manual membership in agriculture has been estimated from the figures given by Kjellberg (1983: 280-281, table 1 and 2). It suffers from underestimation as no breakdown between fishery and merchant shipping of the seamen's union's membership was known. The membership of some recent professional asso-ciations (architects, engineers, economists) has been divided between industry and (business) services (50%).

2.2   Classification by Status

With some adjustments I have followed the classification developed by Bain & Price (1980: 154-155). Of the LO-affiliates the *Handels- og Kontorfunktionærforbund* (HKF, clerical and commercial employees - till 1934 an independent union), the *Funktionærforbund* (technical employees), the *Privatbanefunktionærforbund* (railways) and the *Kommunalarbejderforbund* (municipal workers and employees) have been classified as non-manual, the latter union's membership only partly. Bain & Price classified 50% of its membership as non-manual. This accords with the figures published by Plovsing (1971: 60-61) and Blum & Ponak (1970: 67), but a survey in 1982 (reported in Scheuer, 1987: 237) indicated that this percentage had risen to 80%. The same survey showed that 58% of the membership of the *Husligt Arbejderforbund* is in the non-manual category as well. Originally organizing domestic servants, this union had widened its domain in the 1970s to hospitals and public services. Thus from the 1970s half of this union's membership is in lower-grade white-collar occupations. I have also classified as non--manual the membership of LO-unions in health and nursing, among foremen in the hotel trade (Blum & Ponak, ibid.), of merchant shipping officers, Prison Officials and in the Post Office, but not its railway union as Danish authors (Pedersen, 1977; Scheuer, 1987) sometimes do. Of the recent affiliates of the LO, I did also classify as non-manual the membership of the *Hærens Konstabel og Korporalforening* (military), the *Pædagogisk Medhjælper Forbund* (education), the *Stampersonal i Søvernæt* (navy), and the *Teleforbundet* (telecommunication).

Steuer's survey, relating to 1982, also showed that some (8%) of the HKF's membership belonged in the manual category (warehouses, transport) and that some manual workers unions (in particular, the Metalworkers Union and General Workers' Union) represented some (9% each) white-collar employees. By classifying the membership of these two unions into the manual and that of the HKF into the non-manual category, the overall picture is not greatly distorted.

All members of the FTF, AC, FR and CO-1 (except those already included in the LO or FTF) have been classified in the non-manual category. Of the independent unions, I have classified as non-manual the *Arbejdsledere, Artist Forbund, Børne og Ungdomsforsorgendes Personalforbund, Bygningskonstruktørforening, Centralforening for kontraktansat Stampersonel, Centralorganisation for Telefonstanden, Civiløkonomer, Erhvervssprogligt Forbund, Formandsforening, Handelsrejsende, Hospitalsforbund, Ingeniørsammenslutningen, Jernbaneforeningen, Jordbrukteknikere, Journalistforbund, Kommunale Embedsmænd, Kristelig Funktionær-Organisation, Lægeforening, Musiker Forbund, Post- og Telegrafforening, Prosa, Skolebetjentenes Organisation*, and the *Teknisk Landsforbund.*

2.3 Public Sector Unionism

In Denmark the distribution of union members between the private and public sector of the economy is complicated, especially in the case of the LO unions. Relatively easy to locate are the members of the unions in railways, the Post Office, hospitals, military, education and, of course, the *Kommunalarbejderforbund*, LO's large union of municipal employees. Additionally, 50% of the membership of the *Husligt Arbejderforbund* in 1980 and 1985, and an increasing proportion of the HKF's membership is employed in the public sector, increasing from over 35,000 members in 1970 (Blum & Ponak, 1970: 72) to 35% in 1982 (letter of 25-5-1985 to author by Steen Scheuer) Scheuer also did indicate that some 16-22% of the members of the *Metalarbejder-Forbund* (Metalworkers' Union) and the *Specialarbejderforbundet* (General Workers' Unions) ware now employed in the public sector. Far lack of data on earlier years, I have included members of the latter two union in the public sector.

The distinction is easier to make for the FTF, for this organization has a separate section of white-collar employee unions in the private sector, including unions of clerical staff, technical & managerial staff, and white-collar employees in banking & insurance (see: Blum & Ponak, 1970). The FR-membership is fully placed in the private sector, and that of the CO-I in the public sector. Of the professional associations and the AC-affiliates, those recruiting dentists, veterinarians, doctors, clergymen, military staff, teachers and judges have been placed in the public sector. Additionally, the *Jurist- og økonomforbund, Civilokonomer* and *Ingeniør-sammenslutningen* have also members in the public sector. Approximately half of the AC's membership is employed in the (semi)public sector (see: Floryan & Lindblom, 1982). Of the independent unions the membership in the Postoffice, railways, military, municipal civil servants, hospitals, and among contracted state employees has been allocated to the public sector.

3. LABOUR FORCE STATISTICS

P.J. Pedersen has compiled a yearly series on the dependent labour force in Denmark from 1911 till 1975 (Pedersen,1977). This series is based on social insurance and tax data, and excludes domestic servants and the unemployed. For later years (1975-1984), I have used the series, also based on tax-return data, of the Danish Bureau of Statistics and relating to wage and salary earners in employment(Statistisk Årbog, 1986: 136, table 137). The annual average number of registered unemployed have been added (Statistisk Årbog, 1986: 147, table 148; see also Scheuer, 1986: 15, table 3). It is important to note, that Pederson's series is based upon a rather restricted definition of the labour force. As was mentioned before, domestic servants are excluded. Theirs was a large number, especially before the last world war. Flora, Kraus & Pfenning (1987: 477-484) report on the basis of census data a much larger number of wage and salary earners (excluding assisting spouses and children). It should therefore be noted that a difference exists between table DE 4, which is based on the (updated) series of Pedersen, and table DE 6 which is based on the 1921, 1930, 1940, 1950, 1970 censuses (Flora, Kraus & Pfenning, ibid.) and the labour force sample surveys of 1979 and 1985, as reported in the 1981 and 1987 Yearbook of Labour Statistics of the International Labour Organization (ILO). Note that I compare the union membership of 1979 and 1984 (reported at 1-1-1980 and 1-1-1985) with the survey-data referring to November 1979 and 1985.

To my knowledge, the Danish Bureau of Statistics published only in recent years figures on the total number of employees in the public sector (central and local government). Within its series on wage and salary earners in employment the Bureau distinguishes employment in the Post Office, government-subsidized (and other) services and government services proper. From this statistic it appears that (semi-)public employment rose from 626,836 in 1975 to 892,016 in 1984 (excluding railways which is not given separately). In 1985, the Danish Bureau of Statistics published figures on public employment for 1981-1983, including full-time and part-time employed in central and local government as well as institutions subsidized by central or local government (Statistisk Årbog 1985: 136, table 137). This added up to a number of 933,000 employed persons in 1983, including not only railways but also public utilities and broadcasting.

4. TABLES

table: DE 1/1	Membership by Confederation						DENMARK
year	LO	FTF	FR	CO-1	AC	Other	Total
	1	2	3	4	5		
1913	114,7	.	.	.	.	37,5	152,2
1914	121,6	.	.	.	.	34,6	156,2
1915	133,8	.	.	.	.	41,2	175,0
1916	150,5	.	.	.	.	41,6	192,1
1917	179,3	.	.	.	.	39,3	218,6
1918	255,1	.	.	.	.	61,7	316,8
1919	277,4	.	.	.	.	71,8	349,2
1920	279,3	.	.	.	.	81,9	361,2
1921	244,4	.	.	.	.	76,6	321,0
1922	232,1	.	.	.	.	74,8	306,9
1923	233,1	.	.	.	.	63,1	296,2
1924	237,0	.	.	.	.	67,7	304,7
1925	237,0	.	.	.	.	70,2	307,2
1926	155,6	.	.	.	.	154,2	309,8
1927	156,0	.	.	.	.	160,2	316,2
1928	156,0	.	.	.	.	163,1	319,1
1929	250,2	.	.	.	.	81,5	331,7
1930	259,1	.	.	.	.	84,0	343,1
1931	269,5	.	.	.	.	88,0	357,5
1932	300,0	.	.	.	.	73,3	373,3
1933	301,8	.	.	.	.	106,4	408,2
1934	354,7	.	.	.	.	71,3	426,0
1935	381,3	.	.	.	.	59,9	441,2
1936	423,4	.	.	.	.	41,5	464,9
1937	451,6	.	.	.	.	43,0	494,6
1938	473,1	.	.	.	.	40,0	513,1
1939	509,2	.	.	.	.	32,5	541,7
1940	515,8	.	.	.	.	32,5	548,3
1941	529,5	.	.	.	.	29,6	559,1
1942	547,2	.	.	.	.	29,1	576,3
1943	563,8	.	.	.	.	31,2	595,0
1944	579,4	.	.	.	.	32,3	611,7
1945	604,3	.	.	.	.	34,8	639,1
1946	604,6	.	.	.	.	34,8	639,4
1947	613,9	.	.	.	.	53,6	667,5
1948	623,1	.	.	.	.	54,6	677,7
1949	635,8	.	.	.	.	55,1	690,9

table: DE 1/2	Membership by Confederation						DENMARK
year	LO	FTF	FR	CO-1	AC	Other	Total
	1	2	3	4	5		
1950	656,4	.	.	.	.	120,7	777,1
1951	662,4	.	.	.	.	136,1	798,5
1952	671,1	.	.	.	.	147,2	818,3
1953	687,7	83,9	21,7	14,2	8,3	28,4	844,2
1954	686,6	87,1	20,1	14,5	9,1	28,3	845,7
1955	687,4	88,5	20,8	14,8	10,0	28,2	849,7
1956	705,5	94,7	21,1	14,9	10,8	27,8	874,8
1957	714,9	99,5	21,8	12,6	11,6	27,6	888,0
1958	719,1	102,7	22,4	12,8	12,3	27,6	896,9
1959	753,1	112,7	22,6	12,7	13,2	28,6	942,9
1960	776,5	112,2	23,8	13,0	14,0	29,4	968,9
1961	789,5	110,3	26,1	13,1	15,1	30,6	984,7
1962	802,4	114,1	27,9	13,2	17,8	31,9	1,007,3
1963	817,2	118,0	29,5	12,2	19,7	31,6	1,028,2
1964	834,0	124,7	30,5	12,6	21,6	31,6	1,055,0
1965	829,2	132,1	32,1	13,5	22,7	43,2	1,072,8
1966	835,1	140,4	33,8	13,6	24,0	44,0	1,090,9
1967	849,4	147,0	35,5	12,9	25,4	37,6	1,107,8
1968	865,3	149,1	30,6	14,5	26,0	56,8	1,142,3
1969	894,4	150,0	29,2	13,9	27,8	58,7	1,174,0
1970	896,0	156,1	30,3	10,4	33,3	69,0	1,195,1
1971	909,5	174,5	31,2	1,1	38,1	60,3	1,214,7
1972	924,2	186,8	19,8	1,1	40,2	76,2	1,248,3
1973	930,1	199,8	20,8	3,9	42,6	82,9	1,280,1
1974	947,8	210,3	21,2	3,9	44,0	94,2	1,321,4
1975	1,011,7	227,6	21,7	5,2	45,3	102,4	1,413,9
1976	1,087,2	240,7	21,9	5,3	48,1	109,8	1,513,0
1977	1,141,6	251,5	22,6	5,4	62,5	94,5	1,578,1
1978	1,212,0	265,6	23,3	5,4	65,8	120,8	1,692,9
1979	1,249,6	277,4	24,0	5,7	69,7	129,2	1,755,6
1980	1,279,8	286,1	23,9	5,7	63,1	142,9	1,801,5
1981	1,325,3	295,5	23,1	8,4	64,3	142,3	1,858,9
1982	1,364,7	286,1	23,9	17,1	65,8	161,3	1,918,9
1983	1,380,0	287,9	22,9	17,3	65,6	168,0	1,941,7
1984	1,399,1	309,0	23,7	16,6	74,1	163,5	1,986,0

table: DE 2 Confederal Membership Shares in per centage of total membership			DENMARK
year	LO	FTF	AC	total
	%	%	%	

year	LO	FTF	AC	total
1915	76.5	.	.	100.0
1920	77.3	.	.	100.0
1925	77.1	.	.	100.0
1930	75.5	.	.	100.0
1935	86.4	.	.	100.0
1940	94.1	.	.	100.0
1945	94.6	.	.	100.0
1950	84.5	.	.	100.0
1955	80.9	10.4	1.2	100.0
1960	80.1	11.6	1.4	100.0
1965	77.3	12.3	2.1	100.0
1970	75.0	13.1	2.8	100.0
1975	71.6	16.1	3.2	100.0
1980	71.0	15.9	3.5	100.0
1984	70.4	15.6	3.7	100.0

table: DE 4/1			density rates				DENMARK
year	membership		dep.labour force		density rates		
	total	less pens.	total	employed only	gross	employed only	net
	1	2	3	4	1:3	1:4	2:3
1913	152,2	.	658	.	23.1	.	.
1914	156,2	.	670	.	23.3	.	.
1915	175,0	.	682	.	25.7	.	.
1916	192,1	.	692	.	27.8	.	.
1917	218,6	.	710	.	30.8	.	.
1918	316,8	.	722	.	43.9	.	.
1919	349,2	.	735	.	47.5	.	.
1920	361,2	.	749	.	48.3	.	.
1921	321,0	.	806	.	39.8	.	.
1922	306,9	.	822	.	37.3	.	.
1923	296,2	.	835	.	35.5	.	.
1924	304,7	.	851	.	35.8	.	.
1925	307,2	.	865	.	35.5	.	.
1926	309,8	.	881	.	35.1	.	.
1927	316,2	.	891	.	35.5	.	.
1928	319,1	.	906	.	35.2	.	.
1929	331,7	.	916	.	36.2	.	.
1930	343,1	.	929	.	36.9	.	.
1931	357,5	.	948	.	37.7	.	.
1932	373,3	.	982	.	38.0	.	.
1933	408,2	.	1,002	.	40.7	.	.
1934	426,0	.	1,032	.	41.3	.	.
1935	441,2	.	1,054	.	41.9	.	.
1936	464,9	.	1,080	.	43.0	.	.
1937	494,6	.	1,108	.	44.6	.	.
1938	513,1	.	1,133	.	45.3	.	.
1939	541,7	.	1,163	.	46.6	.	.
1940	548,3	.	1,188	.	46.2	.	.
1941	559,1	.	1,203	.	46.5	.	.
1942	576,3	.	1,219	.	47.3	.	.
1943	595,0	.	1,239	.	48.0	.	.
1944	611,7	.	1,258	.	48.6	.	.
1945	639,1	.	1,278	.	50.0	.	.
1946	639,4	.	1,294	.	49.4	.	.
1947	667,5	.	1,301	.	51.3	.	.
1948	677,7	.	1,316	.	51.5	.	.
1949	690,9	.	1,326	.	52.1	.	.

table: DE 4/2		density rates				DENMARK	
year	membership		dep.labour force		density rates		
	total	less pens.	total	employed only	gross	employed only	net
	1	2	3	4	1:3	1:4	2:3
1950	777,1	.	1,338	.	58.1	.	.
1951	798,5	.	1,356	.	58.9	.	.
1952	818,3	.	1,374	.	59.6	.	.
1953	844,2	.	1,396	.	60.5	.	.
1954	845,7	.	1,417	.	59.7	.	.
1955	849,7	.	1,437	.	59.2	.	.
1956	874,8	.	1,449	.	60.4	.	.
1957	888,0	.	1,463	.	60.7	.	.
1958	896,9	.	1,483	.	60.5	.	.
1959	942,9	.	1,506	.	62.6	.	.
1960	968,9	.	1,535	1,503	63.1	64,5	.
1961	984,7	.	1,573	.	62.6	.	.
1962	1,007,3	.	1,612	.	62.5	.	.
1963	1,028,2	.	1,649	.	62.4	.	.
1964	1,055,0	.	1,684	.	62.7	.	.
1965	1,072,8	.	1,714	1,697	62.6	63.2	.
1966	1,090,9	.	1,741	.	62.7	.	.
1967	1,107,8	.	1,770	.	62.6	.	.
1968	1,142,3	.	1,794	.	63.7	.	.
1969	1,174,0	.	1,823	.	64.4	.	.
1970	1,195,1	.	1,856	1,831	64.4	65.3	.
1971	1,214,7	.	1,913	1,880	63.5	64.6	.
1972	1,248,3	.	1,970	1,937	63.4	64.5	.
1973	1,280,1	.	1,972	1,950	64.9	65.7	.
1974	1,321,4	.	2,011	1,959	65.7	67.5	.
1975	1,413,9	.	2,052	1,924	68.9	73.5	.
1976	1,513,0	.	2,108	1,974	71.8	76.6	.
1977	1,578,1	.	2,160	1,996	73.1	79.1	.
1978	1,692,9	.	2,219	2,028	76.3	83.5	.
1979	1,755,6	.	2,233	2,071	78.6	84.8	.
1980	1,801,5	.	2,257	2,073	79.8	86.9	.
1981	1,858,9	.	2,296	2,043	81.0	91.0	.
1982	1,918,9	.	2,333	2,070	82.3	92.7	.
1983	1,941,7	.	2,368	2,085	82.0	93.1	.
1984	1,986,0	.	2,415	2,139	82.2	92.9	.

Table DE 5/1 Union Membership by Sex, Industry and Status										DENMARK	
year:1921		**total**		**market**			**public**			**status**	
isic	conf.	all	female	b-c	w-c	total	b-c	w-c	total	b-c	w-c
1	LO	15	.	15		15				15	
1	Other	1	.	1		1				1	
		16	.	*16*		*16*				*16*	
2-5	LO	214	.	213	1	214				213	1
2-5	Other	42	.	41	1	42				41	1
		256	.	*254*	*2*	*256*				*254*	*2*
6+8	Other	17	.		17	17					17
		17	.		*17*	*17*					*17*
7	LO	13	.				10	3	13	10	3
7	Other	15	.	3	1	4		12	12	3	13
		28	.	*3*	*1*	*4*	*10*	*14*	*24*	*13*	*15*
9	LO	3	.	2		2	1	1	1	2	1
9	Other	2	.	1		1				1	
		4	.	*3*		*3*	*1*	*1*	*2*	*4*	*1*
	LO	244	44	230	1	230	11	3	14	241	4
	Other	77	13	46	19	65		12	12	46	30
		321	*57*	*276*	*19*	*295*	*11*	*15*	*26*	*287*	*34*

43

Table DE 5/2 Union Membership by Sex, Industry and Status										DENMARK
year:1930		total		market			public			status	
isic	conf.	all	female	b-c	w-c	total	b-c	w-c	total	b-c	w-c
1	LO	14	.	14		14				14	
1	Other	2	.	2		2				2	
		15	.	15		15				15	
2-5	LO	224	.	222	1	224				222	1
2-5	Other	41	.	38	4	41				38	4
		265	.	260	5	265				260	5
6+8	Other	14	.		14	14					14
		14	.		14	14					14
7	LO	10	.				8	2	10	8	2
7	Other	19	.	4	2	7		12	12	4	14
		29	.	4	2	7	8	14	22	13	16
9	LO	12	.	2		2	6	4	10	8	4
9	Other	8	.	2	4	6	2		2	4	4
		20	.	4	4	7	9	4	12	12	8
	LO	259	43	238	1	239	15	6	20	252	7
	Other	84	10	46	24	70	2	12	15	48	36
		343	53	283	25	309	17	18	35	300	43

Table DE 5/3 Union Membership by Sex, Industry and Status										DENMARK
year:1950		total		market			public			status
isic	conf.	all	female	b-c	w-c	total	b-c	w-c	total	b-c	w-c
1	LO	39	.	39		39				39	
1	Other	1	.		1	1					1
		40	.	39	1	40				39	1
2-5	LO	504	.	497	8	504				497	8
2-5	Other	27	.	11	16	27				11	16
		531	.	507	24	531				507	24
6+8	LO	52	.		52	52					52
6+8	Other	10	.		10	10					10
		62	.		62	62					62
7	LO	28	.	5	2	7	11	10	21	17	11
7	Other	20	.	1	1	2		18	18	1	19
		48	.	6	3	9	11	28	39	17	31
9	LO	34	.	12	2	14	10	10	19	22	12
9	Other	57	.	2	6	7		50	50	2	55
		90	.	14	7	21	10	60	69	23	67
0	Other	6	.	.	.		.	.			6
		6	.	.	.		.	.			6
	LO	656	133	553	63	616	21	19	40	574	82
	Other	121	.	13	34	47		68	68	13	108
		777	.	566	97	663	21	88	108	587	190

45

isic	conf.	total		market			public			status	
		all	female	b-c	w-c	total	b-c	w-c	total	b-c	w-c
1	LO	27	.	27		27				27	
1	AC	1	.		1	1					1
		28	.	27	1	28				27	1
2-5	LO	595	.	585	9	595				585	9
2-5	FTF	2	.		2	2					2
2-5	AC	4	.		4	4					4
2-5	FR	24	.		24	24					24
2-5	Other	10	.	10		10				10	
		634	.	595	39	634				595	39
6+8	LO	75	.		75	75					75
6+8	FTF	15	.		15	15					15
		90	.		90	90					90
7	LO	31	.	7	2	8	12	10	22	19	12
7	FTF	13	.		2	2		11	11		13
7	CO1	2	.					2	2		2
7	Other	12	.		2	2		10	10		12
		58	.	7	6	12	12	34	46	19	39
9	LO	50	.	14	2	17	12	21	33	26	23
9	FTF	78	.					78	78		78
9	AC	7	.		2	2		5	5		7
9	CO1	11	.					11	11		11
9	Other	7	.	3	5	7				3	5
		153	.	17	8	25	12	115	127	29	124
0	FTF	4	.	.	.	.	.	.			4
0	AC	2	.	.	.	.	.	.			2
		6	.	.	.	.	.	.			6
	LO	777	167	634	88	722	24	31	55	657	119
	FTF	112	.		19	19		89	89		112
	AC	14	.		7	7		5	5		14
	FR	24	.		24	24					24
	CO1	13	.					13	13		13
	Other	29	6	13	6	19		10	10	13	17
		969	.	646	144	790	24	149	173	670	299

Table DE 5/4 Union Membership by Sex, Industry and Status — DENMARK — year: 1960

Table DE 5/5 Union Membership by Sex, Industry and Status									DENMARK	
year:1970		total		market			public			status
isic	conf.	all	female	b-c	w-c	total	b-c	w-c	total	b-c	w-c
1	LO	24	.	24		24				24	
1	AC	1	.		1	1					1
		25	.	24	1	25				24	1
2-5	LO	634	.	621	12	634				621	12
2-5	FTF	4	.		4	4					4
2-5	AC	8	.		8	8					8
2-5	FR	30	.		30	30					30
2-5	Other	39	.	23	16	39				23	16
		714	.	644	69	714				644	69
6+8	LO	107	.		107	107					107
6+8	FTF	29	.		29	29					29
6+8	Other	6	.		6	6					6
		141	.		141	141					141
7	LO	28	.	4	1	5	11	12	23	15	13
7	FTF	14	.		3	3		11	11		14
7	CO1	2	.					2	2		2
7	Other	16	.	8	1	10		6	6	8	7
		60	.	12	6	18	11	31	42	24	37
9	LO	103	.	22	5	27	20	56	77	42	61
9	FTF	103	.					103	103		103
9	AC	22	.		6	6		16	16		22
9	CO1	8	.					8	8		8
9	Other	9	.		4	4		5	5		9
		245	.	22	15	37	20	188	209	42	204
0	FTF	7	.	.	.	.	.	.			7
0	AC	3	.	.	.	.	.	.			3
		9	.	.	.	.	.	.			9
	LO	896	254	671	126	797	31	68	100	702	194
	FTF	156	.		35	35		114	114		156
	AC	33	.		15	15		16	16		33
	FR	30	.		30	30					30
	CO1	10	.					10	10		10
	Other	69	.	32	27	58		11	11	32	38
		1,195	.	702	233	936	31	219	250	734	461

Table DE 5/6 Union Membership by Sex, Industry and Status											DENMARK
year:1979		total		market			public			status	
isic	conf.	all	female	b-c	w-c	total	b-c	w-c	total	b-c	w-c
1	LO	19	.	19		19				19	
1	AC	2	.		2	2					2
		21	.	*19*	*2*	*21*				*19*	*2*
2-5	LO	753	.	736	17	753				736	17
2-5	FTF	5	.		5	5					5
2-5	AC	23	.		23	23					23
2-5	FR	24	.		24	24					24
2-5	Other	72	.	16	56	72				16	56
		877	.	*753*	*124*	*877*				*753*	*124*
6+8	LO	178	.		178	178					178
6+8	FTF	55	.		55	55					55
6+8	Other	13	.		13	13					13
		247	.		*247*	*247*					*247*
7	LO	25	.				10	15	25	10	15
7	FTF	18	.		5	5		13	13		18
7	CO1	1	.					1	1		1
7	Other	14	.	6	3	9		5	5	6	8
		58	.	*6*	*8*	*14*	*10*	*34*	*44*	*16*	*42*
9	LO	275	.	46	7	54	25	196	221	71	204
9	FTF	192	.					192	192		192
9	AC	43	.		13	13		30	30		43
9	CO1	5	.					5	5		5
9	Other	30	.	1	8	9		21	21	1	29
		544	.	*47*	*29*	*75*	*25*	*444*	*469*	*71*	*473*
0	FTF	7	.	.	.	.	.	.	.		7
0	AC	2	.	.	.	.	.	.	.		2
		9	.	.	.	.	.	.	.		*9*
	LO	1,250	516	802	203	1004	34	211	246	836	414
	FTF	277	.		65	65		205	205		277
	AC	70	.		38	38		30	30		70
	FR	24	.		24	24					24
	CO1	6	.					6	6		6
	Other	129	.	23	80	103		26	26	23	106
		1,756	*516*	*825*	*410*	*1234*	*34*	*478*	*513*	*859*	*897*

Table DE 5/7 Union Membership by Sex, Industry and Status									DENMARK	
year:1984		total		market			public			status	
isic	conf.	all	female	b-c	w-c	total	b-c	w-c	total	b-c	w-c
1	LO	20	.	20		20				20	
1	AC	2	.		2	2					2
1	Other	1	.		1	1					1
		23	.	20	3	23				20	3
2-5	LO	774	.	747	27	774				747	27
2-5	FTF	6	.		6	6					6
2-5	AC	25	.		25	25					25
2-5	FR	24	.		24	24					24
2-5	Other	91	.	16	74	91				16	74
		919	.	763	156	919				763	156
6+8	LO	186	.		186	186					186
6+8	FTF	59	.		59	59					59
6+8	Other	17	.		17	17					17
		262	.		262	262					262
7	LO	33	.				11	22	33	11	22
7	FTF	10	.		8	8		3	3		10
7	CO1	1	.					1	1		1
7	Other	18	.	6	12	18				6	12
		62	.	6	20	25	11	25	36	17	45
9	LO	387	.	63	7	71	24	293	317	87	300
9	FTF	227	.					227	227		227
9	AC	45	.		14	14		31	31		45
9	CO1	16	.					16	16		16
9	Other	38	.	1	14	15		23	23	1	37
		712	.	64	36	99	24	590	613	88	624
0	FTF	6	.	.	.		.	.			6
0	AC	2	.	.	.		.	.			2
		9	.	.	.		.	.			9
	LO	1,399	630	830	220	1,050	35	314	349	865	534
	FTF	309	214		73	73		229	229		309
	AC	74	15		41	41		31	31		74
	FR	24			24	24					24
	CO1	17	1					17	17		17
	Other	164	41	22	118	140		23	23	22	141
		1,986	901	852	476	1,328	35	614	649	887	1,099

49

Table DE 6/1 Dependent Labour Force by Sex, Industry and Status   DENMARK

1921 isic	total all	female	market b-c	w-c	total	public b-c	w-c	total	status b-c	w-c
1	171	.	.	.	.	.	.	.	155	16
2-5	278	.	.	.	.	.	.	.	249	29
6+8	76	.	.	.	.	.	.	.	17	60
7	62	.	.	.	.	.	.	.	29	33
9	268	.	.	.	.	.	.	.	225	43
0	16	.	.	.	.	.	.	.	.	.
	871	*309*	.	.	.	.	.	.	*674*	*181*

Table DE 6/2 Dependent Labour Force by Sex, Industry and Status   DENMARK

1930 isic	total all	female	market b-c	w-c	total	public b-c	w-c	total	status b-c	w-c
1	242	.	.	.	.	.	.	.	217	25
2-5	331	.	.	.	.	.	.	.	297	34
6+8	112	.	.	.	.	.	.	.	23	89
7	69	.	.	.	.	.	.	.	39	30
9	286	.	.	.	.	.	.	.	220	66
0	21	.	.	.	.	.	.	.	.	.
	1,060	*269*	.	.	.	.	.	.	*795*	*244*

Table DE 6/3 Dependent Labour Force by Sex, Industry and Status   DENMARK

1950 isic	total all	female	market b-c	w-c	total	public b-c	w-c	total	status b-c	w-c
1	218	.	206	12	.	.	.	.	206	12
2-5	581	.	511	70	.	.	.	.	511	70
6+8	165	.	32	133	.	.	.	.	32	133
7	121	.	.	.	.	.	.	.	62	60
9	332	.	.	.	.	.	.	.	190	142
0	40	.	.	.	.	.	.	.	24	17
	1,458	*483*	.	.	.	.	.	.	*1,025*	*433*

Table DE 6/4 Dependent Labour Force by Sex, Industry and Status   DENMARK

1960	total		market			public			status	
isic	all	female	b-c	w-c	total	b-c	w-c	total	b-c	w-c
1	146	.	.	.	.	.	.	.	137	9
2-5	674	.	.	.	.	.	.	.	572	101
6+8	195	.	.	.	.	.	.	.	41	153
7	132	.	.	.	.	.	.	.	65	67
9	388	.	.	.	.	.	.	.	179	209
0	56	.	.	.	.	.	.	.	32	24
	1,590	526	.	.	.	.	.	.	1,026	564

Table DE 6/5 Dependent Labour Force by Sex, Industry and Status   DENMARK

1970	total		market			public			status	
isic	all	female	b-c	w-c	total	b-c	w-c	total	b-c	w-c
1	63	.	.	.	.	.	.	.	57	7
2-5	778	.	.	.	.	.	.	.	626	152
6+8	260	.	.	.	.	.	.	.	48	212
7	132	.	.	.	.	.	.	.	58	74
9	573	.	.	.	.	.	.	.	198	375
0	67	.	.	.	.	.	.	.	52	15
	1,873	715	.	.	.	.	.	.	1,038	835

51

Table DE 6/6 Dependent Labour Force by Sex, Industry and Status DENMARK										
1979	**total**		**market**			**public**			**status**	
isic	all	female	b-c	w-c	total	b-c	w-c	total	b-c	w-c
1	52	.	.	.	.	.	.	.	.	.
2-5	705	.	.	.	.	.	.	.	.	.
6+8	306	.	.	.	.	.	.	.	.	.
7	155	.	.	.	.	.	.	.	.	.
9	958	.	.	.	.	.	.	.	.	.
0	49	.	.	.	.	.	.	.	.	.
	2,224	*1,018*	.	.	*1,534*	.	.	*690*	*982*	*1,242*

Table DE 6/7 Dependent Labour Force by Sex, Industry and Status DENMARK										
1984	**total**		**market**			**public**			**status**	
isic	all	female	b-c	w-c	total	b-c	w-c	total	b-c	w-c
1	70	.	.	.	.	.	.	.	.	.
2-5	702	.	.	.	.	.	.	.	.	.
6+8	385	.	.	.	.	.	.	.	.	.
7	170	.	.	.	.	.	.	.	.	.
9	1,067	.	.	.	.	.	.	.	.	.
0	25	.	.	.	.	.	.	.	.	.
	2,419	*1,146*	.	.	*1,630*	.	.	*789*	*1,024*	*1,396*

Chapter 3: FRANCE

LIST OF UNION CONFEDERATIONS: name,abbreviation and foundation year

---

1 *Confédération Générale du Travail* (CGT): 1895-
General Federation of Labour

2 *Confédération Générale du Travail Unitaire* (CGTU): 1920-1935,
Unitarian Federation of Labour (broke away from the CGT in 1920;
the two organizations reunited in 1935)

3 *Confédération Générale du Travail-Force Ouvrière* (FO): 1948-
Reformist Federation of Labour (broke away from CGT in 1948)

4 *Confédération Française du Travailleurs Chrétiens* (CFTC): 1919-
French Federation of Christian Workers (1964-: *CFTC-Maintenue)*

5 *Confédération Française Démocratique du Travail* (CFDT): 1964-
Democratic Federation of French Labour (emerged from CFTC)

6 *Confédération Générale des Cadres* (CGC): 1944-
General Federation of Staff Employee Unions
(in 1980 renamed: *Confédération Française d'Encadrement* (CGC-CFE)

7 *Fédération de l'éducation Nationale* (FEN): 1948-
National Federation of Unions in Education (disaffiliated from
CGT in 1948

---

1. AGGREGATE MEMBERSHIP STATISTICS

1.1 General Series

Judging by the miserable state of union membership statistics in
France, one is tempted to believe that French unions are still deeply
inspired by the classical views and practices of syndicalism. Numbers
bring moderation. Or in the words of Albert Levy - not a theorist
himself but the treasurer (sic!) of the early CGT: 'Le nombre de
syndiqués n'a pas d'importance, le syndicat n'est qu'un entraîner. Le
syndicat, c'est comme un tas de paves, comme une butte de terre sur
laquelle on plante un chapeau et autour duquel on bat le rappel. (...)
Pas besoin de beaucoup de membres dans un syndicat, il vaut mieux qu'il
n'y en ait beaucoup, car le lourde modération entre avec le grand
nombre.' (quoted in: Birien, 1978: 88) But this is of course only
part of the truth. The other side is that French unions are constantly
outcompeting each other in 'inflating' their membership support. In no

other country in Western Europe is the trade union system to such a degree pluralistic and conflictual, and its membership support that much volatile. In no other European country - perhaps with the exception of the new democratic nations: Greece, Portugal and Spain - are union membership data to such a high extent subject to speculation and partis pris by both union organizations and students.

The most careful and methodical study of union membership in France is of Antoine Prost and relates to the CGT and the CGTU in the inter-war years (Prost, 1964). On the basis of this study it is possible to construct a time series of their membership between the wars. I have added the membership of the CGTC and that of three federations of staff associations.

Union membership data since the Second World War have rightly been called a 'disaster area' (Shorter & Tilly, 1974: 149). Their verdict that 'no time series worthy of mention are available' (ibid.) is still true today. Such series as published, for example the series of Lefranc concerning the CGT during the first two decades after the war (Lefranc, 1969), are of a 'precision trompeuse' (Harmel, 1970). Students of French unionism use different methods of calculation for different years and confederations. Contradicting statements abound and there are often large gaps or sudden revisions of the data. France is the only country in this study where there is no statistical agency or research institute - of governments or the unions themselves - which collects and ascertains data on union membership or compiles and evaluates existing sources and reported figures.

By rigorously applying a uniform criterion to all the data found in published sources, I have nevertheless attempted to construct a time series covering the membership of the major confederations between 1913 and 1985 with an exceptions for 1939-1945. Given the method used, the data represent annual averages rather than end-of-year data. Given the wide use of interpolation and estimates, the series cannot, in my opinion, claim to be an exact annual representation of the actual membership. It rather constitutes a starting-point for depicting broad trends on the basis of five-or seven-year moving averages.

In evaluating reported membership claims, I have generally tried to apply the criterion developed in Prost's study of the CGT. His definition of union membership in France, which was also adopted by Annie Kriegel in her analysis of the CGT's membership at the end of the First World War, is based on actual dues payment during a year (Prost, 1964:7-12; Kriegel, 1966: 21-). Membership claims in France relate mainly to the distribution of the annual renewable fee, the so-called carte confédérale. However, these 'cards' are distributed to affiliates and locals as a matter of convenience on the basis of last year's figures, sold at very low fees or given for free, distributed during strikes, etc. and include one-day members (see also: Lorwin, 1954: 171-175; Barjonet, 1968: 64; Caire, 1971: 330-333). It should be recalled that check-off agreements are unknown or even prohibited in France, and that all the sources mentioned specify that dues rates are low, i.e. far less than 0.5% of the gross earnings of an average French worker (Reynaud, 1975: I, 140-). Monthly dues are paid by buying the so-called timbre syndical. Although most rule books specify that full membership requires 12 monthly payments (see the extracts in: Reynaud, 1975: II,31-), 6-9 payments per year is common practice and most confederations have in fact accommodated to 10 (Barjonet, 1968; Reynaud, 1975; Mouriaux, 1982), to 9 in the case of the CFDT (Landier, 1980: 76)

54

or even to 8 (Adam, 1983: 40) monthly payments. For instance, the CGT allocates representation to its congresses on the basis of 10 monthly dues payments, while the CFDT accommodates 9 monthly payments. Both Prost and Kriegel have convincingly argued that, in the case of France, 10 monthly payments constitute a reasonable criterion of 'normal membership', avoiding both under- and overestimation. Thus, membership claims can be recalculated into membership figures which better approach reality - and allow for comparisons with union movements abroad - on the basis of congressional data or by deflating the claims on the basis of the average number of monthly payments per member calculated from financial data.

In short, all the membership figures shown in table FR1-FR5 relate to paying members on the basis of 10 monthly payments per year. Retired and self-employed members are excluded throughout. It should be recalled that my series is entirely based on a secondary analysis of the literature - making comparisons and placing judgments on the data reported in written and, mostly, published sources. I will specify this for each confederation separately:

(1) *Confédération Générale du Travail* (CGT)

- 1918-1920: Labi, 1964: 246.
- 1921-1937: Prost, 1964: 35; the figures for 1922, 1923, 1925, 1927, 1929, 1931 and 1933 are interpolated.
- 1938-1939: my estimate from Prost, 1964: 42-48.
- 1945-1955: Lefranc, 1969: 79; Caire, 1971: 334. Their figures relate to 'cards'. I have deflated the figures on the basis of average annual dues payments in months based on financial statements by the CGT. See for this period and the following years also the reconstruction in Harmel, 1969; Harmel, 1982.
- 1956-68: Lefranc, ibid., and Caire, ibid. both give figures which refer to the number of members 'declared represented' at the CGT congresses taking place every two or three years. One of the problems is that pensioners seem to be included: 210,000 in 1961, 220,000 in 1963, 187,00 both in 1965 and 1967. In this period about 3% of the delegates at the CGT's congresses were retired workers, increasing to 6-7% in the 1970s. I have deflated the membership claims of the CGT by one fifth (assuming on average 8 monthly payments) and subtracted a likewise deflated number of pensioners.
- 1969-1985: based on statements of the CGT made in its periodical Le Peuple. Reported membership included a specified and until the late 1970s increasing number of pensioners (around 300,000 members). These claims (with and sometimes without pensioners) can also be found in: Landier, 1980: 78 (until 1977); Adam, 1983: annex 3 (until 1980); Reynaud, 1984: 79 (until 1980) and Mouriaux, 1986: 29 (until 1983). In deflating these claims I have taken into account that the monthly dues payments have declined to 7 or perhaps 6 times a year. Both Birien (1978: 88) and Landier (1981: 56-60) quote statements made by confederal treasurers deploring the lack of financial discipline in the CGT. A careful analysis of the CGT's claim for 1969 by Harmel (1970) yielded the figure of '1,7 million adhérents a dix timbres' in that year. Mouriaux (1982: 21) states that the CGT's membership after 1975 is falling

off, 'sans que les déclaration officielles permettent de suivre clairement l'évolution'. My reconstruction of the large fall in CGT membership after 1975 is broadly similar to the one made by Jack Kergoat in Le Monde of 18 May 1982. At the time this was contested by the CGT (see: Reynaud, 1984: 79) but Kergoat's series was largely confirmed by later statements of the CGT's general secretary (confessing a loss of 700,000 members between 1977 and 1983, Le Matin of 25 May 1985). Between 1983 and 1985 the CGT suffered a further loss of 145,000 members (Financial Times of 24 July 1986). The CGT's merchant shipping officers union is quoted as having admitted that the CGT as a whole is 'reduced to less than 800,000 members in 1985'.

(2) *Confédération Générale du Travail Unitaire* (CGTU)

- 1921-1934: Prost, 1964: 35-36. I have interpolated the figures for 1922, 1923, 1925 and 1927.

(3) *Confédération Générale du Travail-Force Ouvrière* (FO)

- 1948-1968: The FO is probably the least open organization when it comes to information about its membership or finances. From its very start, in 1948, the FO invariably claimed a support of one million members. As this was not taken seriously by friend or foe, the organization finally began in the 1970s to provide figures on the annual numbers of distributed 'cards' in order to substantiate its claim of being the second-largest confederation in France. At the time of its foundation, the CGT credited its rival with 'at most 200,000 members'. Less partisan observers believe that some 330-340,000 members are likely to have followed the FO in its break away from the CGT (Revue syndicaliste of 2 April 1949; L'économie of 2 November 1949). This figure corresponds with the number of seats in the *Commission Supérieure des Conventions Collective* allocated to the FO at the time. Bergounioux (1979: 115) estimates that the FO had 350,000 paying members in 1950. During the first twenty years of its existence, the FO's membership is believed to have varied between 300,000 and 500,000. Some observers attributed about 400,000 members to the FO in 1958-59 (Entreprise of 16 May 1959; Informations industrielles et commerciales of June 1959). A figure of 500,000 is mentioned for 1967, at the eve of the outburst of student and worker militancy in May 1968 (Reynaud, 1975: I,140; Lefranc, 1969: 205). As the FO's membership was and still is heavily concentrated in the public sector, it is a reasonable assumption that its membership was on a slow growth path during the 1960s.
- 1968-1985: It has been estimated that the FO gained some 100,000 members in the course of 1968 and 1969 (Lefranc, 1969: 205; and Rioux, in Le Nouvel Observateur of 27 April 1970, whose estimates are rather balanced with respect to all confederations and in accordance with later submitted figures). Applying the same method to the FO as we did in the case of the CGT, Harmel calculated that the FO had 617,429 members in 1970, compared with 810,886 'cards' having been distributed (Harmel, 1972). Mouriaux (1986: 29) presents an severely inflated 'membership series' for the FO between 1968 and 1983 based on 'cards' being issued and sales

figures of its journal. The inclusion of retired members adds to the overstatement of the FO's membership. Similar figures can be found in Landier (1980: 77); Landier (1981: 65), but this author adds some partial information on the average number of dues payments in months. This serves to confirm the thesis of Bergounioux (1979: 216) that the FO follows the CGT's practice of accommodating to 6-7 monthly payments. I have deflated the FO's claims accordingly, taking into account that a probably growing number of retired members - the more likely given the FO's over-representation in the public sector - is hidden in its publicized figures. For instance, in 1979 the FO's claim of nearly one million adherents is to be compared with a real paying membership of 720,000 - or 600-650,000 if we are to believe the French employers' association in the metal industry. Finally, between 1983 and 1985 the FO has claimed a further growth from 1,150,000 to 1,180,000 in 1984 (Le Figaro of 8 July 1985) and 'nearly 1,2 million' in 1985 (Financial Times of 24 July 1986), figures which appear to be grossly exaggerated (Le Monde Diplomatique, February 1986).

(4) *Confédération Française du Travailleurs Chrétiens* (CFTC)

- 1919-1939: the membership development of the CFTC in the inter-war years has been reconstructed on the basis of the reports it submitted to the *Confédération Internationale des Syndicats Chrétiens* (CISC - the International Confederation Federation of Christian Trade Unions before World War Two). As a rule, the CFTC overstated its membership by large numbers. My corrected figures correspond with those found - for some years, that is - in other sources: Lorwin (1966: 64) for 1920: 65,000 full paying members as against a claim of 140,000; Prost (1964: 49-50) for 1934-1937; Adam (1964: 49) and Adam (1983: annex 3, table 1) for 1939 and referring to *côtisants* or paying members.
- 1945-1963: Adam (1964: 49) gives a cautious estimate of the CGTC's membership until the eve of its secularization and subsequent split in 1964, especially if one considers the CFTC's claim running as high as three quarters of a million members in the immediate post-war years. Adam's figures are largely confirmed by the index published much later by the CFDT in its revue La CFDT Ajourd'hui (1975-). Recalculations for the years 1948, 1961 and 1963 on the basis of this index and taking into account that the CFDT defines paying membership (*côtisants*) on the basis of 9 monthly payments, show very slight deviations indeed (Adam, 1983: annex 3; however the author now accepts the wider definition of membership).
- 1964-1985: The year before the split between the majority, reconstituting itself as the CFDT, and the minority, also called the *CFTC-Maintenue*, the CFTC had, on my definition, about 500,000 members (see also: Adam, 1983). We know that the unions which supported the majority gained over 70% of the votes at the 1964 congress (Hamon & Rotman, 1982). It is also possible to calculate, with the help of the index mentioned above, that the CFDT did probably take off with 420-440,000 members. On that assumption, the CFTC's membership can have been at most 60-80,000. Unfortunately, the CFTC never published any credible figure on its membership between the mid-1960s and the mid-1970s. Then, it

started to claim 200,000-250,000 members (Landier 1975: 39-40, but most students put the CFTC at much lower figures (for instance, Reynaud, 1975: I,140; II,124-125). The CFTC did actually report some percentages on annual membership growth after 1971 (Landier, 1980: 81; Reynaud, 1983). Between 1964 and 1968 the CFTC's paying membership might have been pretty stable. None of the sources mentions that it gained new strength during the 1968-1969 period (see also Le Nouvel Observateur of 27 April 1970). Thus, starting with 80,000 members in 1970, I have calculated its membership in the 1970s and 1980s on the basis of the annual growth rates which the organization reported. As a result my figures are much lower than the membership figures claimed by the CFTC. But, again, it should be stressed that these claims - as is the case for its competitors - refer normally to a purposely vaguely defined following and are especially instrumental in defending a claim on overall representativity and financial support of the state.

(5) *Confédération Française Démocratique du Travail* (CFDT)

-   1964-85: from 1970 to 1983 an annual series exists dividing the CFDT membership in *côtisants* (paying members) and *adhérents* (Birien, 1978: 109; Landier, 1980: 75-76; Landier, 1981: 62; Adam, 1983: annex 3; Mouriaux, 1986: 29). This series can be extended backwards on the basis of the published index figures for the period 1964-1970, and forwards on the basis of the 1984 and 1985 figures released by Libération of 11/6/1985 and also reported in the Financial Times of 24/7/1986. The CFDT refers to *côtisants* as those members paying 9 monthly dues. I have therefore deflated the published figures for 'paying members' by nine tenth. Apparently, the CFDT calculates its 'following' by simply adding up another 30% to its *côtisants*, assuming that all other organizations do the same. The CFDT's membership does not include pensioners. For some years it has given its membership among retired workers additionally. For instance, in 1977 it reported the membership of 74,560 retired workers, increasing to 78,300 in 1978.

(6) *Confédération Générale des Cadres* (CGC)

-   1945-85: In 1945 the CGC claimed to have 'sold' 78.681 'cards' (Cadres, 1945, no.8). For some years (1946-1952, 1955-1956, 1974--1982) the CGC gave a rough indication of its membership in Le Creuset or in Cadres et Maîtrise. Generally, it has tended to overstate its membership by large numbers: it claimed 100,000--140,000 members between 1946 and 1952, 120,000 in the mid-1950s, 250,000 in 1968 and 1971; it boosted an increase to 280,000 in 1975 and to 325,000 in 1979, followed by a decline to about 300,000 in 1983. Crozier, whose study did not include an estimate of its membership judged the CGC - around 1960 - 'a corporatist and narrow-minded body that works mostly apart from the rest of the labor movement'. According to him the CGC existed 'primarily because of the necessity of presenting candidates for the election to the *comités d'entreprise* (enterprise councils, jv)' (Crozier, 1966: 116). After having been recognized in 1948 as a 'representative organization' with respect to supervisors and technical staff, the CGC seems to have enjoyed a relatively quiet period of

hegemony within this domain until the mid-1960s (Grunberg &
Mouriaux, 1979: 80-; Descostes & Robert, 1984: 207-). Reynaud,
probably referring to the late 1960s, estimated that the CGC organized only half of the 120,000 technicians and supervisors it
claimed to represent, which would still be more than all other
confederations together (Reynaud 1975: I, 141; Groux 1983: 88-).
Around this time, internal conflicts led to disaffiliation of its
unions in the energy sector and the foundation, in 1969, of a new
federation of supervisors and technical staffs, the *Union des
Cadres et Techniciens* (UCT), which however failed to gain representative status under French law and returned to the CGC after
its reform in 1980. The membership of the *Union des Cadres et
Techniciens* (UCT) was put at around 7 to 8 thousand in 1969 by
Reynaud (ibid) and, at maximum, 10-15,000 in the early 1970s
(Grunberg & Mouriaux 1979: 85; Descostes & Robert, 1984: 223). The
total number of unionized 'cadres' has been estimated at 120,000
in 1969 (Groux 1983: 88-). Estimating the CGC's share at about 60%
and allowing for the fact that about one third of its membership
is in other domains (for instance 'commercial agents' (Le Creuset,
1955, no.230), we can put the total membership of the CGC at
maximally 100,000-120,000 in the late 1960s. Rioux, in Le Nouvel
Observateur of 27 April 1970, attributed 150,000 members to the
CGC in early 1970, but that may have included the UCT's members.
Some authors put the growth of the CGC at 12% between 1968 and
1973 (Descostes & Robert, 1984: 214) and at 5,5% from 1975 to 1977
(Landier, 1980: 82). In 1978 the CGC announced a membership of
exactly 322,181, followed by the remark that this figure had been
'calculated according to the customary norms of the unions of wage
and salary earners' (quoted in: Landier 1980: 80). Three observations must be made regarding the CGC's figures. First, they
suffer from the same 'customary' exaggeration as those of the
other organizations. I have put this at 30%. Second, the CGC
membership includes self-employed persons, probably a declining
number over time. Third, the CGC's membership also includes pensioners. For instance, its mining federation included over 35%
retired members in the 1950s (Descostes & Robert, 1984: Chapter
5). In sum, taking only 50-60% of the CGC's reported membership
claims seems a reasonable guess. This corresponds with the difference between the membership (302,122) it claimed and the
membership (215,000, presumably including pensioners), which was
'represented' at its 1980 congress (Landier, 1981: 67). After 1982
the membership of the CGC (now CFE-CGC) seems to have been fairly
constant (Terrain, 1985).

(7) *Fédération de l'éducation Nationale* (FEN)

- 1948-85: The FEN combines some forty unions in education, including some friendly societies, pensioners unions and insurance
  bodies. The Federation experienced a steady growth pattern, from
  130,000 members in 1948 when it disaffiliated from the CGT, to
  over half a million in the late 1970s (Chéramy, 1974; Vivier,
  1985) benefitting from vast expansion in educational services. The
  FEN is the only organization which regularly publicized its
  membership. At the time of its annual or biennial congresses the
  membership of the previous year was made known. In recent years,

the FEN has suffered considerable membership losses, partly because of the stagnation of its domain (primary and secondary schools), and partly because of increased competition from the CFDT and the FO, both of which have started competing unions in education. In 1985, the FEN reported a membership of 451,447 (Vivier, 1985), which is 9% less than in 1982 and 15% less than in 1978. Evaluating the FEN's membership claims is difficult. Given its 'high service' character one may assume that it requires its members to pay full (12 monthly) dues rates; for the same reason, and also given its location in the public sector, reported membership probably includes a sizable proportion of retired teachers. Not having been able to find data on either effect, I have chosen to make no adjustments and simply reproduce the FEN's reported membership.

Additionally, I have included the membership of three union federations of higher technical and managerial staffs before the foundation of the CGC. These are: (a) the *Union Syndicale des Technicienc de l'Industrie, du Commerce et de l'Agriculture* (USTICA), founded in 1919 and later, after statutory changes in 1928 and 1932 also abbreviated UST or USTEI; (b) the *Union Sociale des Ingénieurs Catholiques* (USIC), and (c) the *Union des Syndicats d'Ingénieurs Français* (USIF). The latter two federations also originated in the direct aftermath of the First World War. During the Popular Front the USTEI joined the re-unified CGT. In order to counterbalance militant white-collar unionization, the French employers' association helped constituting a new federation of technical and managerial staff unions. This *Confédération Générale des Cadres de l'économie Française* (CGCEF) was founded in 1937 and embraced both the USIC and USIF. The new organization became the direct predecessor of the postwar *Confédération Générale des Cadres* (CGC). The membership figures are calculated from Descostes & Robert, 1984: 73-81 (for USTICA, UST or USTEI), 81-87 (for USIC) and 66-73 (for USIF), partly interpreted on the basis of the detailed graphs presented. The estimated membership of CGCEF between 1937 and 1939 is derived from the returns to the *Fédération Internationale des Employés et Techniciens* (FIET).

Not included in the series is the membership of friendly societies, the so-called *Amicales*, and of other independent or 'yellow' unions in the pre-war period. Nor is the membership of the federations of revolutionary syndicalists or anarchists. The latter's membership is only known for some years and dwindled from 12,000 to 2,000 between 1927 and 1932 if one is to belief the figures reported by the Anarchist International available in the archives of the International Institute of Social History in Amsterdam. Saposs (1931) mentions some ten thousand members of the revolutionary syndicalists, an offshoot of the communist CGTU, around 1930.

The post-1945 data include only the membership of the five main confederations and of the FEN. Thus, not included is the membership of independent unions and some smaller confederations. Of these 'minor' or 'independent' confederations, which have never been able to gain representative status under the French law (Mouriaux, 1983: 30-31), the most important is probably the *Confédération des Syndicats Libres* (CSL), previously called the *Confédération Française du Travail* (CFT). This confederation was politically inspired by 'Gaullism' and combines a number of company unions, having its stronghold in the car factories of

Peugeot-Talbot and Citroën. Most French students put its membership somewhere around 50,000 members; in 1975 it claimed 82,331 'adhérents verifiés' (Birien, 1978: 71). Another 'rightist' or 'Gaullist' confederation, the *Confédération Générale des Syndicats Indépendents* (CGSI), founded in 1947, seems to have disappeared and its remaining membership has joined the CFTC. It is possible that still some 2,000 members are associated with the anarcho-syndicalist *Confédération Nationale du Travail* (CNT), according to Liaisons Sociales (1980, no.40). The *Confédération Nationale des Salariés en France* (CNSF) has mainly members in road transport, but no figures are known. Neither have I come across any credible figure for the 'reformist' *Confédération Autonome du Travail* (CAT).

Estimates of the combined membership of these confederations and unions vary between 100-150,000 (the latter figure is mentioned by Adam 1983: 41), but nothing is known about the pattern of growth or decline over the years. In Works Council elections, independent union candidates have generally not been able to attract more than 5% of the overall vote. The best we can say is that, by omitting the 'independent' federations and unions, the figures underestimate union membership in France by at maximum 5%.

1.2 Retired Members

All figures are calculated so as to exclude retired members

1.3 Female Members

See under 2.4

2. MEMBERSHIP BY INDUSTRY AND STATUS

Only for the period between both World Wars is it possible, on the basis of the study of the CGT(U)'s membership (Prost, 1966: 178-194, tables I-VIV), to disaggregate union membership by major industrial sector and status groups. My tables are derived from this study. Note that the following list does not apply to the CFTC or the white-collar and staff associations. No disaggregation by industry of the membership is possible for the latter organizations.

2.1 Classification by Industry

   1 Agriculture: *agriculture et fôrets*

2-4 Mining, manufacturing, gas, water & electricity: *alimentation; allumettes, ameublement; bijouterie; bois; céramique; chapeliers; cuirs et peaux; dessinateurs; éclairage; établiisements d'état; feuillardiers; habillement; journalistes; livre; livre et papier; magazins de guerre; métaux, papier; papier et carton; poudreries; produits chimiques; sciage et tabletterie; sous-sol; tabac; tabacs et allumettes; teinturiers; techniciens; textile; textile et vête-*

ment; tonneau; verriers

5 Construction: *bâtiment*

6+8 Commerce, Banking & Insurances: *employés* (50% in industry); *finances; monaie; pharmacie et droguerie; voyageurs et représentants*

7 Transport & communication: *cheminots; chemins de fer; incrits maritimes; marins; mécaniciens marine; officiers marine; PTT; employés de la PTT; ouvriers de la PTT; agents de la PTT; officiers radio; ports et docks; transports; voiture et aviation*

9 Other services: *blanchisseurs et nettoyage; coiffeurs; enseignement; enseignement secondaire; fonctionnaires; instituteurs; police; personnel civil de guerre; marine et Etat; services de santé; services publics; spectacle*

2.2. Classification by Status

Of the federations belonging to the CGT and the CGTU, I have classified as non-manual: *dessinateurs, journalistes, techniciens, employés, pharmacie et droguerie, voyageurs et représentants, employés et agents de la PTT, aviation, officiers et mécaniciens marine, officiers radio, finances, monnaie, enseignement, fonctionnaires, instituteurs, personnel civil de guerre, marine et Etat, police, services publics* (50%), *services de santé, spectacle.* A rather rough classification by status can also be given for the membership of the *Confédération Française du Travailleurs Chrétiens* (CFTC). We know that this confederation was founded by a union of white collar employees, and that at the time of its foundation, in 1919, 60-70% of its membership was in this union. At the eve of the Popular Front, the CFTC's union of employees still was the largest affiliate and held 27.7% of the confederation's total membership (Prost, 1964: 49). Only during the 1936-1939 years did the CFTC start to rally manual workers in industry in great numbers and outside the strongholds it previously had in mining, textiles and railways. Also in the non-manual category are of course the members of the various association of technical and managerial staffs.

2.3. Public Sector Unionism

Still on the basis of Antoine Prost's study (in particular his tables XVII and XXII) it is possible to calculate the presence of the CGT and CGTU in the public sector. The following national federations organize members in the pubic sector: *enseignement, établissements d'état, fonctionnaires, instituteurs, police, personnel civil de guerre, marine et Etat, services de santé, services publics, chemin de fer, PTT.*

2.4. Classification of Membership after 1945

It is not possible to arrive at similarly disaggregated figures for the years after 1945. Unlike other countries, I do not have membership figures for each of the (affiliated) unions individually. Moreover, in contrast to the pre-war period no systematic data on the distribution of votes or delegates per affiliate in congress is available. To my knowledge there exists no serious study either. Thus, only for some years and some confederations we can make an estimate on the basis of surveys among congress delegates. However, it is very hazardous to infer from knowledge about the composition of delegate conferences statements on the composition of the membership at large. First, we do know little about the ways these surveys are conducted and it is normally not possible to ascertain their reliability or validity.

Second, certain groups - for instance female members or the unskilled - are likely to be under-represented in congresses, whereas the opposite is often true for categories such as civil servants and professional employees (see Crozier, 1966 about this distortion in French unionism in particular). Unfortunately, French union confederations have used the method of surveying their entire membership only very rarely.

From the Congress Reports of the *Confédération Générale du Travail* (CGT), it follows that between 1948 and 1963 the percentage of female delegates rose from 7.8 to 14%, then remained rather constant (14-16%) until 1972, and rose again to around 25% after 1975. The percentage of pensioners among delegates rose from 2% in 1963 to 7% in 1972 and remained at about that level since. Youths under the age of 25 were represented with 12-15% until 1975. In the past ten years their share fell to less than 7% in 1985. Similarly, until 1975 more than 60% of the congress delegates reportedly were blue collar workers in private industry; in 1978, 1982 and 1985 their share had fallen to 52.5%, 49.6% and 46.4% respectively. The share of state employees, without the nationalized sector, stood at about 16-17% between 1948 and 1972, rose to 21.8% in 1975 and 25.4% in 1985.

Only in 1975, the CGT commissioned a membership survey to the French Institute of Public Opinion, the results of which were published in Le Peuple (no.972 of 1-15 September 1975). It appeared that of its 'active members' 15% were below the age of 25 and 3.3% were 65 years or older. A further 7.8% of its members had retired. 25.5% of the CGT's membership were females and 69.6% manual workers (*manuoevres, OS, OP, and OHQ*). 22.8% of its members classified as clerical and administrative employee, and 7.7% as supervisors, technical and managerial staffs. The same survey placed 26.5% in the government sector and a further 16.1% in nationalized industries and public enterprises. 57.4% of the members were in the private sector of the economy. By broad sector of economic activity, the 1975 CGT survey showed the following distribution: 1.7% of its members were employed in agriculture; 58.5% in industry, mining and construction; 10.3% in transport & communication; 4.0% in commerce & retail; 1.3% in banking; and 23.6% in non-commercial services and public administration (see also: Birien, 1978: 89-92; Adam, 1983: 52-59). The metal workers federation was with 22% of the total confederal membership the single most important affiliate of the CGT, followed by the public service federation (10.3%), its railway federation (6.3%), the federation for Post Office workers (5.4%) and the one in chemical industry (5.1%). The 10 largest CGT federations represented 69.5% of the CGT's overall membership. From other sources (Smid, 1979: 198-9; Landier, 1980: 79; Landier, 1981: 57; Reynaud, 1983: 90; and Adam, 1983: 50), we know that the CGT Metalworkers' Federation lost a quarter of its membership between 1974 and 1978. Its reported (inflated) membership fell from 800,000 in 1945-7 to 287,000 in 1967. Late 1968 it claimed 391,000 and in 1974 420,000 members. Its membership fell to 320,000 in 1978 and less than 280,000 in 1980/81.

George Ribeil reports that the CGT railway federation has lost 39% of its members between 1974 and 1983 (Ribeil, 1986).

The *Confédération Française Démocratique du Travail* (CFDT), and its predecessor CFTC, did never conduct a similar survey of its membership. On the other hand, they seem to be better represented in general opinion polls about trade union membership in France than the CGT which normally fares badly in such polls (see: Adam, 1983: 58 on this point). The CFDT conducted a survey among congress delegates in 1976, 1979, 1982 and 1985, the results of which were published in La CFDT Ajourd'hui. From this material it is, however, difficult to conclude anything definite about the composition of its overall membership. In the late 1970s the CFDT claimed that 35-40% of its members were females (reported by Maruani, 1979: 16). If that is true, female members were extremely under-represented among congress delegates: only 14% in 1976, rising to 21% in 1985. Surveys in 1970 and 1977 (reported by Adam 1983: 54) indicated that the CFDT had a somewhat younger membership than the CGT. However, between 1979 and 1985 the share of the membership in the younger age groups (under the age of 30) fell from 25% to 18% of all delegates under 65. 2-3% of the delegates were 65 years or older.

The public and nationalized sector is well represented and increasingly important among the CFDT's congress delegates: 46.5% in 1976, 47.3% in 1979, over 50% in 1982 and 62.5% in 1985. The share of delegates from the private sector fell from 50.3% in 1976 and 50.8% in 1979 to 46% in 1982 and a mere 33% in 1985. 3-5% of the delegates had retired or were out of employment. Another feature of the CFDT's congresses is the small share of *manuoevres* or unskilled workers: 5% in 1976, 8% in 1982 and again 5% in 1985. The share of all manual workers fell from over 44% in 1976 to 34% in 1985. About 7-8% of the CFDT's congress delegates belonged to the category of higher staff and civil servants in leading positions.

The CFTC in 1950 and the CFDT in 1972 did provide some figures on its membership composition by broad economic sector (Adam, 1983: 58). It shows that the bulk of the membership was in services, both public and private. In 1950 less than a quarter of the CFTC's members were employed in the primary and secondary sectors of the economy (agriculture, mining, manufacturing and construction). In 1972 their share (47,2%) was still less than half of the CFDT's membership. Hamon & Rotman (1984:133) mention 40% in 1969 against 25% ten years earlier. The share of the government sector, including the professional armed forces and education, increased from 21.7% in 1950 to 25.3% in 1972; the semi-public sector (including health services) from 4.9% to 8.2%. There was a sharp fall in the membership share of the private service sector (commerce & retail, private transport, financial services) from 24.3% in 1950 to 9.4% in 1972, and in the nationalized sector (gas, water, electricity, public industry and public transport) from 20.5% to 9.1%. Finally, the CFDT's metalworkers' union did suffer a similar process of decline after the mid-1970s as its CGT sister organization. Its reported membership appears to have declined from 145,000 in 1976 to 118,000 in 1979 and less than 100,000 in 1981. With respect to the CFDT's railway federation, Ribeil (1986) reports a membership loss of 32.2% between 1974 and 1983.

The membership of *Force Ouvrière* (FO) is highly concentrated in the public sector. At the time of its foundation, in 1948, five among its ten largest affiliates, together representing 70% of the FO's overall membership, were public sector unions (Adam, 1965; Bergounioux,

64

1979; Adam, 1983). With the passing of time their position has only become stronger. In 1969 the ten largest FO affiliates represented 71.5% of total membership; among them were five public sector unions representing 45% of all FO members. From Bergounioux's study it can be calculated that the public sector unions together represented 56% of the total membership of the FO. The by far largest FO-affiliate is its public service federation (almost one-fifth of the FO's membership in 1969), followed by its Post Office federation (14%). The FO's federation of employees and supervisors held the third position with 8%, followed by the metalworkers' (7%) and the railway federation (4.5%). In 1969 4% of the FO members were employed in agriculture, 27% in mining, industry and construction, and 13% in private services (commerce, private transport, financial and other services) (Bergounioux, 1979: 230-231).

Unfortunately, data for the 1970s or 1980s are not known. It was estimated (Smid, 1979: 199) that the FO's metal workers federation had about 40-50,000 members in the mid-1970s, and that the FO had approximately 30,000 members in the category of technical and managerial staff. As far as I know, the FO never conducted a survey of its membership. Data on membership by sex, age or occupational status are therefore not available. From the 1969 list of affiliates, it appears that about 55% of the FO's membership were in the non-manual category. This can only be a rough estimate, however, as some unions are organizing non-manual employees alongside blue-collar workers.

Nothing is known that does permit a further disaggregation of the membership in the *Confédération Française du Travailleurs Chrétiens* (CFTC) after 1964. All we can guess is that its membership profile is likely to resemble that of the CFTC in the 1950s and 1960s. The membership of the *Confédération Générale des Cadres* (CGC) is all in the category of higher white-collar employees in the private (and nationalized) sector. The membership of the *Fédération de l'éducation Nationale* (FEN) is in the public sector and in the white-collar category.

It is a risky enterprise to estimate union density rates from such scattered data. A few general points can be made, though. All students of postwar unionism in France have stressed that the extent of unionization in the public sector is probably double as high as in the private sector. Secondly, unionization among non-manual employees, and in particular among technical and managerial staffs, is probably as high (or rather as low) as among manual workers. Union density in manufacturing industries is very low by international standards - for instance, a mere 18-20% was estimated by Smid (1979: 199), a similar figures appears in Adam (1983) for the metal industry in the 1970s, not counting the recent decline. Union density in commerce, financial and other private services is probably way below 10% (compare: Adam, 1983: 60-61).

3. LABOUR FORCE STATISTICS

The employment data are based on the 1921, 1926, 1931 and 1936, 1945, 1954, 1962, 1968 and 1975 population censuses (Flora, Kraus & Pfenning, 1986: 501-504). They include salaried employees, workers, casual workers and apprentices, and the unemployed. The breakdown of the unemployed by status group in 1975 is added on the basis of the results of the survey conducted by the French National Bureau of Statistics INSÉE and refer to April of that year. From 1968 the INSÉE has constructed an annual series, which was slightly revised in 1975, and gives also the necessary breakdowns by sex, industry and public or private sector. This series is published, and extended from year to year, in the Annuaire Statistique de la France (Statistical Yearbook of France), Paris, annual.

4. TABLES

table: FR 1/1	Membership by Confederation					FRANCE
year	CGT	CGTU	CFTC	Staff Ass	Other	total
	1	2	4			
1913	276			7	.	283
1914	206			8	.	214
1915	40			8	.	48
1916	77			8	.	85
1917	238			8	.	246
1918	490			9	.	499
1919	995		70	10	.	1,075
1920	1,193		65	6	.	1,264
1921	489	349	90	7	.	935
1922	490	365	73	8	.	936
1923	491	380	65	8	.	944
1924	491	396	63	10	.	960
1925	505	413	62	10	.	990
1926	525	431	65	11	.	1,032
1927	535	405	72	11	.	1,023
1928	555	370	79	12	.	1,016
1929	566	411	86	13	.	1,076
1930	577	323	85	15	.	1,000
1931	560	294	84	15	.	953
1932	533	259	88	15	.	895
1933	510	260	92	13	.	875
1934	491	264	97	13	.	865
1935	786		106	13	.	905
1936	2,584		275	20	.	2,879
1937	3,959		320	41	.	4,320
1938	3,469		305	40	.	3,814
1939	2,500		270	40	.	2,810

table: FR 1/2			Membership by Confederation					FRANCE
year	CGT	FO	CFTC	CFDT	CGC	FEN	ohter	total
	1	3	4	5	6	7		
1945	4,473		300		59		.	4,832
1946	4,979		365		80		.	5,424
1947	4,549		380		88		.	5,017
1948	2,856	350	320		88	163	.	3,677
1949	2,823	350	330		90	156	.	3,749
1950	2,915	350	335		105	156	.	3,861
1951	2,746	350	350		100	150	.	3,696
1952	2,337	350	350		95	173	.	3,305
1953	1,979	350	340		90	182	.	2,941
1954	1,657	350	323		90	185	.	2,605
1955	1,579	350	333		90	202	.	2,554
1956	1,500	360	366		90	208	.	2,524
1957	1,239	370	403		90	220	.	2,322
1958	1,350	380	415		95	232	.	2,472
1959	1,398	390	408		100	244	.	2,540
1960	1,410	400	422		105	255	.	2,592
1961	1,411	415	433		110	267	.	2,636
1962	1,415	430	455		115	281	.	2,696
1963	1,405	445	500		120	303	.	2,773
1964	1,422	460	75	420	120	322	.	2,819
1965	1,432	475	70	471	120	346	.	2,914
1966	1,433	490	70	480	110	368	.	2,951
1967	1,434	500	70	492	110	379	.	2,985
1968	1,600	560	80	565	130	393	.	3,328
1969	1,685	600	80	594	120	407	.	3,486
1970	1,693	617	80	611	120	428	.	3,549
1971	1,679	627	83	635	130	449	.	3,603
1972	1,669	616	84	669	140	475	.	3,653
1973	1,682	629	87	699	150	501	.	3,748
1974	1,685	630	87	703	168	513	.	3,786
1975	1,708	640	90	738	180	526	.	3,882
1976	1,665	639	94	746	183	538	.	3,865
1977	1,607	649	96	745	186	550	.	3,833
1978	1,475	649	99	726	193	535	.	3,677
1979	1,359	661	102	698	195	520	.	3,535
1980	1,249	665	105	667	181	507	.	3,374
1981	1,257	683	109	657	184	493	.	3,383
1982	1,117	686	111	664	179	480	.	3,231
1983	1,046	705	114	613	175	465	.	3,118
1984	998	712	117	623	178	451	.	3,079
1985	901	715	120	588	180	440	.	2,944

table: FR 2	Confederal Membership Shares in per centage of total members					FRANCE
year	CGT	FO	CFTC	CFDT	CGC	total
	1	3	4	5	6	
1915	83.3					100.0
1920	94.4		5.1			100.0
1925	51.0		6.3			100.0
1930	57.7		8.5			100.0
1935	86.9		11.7			100.0
1939	89.0		9.6			100.0
1945	92.6		6.2		1.2	100.0
1950	75.5	9.1	8.7		2.7	100.0
1955	61.8	13.7	13.0		3.5	100.0
1960	54.4	15.4	16.3		4.1	100.0
1965	49.1	16.3	2.4	16.2	4.1	100.0
1970	47.7	17.4	2.3	17.2	3.4	100.0
1975	44.0	16.5	2.3	19.0	4.6	100.0
1980	37.0	19.7	3.1	19.8	5.4	100.0
1985	30.6	24.3	4.1	20.0	6.1	100.0

table: FR 4/1	density rates						FRANCE

year	membership		dep.labour force		density rates		
	total	less pens.	total	employed only	gross	net	employed only
	1	2	3	4	1:3	2:3	2:4
1913	.	283	.	.	.	.	.
1914	.	214	.	.	.	.	.
1915	.	48	.	.	.	.	.
1916	.	85	.	.	.	.	.
1917	.	246	.	.	.	.	.
1918	.	499	.	.	.	.	.
1919	.	1,075	.	.	.	.	.
1920	.	1,264	.	.	.	.	.
1921	.	935	12,987	12,449	.	7.2	7.5
1922	.	936	.	.	.	.	.
1923	.	944	.	.	.	.	.
1924	.	960	.	.	.	.	.
1925	.	990	.	.	.	.	.
1926	.	1,032	13,031	12,787	.	7.9	8.1
1927	.	1,023	.	.	.	.	.
1928	.	1,016	.	.	.	.	.
1929	.	1,076	.	.	.	.	.
1930	.	1,000	.	.	.	.	.
1931	.	953	13,250	12,797	.	7.2	7.4
1932	.	895	.	.	.	.	.
1933	.	875	.	.	.	.	.
1934	.	865	.	.	.	.	.
1935	.	905	.	.	.	.	.
1936	.	2,879	12,193	11,329	.	23.6	25.4
1937	.	4,320	.	.	.	.	.
1938	.	3,814	.	.	.	.	.
1939	.	2,810	.	.	.	.	.
.							
.							
1945	.	4,832	.	.	.	.	.
1946	.	5,424	11,738	.	.	46.2	.
1947	.	5,017	.	.	.	.	.
1948	.	3,677	.	.	.	.	.
1949	.	3,749	.	.	.	.	.

table: FR 4/2			density rates			FRANCE	
year	membership		dep.labour force		density rates		
	total	less pens.	total	employed only	gross	net	employed only
	1	2	3	4	1:3	2:3	2:4
1950	.	3,861	.	.	.	.	.
1951	.	3,696	.	.	.	.	.
1952	.	3,305	.	.	.	.	.
1953	.	2,941	.	.	.	.	.
1954	.	2,605	12,679	12,352	.	20.5	21.1
1955	.	2,554	.	.	.	.	.
1956	.	2,524	.	.	.	.	.
1957	.	2,322	.	.	.	.	.
1958	.	2,472	.	.	.	.	.
1959	.	2,540	.	.	.	.	.
1960	.	2,592	.	.	.	.	.
1961	.	2,636	.	.	.	.	.
1962	.	2,696	13,953	13,745	.	19.3	19.6
1963	.	2,773	14,493	14,220	.	19.1	19.5
1964	.	2,819	14,937	14,721	.	18.9	19.1
1965	.	2,914	14,989	14,720	.	19.4	19.8
1966	.	2,951	15,263	14,983	.	19.3	19.7
1967	.	2,985	15,366	15,001	.	19.4	19.9
1968	.	3,328	16,148	15,711	.	20.6	21.2
1969	.	3,486	16,357	15,880	.	21.3	22.0
1970	.	3,549	16,653	16,143	.	21.3	22.0
1971	.	3,603	16,920	16,411	.	21.3	22.0
1972	.	3,653	17,308	16,713	.	21.1	21.9
1973	.	3,748	17,642	17,065	.	21.2	22.0
1974	.	3,786	17,869	17,254	.	21.2	21.9
1975	.	3,882	18,150	17,248	.	21.4	22.5
1976	.	3,865	18,572	17,579	.	20.8	22.0
1977	.	3,833	18,924	17,802	.	20.3	21.5
1978	.	3,677	19,121	17,915	.	19.2	20.5
1979	.	3,535	19,361	17,990	.	18.3	19.7
1980	.	3,374	19,527	18,057	.	17.3	18.7
1981	.	3,383	19,702	17,973	.	17.2	18.8
1982	.	3,237	19,986	18,067	.	16.2	17.9
1983	.	3,118	20,011	18,050	.	15.6	17.3
1984	.	3,079	20,219	17,907	.	15.2	17.2
1985	.	2,944	20,287	17,872	.	14.5	16.5

year:1921		total		market			public			status	
isic	conf.	all	female	b-c	w-c	total	b-c	w-c	total	b-c	w-c
1	CGT	5	.	5		5				5	
1	CGTU	1	.	1		1				1	
		6	.	*6*		*6*				*6*	
2-4	CGT	277	.	267	7	274	3		3	271	7
2-4	CGTU	173	.	167	2	169	4		4	171	2
		451	.	*435*	*9*	*443*	*8*		*8*	*442*	*9*
5	CGT	18	.	18		18				18	
5	CGTU	41	.	41		41				41	
		59	.	*59*		*59*				*59*	
6+8	CGT	16	.		16	16					16
6+8	CGTU	5	.		5	5					5
		21	.		*21*	*21*					*21*
7	CGT	123	.	64		64	44	16	60	108	16
7	CGTU	92	.	20		20	67	5	73	87	5
		215	.	*83*		*83*	*111*	*21*	*132*	*194*	*21*
9	CGT	49	.		7	7	16	26	42	16	33
9	CGTU	37	.	1	2	3	4	31	35	5	33
		86	.	*1*	*9*	*10*	*20*	*57*	*77*	*21*	*66*
0	CFTC	90	.	.	.	.	.	.	.	30	60
0	ITC	7	.		7	7					7
		97	.	.	*(7)*	*(7)*	.	.	.	*30*	*67*
	CGT	488	.	354	30	383	63	41	105	417	71
	CGTU	349	.	229	9	238	76	36	111	304	45
	CFTC	90	.	.	.	.	.	.	.	30	60
	ITC	7	.		7	7					7
		935	.	*(583)*	*(46)*	*(628)*	*(139)*	*(77)*	*(216)*	*751*	*183*

Table FR 5/2 Union Membership by Sex, Industry and Status									FRANCE	
year:1930	total		market			public			status	
isic	conf.	all	female	b-c	w-c	total	b-c	w-c	total	b-c	w-c
1	CGT	2	.	2		2				2	
1	CGTU	3	.	3		3				3	
		5	.	*5*		*5*				*5*	
2-4	CGT	223	.	190	9	199	25		25	215	9
2-4	CGTU	90	.	81	2	83	7		7	88	2
		313	.	*271*	*10*	*281*	*32*		*32*	*303*	*10*
5	CGT	9	.	9		9				9	
5	CGTU	31	.	31		31				31	
		40	.	*40*		*40*				*40*	
6+8	CGT	12	.		12	12					12
6+8	CGTU	2	.		2	2					2
		14	.		*14*	*14*					*14*
7	CGT	185	.	54		54	83	49	132	137	49
7	CGTU	151	.	31		31	107	13	120	139	13
		337	.	*85*		*85*	*190*	*61*	*252*	*275*	*61*
9	CGT	145	.	1	4	5	17	124	140	17	128
9	CGTU	47	.	2	1	3	19	25	44	21	26
		192	.	*3*	*5*	*8*	*35*	*149*	*184*	*38*	*154*
0	CFTC	85	.	.	.	.	.	.	.	27	58
0	ITC	15	.		15	15					15
		100	.		*(15)*	*(15)*				*27*	*73*
	CGT	577	.	255	25	281	124	172	297	380	198
	CGTU	323	.	148	4	152	134	38	171	281	41
	CFTC	85	.	.	.	.	.	.	.	27	58
	ITC	15	.		15	15					15
		1,000	.	*(403)*	*44*	*(448)*	*(258)*	*(210)*	*(468)*	*688*	*312*

Table FR 5/3 Union Membership by Sex, Industry and Status										FRANCE	
year:1935		total		market			public			status	
isic	conf.	all	female	b-c	w-c	total	b-c	w-c	total	b-c	w-c
1	CGT	5	.	5		5				5	
		5	*.*	*5*		*5*				*5*	
2-4	CGT	275	.	239	7	246	28		28	268	7
		275	*.*	*239*	*7*	*246*	*28*		*28*	*268*	*7*
5	CGT	33	.	33		33				33	
		33	*.*	*33*		*33*				*33*	
6+8	CGT	10	.		10	10					10
		10	*.*		*10*	*10*					*10*
7	CGT	249	.	66		66	107	76	183	173	76
		249	*.*	*66*		*66*	*107*	*76*	*183*	*173*	*76*
9	CGT	214	.	3	6	9	29	176	205	31	182
		214	*.*	*3*	*6*	*9*	*29*	*176*	*205*	*31*	*182*
0	CFTC	106	.	.	.	.	.	.	.	53	53
0	ITC	13	.		13	13					13
		119	*.*		*(13)*	*(13)*				*53*	*66*
	CGT	786	.	346	23	370	164	252	416	511	275
	CFTC	106	.	.	.	.	.	.	.	53	53
	ITC	13	.		13	13					13
		905	*.*	*(346)*	*(36)*	*(383)*	*(164)*	*(252)*	*(416)*	*564*	*341*

Table FR 5/4 Union Membership by Sex, Industry and Status										FRANCE
year:1937		total		market			public			status
isic	conf.	all	female	b-c	w-c	total	b-c	w-c	total	b-c	w-c
1	CGT	48	.	48		48				48	
		48	*.*	*48*		*48*				*48*	
2-4	CGT	2,433	.	2,219	142	2,361	73		73	2,291	142
		2,433	*.*	*2,219*	*142*	*2,361*	*73*		*73*	*2,291*	*142*
5	CGT	343	.	343		343				343	
		343	*.*	*343*		*343*				*343*	
6+8	CGT	97	.		97	97					97
		97	*.*		*97*	*97*					*97*
7	CGT	676	.	218	3	222	359	95	454	578	98
		676	*.*	*218*	*3*	*222*	*359*	*95*	*454*	*578*	*98*
9	CGT	362	.	7	17	25	77	261	337	84	278
		362	*.*	*7*	*17*	*25*	*77*	*261*	*337*	*84*	*278*
0	CFTC	320	.	.	.	.	.	.	.	200	120
0	ITC	41	.		41	41					41
		361	*.*		*(41)*	*(41)*				*200*	*161*
	CGT	3,959	.	2,835	260	3,095	509	355	864	3,344	615
	CFTC	320	.	.	.	.	.	.	.	200	120
	ITC	41	.		41	41					41
		4,320	*.*	*(2,835)*	*(301* | *3,136)*	*(509)*	*(355)*	*(864)*	*3,544*	*776*

Table FR 5/5 Union Membership by Sex, Industry and Status										FRANCE

year:1975		total		market			public			status	
isic	conf.	all	female	b-c	w-c	total	b-c	w-c	total	b-c	w-c
1	CGT	29	.	.	.	.	.	.	.	.	.
1	FO	25	.	.	.	.	.	.	.	.	.
1	CFTC	5	.	.	.	.	.	.	.	.	.
1	CFDT	22	.	.	.	.	.	.	.	.	.
		81	.	.	.	.	.	.	.	.	.
2-5	CGT	1,000	.	.	.	.	.	.	.	.	.
2-5	FO	160	.	.	.	.	.	.	.	.	.
2-5	CFTC	41	?	?	?	?	?	?	?	?	?
2-5	CFDT	323	.	.	.	.	.	.	.	.	.
2-5	CGC	120	.		.	.		.	.		120
		1,644	.	.	.	.	.	.	.	.	.
9	CGT	579	.	.	.	.	.	.	.	.	.
9	FO	455	.	.	.	.	.	.	.	.	.
9	CFTC	44	.	.	.	.	.	.	.	.	.
9	CFDT	385	.	.	.	.	.	.	.	.	.
9	CGC	60	.	.	.	.		.	.		60
9	FEN	526	.					526	526		526
		2,049	.	.	.	.	.	.	.	.	.
	CGT	1,708	435	.	.	980	.	.	728	1,189	519
	FO	640	.	.	.	256	.	.	384	352	288
	CFTC	90	.	.	.	49	.	.	41	54	36
	CFDT	738	255	.	.	410	.	.	328	482	256
	CGC	180	.		144	144		36	36		180
	FEN	526	.					526	526		526
		3,882	.	.	.	*1,839*	.	.	*2,043*	*2,077*	*1,805*

Table FR 6/1 Dependent Labour Force by Sex, Industry and Status FRANCE										
1921	total		market			public			status	
isic	all	female	b-c	w-c	total	b-c	w-c	total	b-c	w-c
1	3,416	.	.	.	.	.	.	.	3,410	6
2-4	3,984	.	.	.	.	.	.	.	3,596	388
5	454	.	.	.	.	.	.	.	431	24
6+8	910	.	.	.	.	.	.	.	225	685
7	1,177	.	.	.	.	.	.	.	853	324
9	2,509	.	.	.	.	.	.	.	1,237	1,272
0	537	.	.	.	537	.	.	.	537	.
	12,986	4,466	.	.	11,309	.	.	1,678	10,288	2,699

Table FR 6/2 Dependent Labour Force by Sex, Industry and Status FRANCE										
1931	total		market			public			status	
isic	all	female	b-c	w-c	total	b-c	w-c	total	b-c	w-c
1	2,518	.	.	.	.	.	.	.	2,512	7
2-4	4,871	.	.	.	.	.	.	.	4,332	539
5	617	.	.	.	.	.	.	.	588	30
6+8	1,186	.	.	.	.	.	.	.	303	883
7	1,101	.	.	.	.	.	.	.	822	280
9	2,503	.	.	.	.	.	.	.	1,216	1,287
0	453	.	.	.	453	.	.	.	453	.
	13,250	4,139	.	.	11,589	.	.	1,660	10,225	3,025

Table FR 6/3 Dependent Labour Force by Sex, Industry and Status FRANCE										
1936	total		market			public			status	
isic	all	female	b-c	w-c	total	b-c	w-c	total	b-c	w-c
1	2,255	.	.	.	.	.	.	.	2,250	5
2-4	3,905	.	.	.	.	.	.	.	3,446	459
5	413	.	.	.	.	.	.	.	389	24
6+8	1,083	.	.	.	.	.	.	.	275	808
7	996	.	.	.	.	.	.	.	769	227
9	2,678	.	.	.	.	.	.	.	1,222	1,456
0	864	.	.	.	864	.	.	.	864	.
	12,193	3,735	.	.	10,502	.	.	1,692	9,216	2,978

| Table FR 6/4 Dependent Labour Force by Sex, Industry and Status   FRANCE | | | | | | | | | | |
| 1954 | total | | market | | | public | | | status | |
isic	all	female	b-c	w-c	total	b-c	w-c	total	b-c	w-c
1	1,197	.	.	.	.	.	.	.	.	.
2-4	4,805	.	.	.	.	.	.	.	.	.
5	1,106	.	.	.	.	.	.	.	.	.
6+8	1,146	.	.	.	.	.	.	.	.	.
7	945	.	.	.	.	.	.	.	.	.
9	2,927	.	.	.	.	.	.	.	.	.
0	553	.	.	.	.	.	.	.	.	.
	12,679	4,100	.	.	.	.	.	.	.	.

| Table FR 6/5 Dependent Labour Force by Sex, Industry and Status   FRANCE | | | | | | | | | | |
| 1975 | total | | market | | | public | | | status | |
isic	all	female	b-c	w-c	total	b-c	w-c	total	b-c	w-c
1	894	.	.	.	.	.	.	.	.	.
2-4	5,455	.	.	.	.	.	.	.	.	.
5	1,604	.	.	.	.	.	.	.	.	.
6+8	2,295	.	.	.	.	.	.	.	.	.
7	1,175	.	.	.	.	.	.	.	.	.
9	5,742	.	.	.	.	.	.	.	.	.
0	834	.	.	.	834	.	.	.	672	162
	18,000	6,840	.	.	13,200	.	.	4,800	9,890	8,110

Chapter 4: GERMANY

LIST OF UNION CONFEDERATIONS: name, abbreviation and foundation year

1 *Allgemeiner Deutscher Gewerkschaftsbund* (ADGB): 1875-1933
General Confederation of German Unions

2 *Gesamtverband der Christlichen Gewerskschaften Deutschlands*
(GCGD): 1899-1933, German Confederation of Christian Trade Unions

3 *Verband der Deutschen Gewerkvereine (Hirsch-Dunckersche Vereine)*
(H-D): 1868-1933, Liberal Confederation of German Unions

4 *Allgemeneiner freier Angestelltenverbände* (AFA): 1919-1933
Central Organization of Free White-Collar Unions
(associated with ADGB)

5 *Gesamtverband Deutscher Angestellten-Gewerkschaften* (GEDAG):
1919-1933, Central Organization of Christian White-Collar Unions
(associated with GCGD)

6 *Liberaler Gewerkschaftsring* (RING): 1919-1933
Central Organization of Liberal White-Collar Unions
(associated with H-D)

7 *Deutscher Gewerkschaftsbund* (DGB): 1949-
German Confederation of Trade Unions

8 *Deutsche Angestellten-Gewerkschaft* (DAG): 1945-
German Union of White-Collar Employees

9 *Christlicher Gewerkschaftsbund* (CGB): 1959-
Christian Union Confederation

10 *Deutscher Beamtenbund* (DBB): 1949-
German Civil Servants Federation

---

1. AGGREGATE MEMBERSHIP STATISTICS

1.1 General Series

Trade union history in Germany divides into two periods. The first ends
in 1933 with Nazism and the compulsory enrollment of trade unionists in
the *Deutsche Arbeitsfront*. The second begins with the foundation of the

79

Federal Republic and the reconstitution of a free and democratic union movement after the Second World War.

As to the first period I have chosen to include in the aggregate series only the membership of the three main confederations together with the membership of the *Angestelltenverbände* (associations of salaried employees -listed under the numbers 4, 5 and 6 above). The membership of the three main confederations, the so-called 'Big Three', was published by the Reichsarbeitsverwaltung (the Central Labour Office) in special editions on professional associations of the Reichsarbeitsblatt (Berlin, several years). As to the associations of salaried employees I have relied upon the data provided by Ebbinghaus (1988), who has painstakingly adjusted the published series for double membership, self-employed members, double affiliations and membership outside the than existing boarders of the German Reich. This series differs from the ones published by G.Hartfiel (1966) and also from the figures of Bain & Price (1980: 130-).

I have decided to 'group' the total membership of the three central organizations of salaried employees in one series. Outside these federations, but included in the figures presented, is the membership of the *Vereinigung Leitender Angestellten Berufsverbände* (VELA) and the *Reichsbund Deutscher Angestellten Berufsverbände* (RDAB). Not included is the membership of the *wirtschaftsfriedlicher* or 'yellow' unions, and that of the independent civil servant's organizations (for further detailed figures: Ebbinghaus, 1988).

From 1950, the membership of the DGB, the DAG and the DBB is published annually by the Federal Bureau of Statistics in the Statistische Jahrbuch für die Bundesrepublik Deutschland (Statistical Yearbook of the Federal Republic of Germany), Wiesbaden. It should be observed that the DAG is rather a union than a confederation, although some small organizations have 'affiliated' with the DAG (see below). The membership figures of the Christian Union Confederation, the CGB, are with certain intervals published in Jühe, Niedenhoff & Pege (1982: 183) and for recent years in Niedenhoff & Pege (1987: 265). Membership in intermediate years has been interpolated by the author. The Statistische Jahrbuch also publishes the annual membership figures of the *Deutscher Handels- und Industrieangestelltenverband* (DHV, or German Union of Clerical Employees), which is the main affiliate of the CGB. The DHV was the main Christian employee organizations in Imperial Germany and in the Weimar Republic, and was refounded in 1950. Its membership after 1959 is included in the CGB figure; before 1959 the data are taken from a DHV publication (DHV, 1960) and reported under 'Other Unions' in the tables.

In addition to the DHV before 1959, this rubric 'Other Unions' combines 1) the membership of the *Gewerkschaft der Polizei* (GdP, the main union of police officers) from 1950 until its affiliation with the DGB in 1978; 2) the *Richterbund* (RB) from 1955 when it first reported membership; 3) the main industrial affiliate (AFA) of the *Union Leitender Angestellten* (ULA, the main association of managerial staff) from 1960 onwards and, from 1976, the ULA as a whole; 4) the *Marburger Bund* (MB), which is an association of doctors and medical specialists in state hospitals, from 1974, and 5) the *Deutsche Journalisten-Verband* (DJV, or German Federation of Journalists) from 1976 onwards. The RB, MB and ULA are clearly federations of unions. The RB combines associations in the different states or Länder; the MB combines 10 staff associations; and the ULA, which is a continuation of the pre-war VELA,

7 unions of managerial staff. Niedenhoff & Pege (1987: 282,296-297) report the membership of the *Gewerkschaft der Polizei*, the *Marburger Bund* (1978-1985), and the *Deutsche Journalisten-Verband* (1976-1985). For earlier years the membership of the *Marburger Bund* is mentioned in a report of the DGB's public employee and transport union (ÖTV, 1977: 19). The *Richterbund* reported its membership to the Federal Bureau of Statistics from 1955 to 1969. Membership in recent years is given in Ganser & Herberz (1985: 43), and was interpolated for intermediate years by the author. The membership of the AFA from 1960 onwards is reported in Bayer, Streeck & Treu (1981: 217). The estimate of the 1976 membership of the *Union Leitender Angestellten* (ULA) was taken from the same source. With respect to recent years I have relied upon Ganser & Herberz (1985: 42) and Niedenhoff & Pege (1987: 171-2), with inter-polations for intermediate years.

There are still a considerable number of independent unions which could not be included in the series as their existence, trade union character or membership was unknown in all but a few years. Still existing union organizations are the *Deutsche Arbeitnehmer-Verband* (15,000 members) which started in 1960 as a mining union; the *Deutsche Bankangestellten Verband* (20,000 members), founded in 1952; the *Verein-igung Cockpit* (2,000 members), founded in 1969; the *Verband Deutscher Flugleiter* (2,100 members); the *Union Hohere Beamten der Bundesbahn* (2,350 members); the *Deutscher Postgilde* (12,500 members); the *Deutsche Posthalter* (10,000 members); the *Verband Strassenwarter* (3,000 members); the *Verband Deutscher Meteriologen* (395 members); the *Anwaltsverein* (700 members); the *Deutscher Vereinigung der Rechts-anwalts- und Notariatsangestellten* (?); the *Bund Deutscher Kriminal-beamter* (10,900 members), founded in 1968; the *Verein der Auslands-beamten* (900 members); the *Patentamt-beamten* (650 members) and the *Deutscher Hochschul-Verband* (8,000 members). The quoted membership figures relate to 1984 or 1985, and are reported in Ganser & Herberz (1985: 43-) or in Niedenhoff & Pege (1987: 120-). Together these unions represent some 100,000 members in 1984 or 1985 (including pensioners), which is about 1% of total membership in the Federal Republic of Germany. A further observation is that these unions mainly cater for white collar employees and civil servants. Some organizations take part in the bargaining cartels for salaried employees in combi-nation with DBB- or CGB- unions or with the DAG (Keller,1983: 146-). Also not included in the series are the associations representing the professional military and military conscripts. The most important of these organizations is the *Deutsche Bundeswehr-Verband*, which was founded after the remilitarization of the Federal Republic (see Niedenhoff & Pege (1987: 296) for membership figures and Schössler (1968) with respect to interest representation and union character).

It should be noted that the membership of the ADGB and of the GCGD is given as an annual average; all other pre-war membership figures are end-of-year data. The reporting date of the DGB was 30 September each year from 1950 to 1959 and was changed to 31 December since. From 1950 to 1977 the DAG reported its membership at 30 September each year, but from 1978 onwards its membership is reported at 31 December. The DBB reports its membership still at 30 September each year. The membership of the CGB (1959-61, 1964, 1968, 1972 and 1975-1985) is reported at 31 December. The DHV reported its membership also at 31 December, but the Statistical Yearbook presents the DHV membership figures as of 31 September. Most other unions and federations report at 31 December, except the AFA which until 1966 reported at 1 April and than changed to end-of-year data.

1.2   Retired Members

Retired members are included in the reported membership of all unions and confederations. On the basis of the annual reports of the DGB--affiliates and information given by union officials, I have made an estimate of the number of pensioners in all DGB-affiliates, except the *Gewerkschaft Erziehung und Wissenschaft* and the small *Gewerkschaft Kunst*. My figures correspond with the estimates given for 1960-1975 in Bayer, Streeck & Treu (1981, detailed tables). Recently, Armingeon has also provided estimates of retired members in DGB unions (Armingeon, 1987). Hagelstange, who gives figures for 'workers in employment in DGB-unions' seems to have excluded also the unemployed although that is not fully clear from his text (Hagelstange, 1979). I have excluded only pensioners and military conscripts (the latter category is small and amounts to less than 1% of the membership in DGB-unions). The table on page 83 summarizes the data on retired members in the DGB unions.

   Reported membership of the DAG also comprises retired members and conscripts, probably in the same proportion as in the DGB-membership. Mid-1974 52,336 of the 454,811 DAG-members were retired employees, and a further 4,792 members were military conscripts (calculated from internal financial statistics of the DAG, as published in ÖTV, 1977: 17,39). This corresponds with DGB-average. I have therefore assumed that the DGB and the DAG are in this respect similar. Of the DBB's reported membership one-fifth or even more have retired from the labour force. The DBB probably compares with the public employee unions of the DGB. One of the largest affiliates of the DBB is its pensioner union, the *Gewerkschaft der Ruhestandsbeamten und Hinterbliebenen*, with 90,000 members in 1984 (Ganser & Herberz 1985: 45-). I have found no information on retired members included in reported membership of the CGB. Of the other union organizations, it was possible to separate retired members in the GdP on the basis of its Congress Reports, and also to specify the student-members in the MB (Niedenhoff & Pege 1987: 296).

1.3   Female Membership

The DGB and the DAG report male and female membership from 1950 (Statistische Jahrbuch); the DBB from 1971 (Statistische Jahrbuch) and the CGB only from 1980 (Niedenhoff & Pege 1987: 288,265). I have extrapolated backwards the female membership in the DBB for 1970 and in the CGB for 1961 and 1970, the latter on the basis of the female membership in its largest affiliate, the DHV, which was known (Statistische Jahrbuch, 1962, 1971). Female membership in the other unions is not known. I have not been able to calculate male and female membership exclusive pensioners; hence both figures are overstated, but it may be safely conjectured that this overstatement regards in particular male membership.

82

Retired members included in DGB-unions (in % of total membership)					
DGB - affiliates	1951	1961	1970	1979	1985
IGBE (mining)	8.6	21.4	35.0	35.0	36.1
GED (railways)	16.0	22.9	29.9	33.3	33.7
GdP (police)				17.6	18.3
DPG (post office)	8.4	14.2	16.2	15.3	14.7
DGLF (agriculture)	10.0	15.0	20.4	20.6	14.6
IGC (chemicals)	4.0	8.5	11.3	11.9	13.6
ÖTV (public & transport	5.2	10.4	12.8	11.5	12.7
NGG (food, hotels)	4.5	7.6	11.4	11.1	12.0
BSE (construction)	5.0	7.5	10.0	10.0	10.0
IGM (metal)	5.0	5.2	9.0	9.6	9.9
IGD (printing)	8.1	11.0	13.6	6.4	6.5
GL (leather)	5.8	7.7	5.3	6.0	6.4
GHK (wood)	7.0	10.0	14.5	7.1	6.3
HBV (commerce, banking	5.7	4.4	7.0	3.5	5.0
GTB (textile & cloth)	0.0	0.0	0.0	0.0	0.0
GEW (education)	.	.	.	.	.
GK (art & entertainment)	.	.	.	.	.
DGB (total)	6.0	9.5	12.7	12.1	12.5

2. MEMBERSHIP BY INDUSTRY AND STATUS

2.1. Classification by Industry

2.1.1 Classification in 1925

1   Agriculture:
-- Socialist: *Verband der Gärtner; Landarbeiter-Verband*
-- Christian: *Gärtner-Verband; Zentralverband der Landarbeiter; Reichsverband Guts- und Forstbeamten*

2-5 Mining, Industry, Construction, Gas, Water & Electricity:
-- Socialist: *Baugewerkschaft; Bekleidungsarbeiter-Verband; Verband der Bergarbeiter; Verband der Böttcher und Weinküfer; Verband der Buchbinder; Zentralverband der Dachdecker; Verband der Fabrikarbeiter; Zentralverband der Fleischer; Zentralverband der Glasarbeiter; Verband der graphische Hilfsarbeiter; Holzarbeiter-verband; Deutscher Hutarbeiter-Verband; Verband der Kupfer-schmiede; Verband der Lebensmittel und Getränkearbeiter; Zentral-verband der Lederarbeiter; Verband der Lithographen und Stein-drucker, Verband der Maler und Lackierer; Zentralverband der Machinisten und Heizer, Metallarbeiter-Verband; Nahrungs und Genussmittelarbeiter-Verband; Verband der Porzellanarbeiter; Sattler und Tappezierer-Verband; Zentralverband der Schuhmacher; Zentralverband der Steinarbeiter; Tabakarbeiter-Verband; Textil-arbeiterverband; Zentralverband der Zimmerer; Fördermachinisten--Verband; Polier-, Werk- und Schachtmeister-Bund; Bund technische Angestellten und Beamten; Werkmeisterverband; Werkmeister-Verband der Schuhindustrie; Verband der Zuschneider*
-- Christian: *Zentralverband christl. Bauarbeiter; Verband christl. Arbeitnehmer des Bekleidungsgewerbe; Gewerkschaft von christl. Bergarbeiter; Zentralverband christl. Tekstil-und Transportarbeiter; Gutenberg-Bund; Graphischer Zentralverband; Zentralverband christl. Holzarbeiter; Zentralverband christl. Lederarbeiter; Zentralverband christl. Maler; Christl. Metall-arbeiter-Verband; Zentralverband der Nahrungs- und Genussmittel-industrie-Arbeiter; Zentralverband christl. Tabakarbeiter; Zentralverband christl. Tekstilarbeiter; Werkmeisterbund; Verband Deutscher Techniker; Bund angestellte Akademiker techn-naturwiss. Berufe; Reichsverband Deutscher Bergbauangestellter; Reichsverband der Molkerei und Käsereiangestellten; Verband des Strassen- und Wasserbaupersonals*
-- Liberal: *Gewerkverein der Bäcker und Konditoren; Gewerkverein der Bekliedungsarbeiter; Bund Deutscher Brauer; Gewerkverein der Deutschen Fabrik- und Handarbeiter; Fleischergesellenbund; Gewerk-verein der Holzarbeiter; Gewerkverein der lederarbeiter; Gewerk-verein der maler und graphische Berufe; Gewerkverein Deutscher Metallarbeiter; Gewerkverein Deutscher Tabakarbeiter; Gewerkverein Deutscher Textilarbeiter*

6+8 Commerce, Banking & Insurances:
-- Socialist: *Zentralverband der Angestellten (ZdA); Allgem. Verband der Deutschen Bankangestellten*
-- Christian: *Deutschnationaler Handlungsgehilfen-Verband (DHV); Verband der weibliche Handels- und Büroangestellten; Reichsverband*

der Büroangestellten und Beamten
-- Liberal: *Gesamtverein der Angestellten (GdA); Bankangestellten-verein*

7   Transport & Communication:
-- Socialist: *Einheitsverband der Eisenbahner; Verkehrsbund; Verband Deutscher Kapitäne und Steuerleute; Verband Deutscher Schiffsingenieure; Allgem. Deutsche Postgewerkschaft*
-- Christian: *Fachverband der Privateisenbahner; Gewerkschaft Deutscher Eisenbahner; Bayer.Eisenbahnerverband; Verkehrsbeamten-gewerkschaft; Gewrkschaft technische Eisenbahnbeamten; Württ. Eisenbahnbeamten-Verband; Postgewerkschaft; Verband Deutscher Postagenten; Bund Deutscher Post- und Telegraphenbeamten; Wasser-strassengewerkschaft*
-- Liberal: *Berufsvereinigung Deutscher Kraftfahrer; Verband Deut-scher Schiffahrtsangestellten; Reichsbund kommunaler Strassen-bahner; Hamburger Verband der Machinisten; Algem.Deutscher Eisen-bahner Verband*

9   Other Services:
-- Socialist: *Verband Deutscher Berufsfeuerwehrmänner; Deutsche Filmgewerkschaft; Arbeitnehmer-Verband des Friseur- und Haar-gewerbe; Verband der Gemeinde- und Staatsarbeiter; Zentralverband der Hotel-, Restaurant- und Café-Angestellten; Musiker-Verband; Schornsteinfegergesellen; Chorsänger und Ballet-Verband; Genossen-schaft Deutscher Bühnenangehörigen; Arbeitsgemeinschaft Deutscher Justiz- und Strafanstalts-Beamten; Bund der Gefängnis-, Straf- und Erziehungsanstallts-Beamten; Bayer.Justizbeamtenbund; Reichs-gewerkschaft Deutscher Verwaltungsbeamten; Reichsgewerkschaft Kommunalbeamten; Gewerkschaft Deutscher Volkslehrer und Volks-lehrerinnen; Bund Sächsischer Staatsbeamten, Verband Thüringer Polizeibeamten; Algem. Preuszischer Polizeibeamten-Verband; Arbeitsgemeinschaft der Verwaltungsbeamten*
-- Christian: *Bund der Hotel-, Restaurant- und Cáfe-Angestellten; Reichsverband weibliche Hausangestellten; Gewerkverein der Heim-arbeiterinnen; Reichsverband Deutscher Berufsmusiker; Bund Deutscher Assistenzärzte; Berufsverband Deutscher Dentisten; Verband angestellter Zahnärzte; Gewerkschafts Deutscher Verwaltungssekretäre und Anwärter; Zentralverband Arbeitnehmer öffentliche Betriebe und Verwaltung; Finanzbeamtengewerkschaft; Bayer. Landesverband Deutscher Zollbeamten, Gestütbeamtenbund; Interessengemeinschaft der Schutzpolizeibeamten Preuszens; Preuszischer Justizbeamtenbund; Reichsverband evangelische Kirchenbeamten; Reichsverband katholische Kirchenbeamten; Verband für das mittlere Schulwesen; Verband der evangelische Lehrer- und Lehrerinnen-vereine; Verband der Beamten der Reichsversicherungs-anstalt für Angestellte; Interessengemeinschaft ehemalige Hof-beamten; Reichsverband der Kommunalbeamten; Akademische Assistenten-Verband*
-- Liberal: *Genfer Verband der Hotel- und Restaurant-Angestellten; "Gasterea"; Berliner Kellner-verein; Verband der Portiers und Berufsgenossen; Gewerkverein der Deutschen Frauen und Mädchen; Ring Deutscher Beamtenverbände*

0   Not classified: *Schweizerbund; AFA-bund Polnisch Oberschlesien*

With respect to 1925 I have relied on the Jahrbuch der Berufs-verbände im Deutschen Reiche. Sonderheft 36 zum Reichsarbeitsblatt, published by the Reichsarbeitsverwaltung (Central Labour Office) in Berlin, 1927, Charts 11-13. The membership of affiliated union is reported for each of the tree main confederations: the socialist ADGB, the christian GCGD and the liberal H-D.

All members who belonged to the three main confederations have been placed in the manual category, with two exceptions. The first is that two of the ADGB's affiliates - its unions of musicians, and the union of film operators - recruited white-collar employees really. The second exception relates to the separate 'union sections' for civil servants. When such 'sections' existed, the specified membership in them has been placed in the 'non-manual' category. As in the case of Austria, the distinction between manual and non-manual workers in Germany is not directly comparable to the Anglo-saxon variety.

For each of the 'Big Three' the Jahrbuch der Berufsverbände of 1927 reported the membership by status and affiliate, and, if it did apply, the membership in the sections for *Beamte* in each affiliate. Double counting could therefore be avoided by subtracting the member-ship in the sections for *Beamte* from their parent unions in the 'worker' or 'employee' category. For the breakdown of membership in the general unions of salaried employees - the *Zentralverband der Ange-stellten* (ZdA), the *Deutschnationaler Handlungsgehilfen-Verband* (DHV) and the *Gesamtverband der Angestellten* (GdA) - I have relied on the analysis of Ebbinghaus (1988). For the remaining unions, the classifi-cation by industry, status and pubic or private employment was relati-vely uncomplicated. Note however that the figures in tables GE 5/1 differ from the time series (tables GE 1, GE 4) because of the inclu-sion of the 'sections' of civil servants, and the use of a different reporting date.

2.1.2 Classification of membership after 1945

1 Agriculture:
   -- DGB: *Gewerkschaft Gartenbau, Land- und Forstwirtschaft* (GGLF)
   -- DBB: *Bund deutscher Forstmänner*
   -- other: *Föderation Landbau* (affiliated with ULA)

2-4 Mining, industry and energy:
   -- DGB: *IG.Bergbau und Energie; IG.Chemie, Papier, Keramiek; IG. Druck und Papier* (IGD - inclusive journalists but excluding a small section of writers); *IG.Holz und Kunststoff; IG.Leder; IG.Metall; IG.Nahrung, Genuss und Gaststätten* (NGG - excluding its sections 'co-ops' and 'hotel & restaurants'); *IG.Textil und Bekleidung*; and the section '(semi-)public energy' in the *Gewerk-schaft öffentliche Dienst, Transport und Verkehr* (ÖTV).
   -- DAG-sections *'Bergbauangestellte', 'Werkmeister', 'Technische Angestellte und Beamte'* (50%), and *'Kaufmännische Angestellte'* (35%); and one union affiliated to the DAG: the *Fördermachinisten-verein für das Saarland*
   -- other: ULA-unions (minus agriculture and construction); *Deutscher Journalisten-Verband*

5   Construction:
-- DGB: *Gewerkschaft Bau, Stein und Erde*
-- DAG: section *'Technische Angestellte und Beamte'* (50%)
-- other: *Föderation Bau* (affiliated with ULA).

6+8 Commerce, Banking & Insurances:
-- DGB: *Gewerkschaft Handel, Banken und Versicherungen* (HBV);
section 'co-ops' in the NGG and section 'commerce & warehouses' in
ÖTV.
-- DAG: sections *'Bank und Sparkassenangestellte'*, *'Versicherungs-angestellte'*, *'Kaufmännische Angestellte'* (65%).

7   Transport & Communication:
-- DGB: *Gewerkschaft der Eisenbahner Deutschlands; Deutsche Post-gewerkschaft; Gewerkschaft Öffentliche Dienst, Transport und Verkehr* (öTV - only the sections '(semi-)public transport, road,
port, sea, air and allied services').
-- DAG: section *'Schifffahrtangestellte'*
-- DBB: *Deutscher Postverband; Gewerkschaft Deutscher Bundesbahn-beamter und Lokomitivführer*

9   Other Services:
-- DGB: *Gewerkschaft Öffentliche Dienst, Transport und Verkehr*
(ÖTV - except for 'sections' in mining, commerce and transport);
*Gewerkschaft Erziehung und Wissenschaft; Gewerkschaft Kunst;
Gewerkschaft der Polizei* (GdP - affiliated from 1978); the section
'hotel & restaurants' in the NGG; and the section 'writers' in the
IGD.
-- DAG: section *'Angestellte im öffentliche Dienst'*, including a
number of small unions which are affiliated with the DAG: *Verein
Deutscher Opernchore und Buhnentänzer; Verein angestellter Bühnen-künstler; Verein Krankengymnastinnen; Verband Deutscher Muzik-erzieher und konzertierender Künstler; Bund Deutscher Fussbal-lehrer; Verband Deutscher Schwimmeister*
-- DBB: all affiliates except those listed under 1 and 7
-- other: all members of the *Richterbund, Marburger Bund* and the
Gewerkschaft der Polizei before its affiliation with the DGB.

Membership by sections in DGB-unions which needed further dis-aggregation has been calculated on the basis of the Annual Reports of
these unions. The DAG reports its membership by broad industrial or
occupational category, in recent years by sectors only (Statistical
Yearbook). The further breakdown of the membership in these sections -
in particular between industry, construction and commerce - is based on
the studies of Bayer (1980), and Bayer, Streeck & Treu (1981). The
membership by affiliate of the DBB is published only for 1951 (Statis-tical Yearbook 1952) and for 1984 (Ganser & Herberz, 1985: 45-). It
have found no way to calculate or estimate the membership in the
Christlicher Gewerkschaftsbund (CGB) by industry. The difficulty is
that the membership of (and within) its affiliates is unknown with few
exceptions, and unlike the other organizations no information about
retired members could be obtained.

2.2. Classification by Status

The Statistical Yearbook makes a three-fold distinction of manual workers (*Arbeiter*), salaried employees *Angestellte*) and civil servants (*Beamte*). Note that the latter category is smaller than 'public employees': *Beamten* or civil servants are those with special legal status within the public sector (job tenure rights, special insurance and pension funds). Although not all *Beamten* are white-collar employees, I have identified the categories of *Angestellte* and *Beamte* with non-manual employees at large.

All affiliates of the DGB apply this three-fold classification. Some DGB unions also report the membership by category excluding retired members; for the others I have estimated 'active membership' by status group on the basis of the distribution of male membership by status groups. The membership of the DAG has been deemed in the category of *Angestellte, some of them in the public sector. The DBB orga* nizes overwhelmingly *Beamte*, but also two small sections of *Arbeiter* and *Angestellte* in the public service (Niedenhoff & Pege 1987: 288-289 give figures for 1972-1985, which I have extrapolated backwards). The CGB divides it membership also in three broad groups: 1) the *Gesamtverband der Christlichen Gewerkschaften Deutschland* (GCD - which combines seven unions of mainly workers in agriculture, mining & industry, construction, and hotel & restaurants); 2) the *Gesamtverband Deutscher Angestellten-Gewerkschaften* (GEDAG - with five unions of salaries employees among which the *Deutscher Handels- und Industrieangestelltenverband* (DHV), the *Verband weiblichen Angestellten* and the *Verband Deutscher Techniker*); and 3) the *Gesamtverband Christlichen Gewerkschaften der öffentlichen Dienst, Bahn und Post* (GCÖD - also with five affiliates). I have identified the membership in the third group with *Beamte*, although the GCÖD comprises also some workers and salaried employees in the public sector (ÖTV, 1977; Jühe, Niedenhoff & Pege, 1982; Niedenhoff & Pege, 1987). The membership of the *Union Leitender Angestellte* (ULA) and of the *Deutsche Journalisten-Verband* was placed in the category of salaried employees; the membership of the *Gewerkschaft der Polizei, Richterbund* and *Marburgerbund* in the civil servants category, although some of these members are salaried employees.

1.3 Public Sector Unions

Of the DGB-affiliates the *Gewerkschaft der Eisenbahner Deutschlands, Deutsche Postgewerkschaft, Gewerkschaft Erziehung und Wissenschaft,* and *Gewerkschaft der Polizei* recruit only public employees. With the exception of its members in private and nuclear energy, in private transport and warehouses, the large majority of the membership of the *Gewerkschaft Öffentliche Dienst, Transport und Verkehr* (ÖTV) is employed in the public sector (ÖTV, Annual Reports). Almost half of the membership of the *Gewerkschaft Gartenbau, Land- und Forstwirtschaft* is employed in the public (state forestry) sector (GGLF, Annual Reports). The DAG--membership in the public sector is organized in a separate section; the same is true for the CGÖD in the CGB. Furthermore, the total membership of the DBB, the RB, and the MB was allocated to the public sector.

3. LABOUR FORCE STATISTICS

The time series of the dependent labour force before 1933 is taken from Bain & Price (1980: 133). Before the census of 1925 this series is however carried out over too long a period and therefore only a rough indication of the development of the German labour force (Bain & Price, 1980: 131). The figures on unemployment (1926-1933) are based on Niess (1979: 223) and relate to the month of April each year; they are slightly lower than the annual averages given by Moses (1982, vol.2: appendix VII) for 1928-1936.

The postwar series refers to annual averages derived from census data and, after 1962, from the annual labour force sample surveys. They exclude employers, self-employed persons, family workers and the armed forces, but include the (annual average number of) unemployed. All data are taken from the Statistische Handbuch; there is a slight break in the series in 1971 but that does not affect the series on aggregate employment or unemployment (see: OECD, Labour Force Statistics, Paris 1985). As a consequence of using annual averages in stead of (micro-)census data, referring to April, May or June each year, my series deviates slightly from the one used by Bain & Price (1980: 134-5). Both the labour force and union membership figures include West Berlin and the Saarland throughout.

The disaggregation of the dependent labour force by industry, status and sex is based on the censuses of 1925, 1950, 1961 and 1970, and the micro-census results of 1979 and 1985. For the four censuses I have relied on the data published in Flora, Kraus & Pfenning (1987: 516-521). The number of civil servants in 1925 is based on the reclassification of that census on the basis of the results of the 1933--census (Dittrich, 1939: 64); for other years this was entered as a separate category. The figures given include apprentices (Lehrlinge), which I have allocated to status groups according to the sector in which they are employed (which, in fact, is only an approximation). I have excluded the armed forces (included in the civil servants category from 1970 in Flora, Kraus & Pfenning, 1987: 521-523, and in the Statistische Handbuch. The micro-census results (1979, 1985) are reported in the Yearbook. The disaggregation of the unemployed by status and industry is based on the data of the Federal Bureau Statistics and the Federal Labour Market Board, the Bundesanstalt für Arbeit, which publishes disaggregated figures on unemployment in September each year in the official monthly statistical bulletin Wirtschaft und Statistik, Wiesbaden. Note that the census-figures deviate from the annual averages used elsewhere. A smaller number of unemployed, in particular those seeking a first job appears to be included in these figures, and a somewhat greater number of them could not be classified by either industry or status.

The figures on public employment are also from the Statistische Handbuch (table: 'Personal der öffentliche Haushalte') and includes the full-time and part-time employed in the 'direct' (central, state and local government, education, Postoffice and railways; but not armed forces) and 'indirect' pubic services (part of health and welfare services, and social insurance). The armed forces (professional military and conscripts) are excluded throughout. The 1950 figures relate to September, the 1961 figures to October 1960, the 1970 figures to October of that same year; the 1979 and 1985 figures to 30 June. Unfortunately, these figures do not fully include the semi-public sector (that part of, in particular, energy production, public works and health and research activities that is fully or mainly financed by the public sector). As the nearest approximation, I have included those with special 'civil servant' status in these sub-sectors.

4. TABLES

table: GE 1/1	Membership by Confederations				GERMANY
year	ADGB	GCGD	H-D	Angestellte	total
	1	2	3	(4-5-6)	
1913	2,573,7	342,8	106,6	941,3	3,964,4
1914	2,075,8	282,8	77,7	759,2	3,195,5
1915	1,159,5	176,1	61,1	531,6	1,928,3
1916	966,7	174,3	57,8	479,9	1,678,7
1917	1,106,7	243,9	79,1	425,3	1,855,0
1918	1,665,0	404,7	113,8	871,8	3,055,3
1919	5,479,1	858,3	189,8	1,323,3	7,850,5
1920	7,890,1	1,076,8	226,0	1,491,7	10,684,6
1921	7,568,0	986,3	224,6	1,540,3	10,319,2
1922	7,895,1	1,049,4	230,6	1,544,9	10,720,0
1923	7,138,4	937,9	216,5	1,501,2	9,794,0
1924	4,618,4	613,0	147,3	1,217,4	6,596,1
1925	4,156,5	587,7	157,6	1,222,0	6,123,8
1926	3,977,3	531,6	163,5	1,210,3	5,882,7
1927	4,150,2	605,8	167,6	1,252,8	6,176,4
1928	4,653,6	647,4	168,7	1,338,8	6,808,5
1929	4,906,2	673,1	168,7	1,449,4	7,197,4
1930	4,821,8	658,7	163,3	1,506,5	7,150,3
1931	4,417,9	577,5	149,8	1,471,4	6,616,6
1932	.	.	.	.	.

table: GE 1/2		Membership by Confederation				GERMANY (-FRG)	
year	DGB	DAG	DBB	DHV	CGB	other	total
	7	8	9		10		
1950	5,278,6	307,2	120,0	2,8		42,5	5,751,1
1951	5,912,1	343,5	234,4	6,3		44,5	6,540,8
1952	6,004,5	360,4	350,0	13,2		49,4	6,777,5
1953	6,051,2	384,4	447,1	21,3		54,4	6,958,4
1954	6,103,3	406,5	567,8	27,0		58,5	7,163,1
1955	6,104,9	420,5	517,0	33,1		71,8	7,147,3
1956	6,124,5	431,5	545,0	46,1		76,0	7,223,1
1957	6,244,4	437,1	598,6	49,4		79,9	7,409,4
1958	6,331,7	438,1	620,5	51,9		85,6	7,527,8
1959	6,273,7	440,0	634,2	└─────198,0		88,9	7,634,8
1960	6,378,8	450,4	650,0		200,0	99,4	7,778,6
1961	6,382,0	461,5	656,6		230,0	104,1	7,834,2
1962	6,430,4	471,9	669,4		231,5	108,6	7,911,8
1963	6,431,0	479,5	680,7		233,0	113,7	7,937,9
1964	6,485,5	475,4	692,2		234,7	119,0	8,006,8
1965	6,574,5	475,6	703,1		223,8	121,4	8,098,4
1966	6,537,2	478,0	710,2		212,9	126,4	8,064,7
1967	6,407,7	481,3	724,8		202,0	131,1	7,946,9
1968	6,376,0	471,1	717,6		190,9	136,3	7,891,9
1969	6,482,4	467,8	718,1		193,0	138,5	7,999,8
1970	6,712,5	461,3	721,0		195,1	143,0	8,232,9
1971	6,868,7	469,9	706,6		197,1	145,2	8,387,5
1972	6,985,5	468,9	713,2		199,2	150,2	8,517,0
1973	7,167,5	463,4	718,0		207,6	153,1	8,709,6
1974	7,405,8	472,0	720,5		216,0	177,1	8,991,4
1975	7,364,9	470,5	726,9		224,4	183,7	8,970,4
1976	7,400,0	471,8	803,7		232,1	203,7	9,111,3
1977	7,471,0	473,4	793,2		245,0	213,5	9,196,1
1978	7,751,5	481,6	800,7		249,2	92,7	9,375,7
1979	7,843,6	487,7	824,4		266,6	97,1	9,519,4
1980	7,882,5	494,9	821,0		288,2	103,4	9,590,0
1981	7,957,5	499,4	820,3		294,9	107,2	9,679,3
1982	7,849,0	501,0	812,5		297,2	112,5	9,572,2
1983	7,745,9	497,3	801,4		299,8	114,5	9,458,9
1984	7,660,3	497,7	794,6		306,3	117,4	9,376,3
1985	7,719,5	500,9	796,3		307,1	119,6	9,443,4

92

table: GE 2/1	Confederal Membership Shares in per centage of total members			GERMANY
year	ADGB	GCGD	H-D	total
	%	%	%	
1915	60.1	9.1	3.2	100.0
1920	73.8	10.1	2.1	100.0
1925	67.9	9.6	2.6	100.0
1930	67.4	9.2	2.3	100.0

table: GE 2/2	Confederal Membership Shares in per centage of total members				GERMANY (-FRG)
year	DGB	DAG	DBB	CGB	total
	%	%	%	%	
1950	91.8	5.3	2.1		100.0
1955	85.4	5.9	7.2		100.0
1960	82.0	5.8	8.4	2.6	100.0
1965	81.2	5.9	8.7	2.8	100.0
1970	81.5	5.6	8.8	2.4	100.0
1975	82.1	5.2	8.1	2.5	100.0
1980	82.2	5.2	8.6	3.0	100.0
1985	81.7	5.3	8.4	3.3	100.0

table: GE 3	Retired workers among membership						GERMANY (-FRG)		
year	DGB		DAG		DBB		other	total	
	abs	%	abs	%	abs	%	abs	abs	%
1950	316,7	6.0	18,4	6.0	10,0	8.3	.	345,1	6.0
1951	354,7	6.0	20,6	6.0	21,1	9.0	.	396,4	6.1
1952	381,3	6.4	22,9	6.4	32,9	9.4	4,0	441,1	6.5
1953	408,9	6.8	25,8	6.7	44,5	10.0	5,7	484,9	7.0
1954	430,4	7.1	28,7	7.1	49,1	8.6	6,4	514,6	7.2
1955	453,2	7.4	31,1	7.4	57,1	11.0	7,3	548,7	7.7
1956	483,9	7.9	32,4	7.5	63,2	11.6	8,1	587,6	8.1
1957	505,4	8.1	35,4	8.1	72,7	12.1	8,9	622,4	8.4
1958	535,0	8.4	37,6	8.6	78,8	12.7	10,0	661,4	8.8
1959	552,1	8.8	39,6	9.0	84,0	13.2	10,8	686,5	9.0
1960	583,7	9.2	41,2	9.1	89,7	13.8	12,4	727,0	9.3
1961	604,7	9.5	43,8	9.5	94,2	14.3	13,0	755,7	9.6
1962	633,4	9.9	46,5	9.9	97,8	14.6	13,8	791,5	10.0
1963	656,0	10.2	48,9	10.2	101,8	15.0	14,8	821,5	10.3
1964	684,2	10.5	50,2	10.6	105,5	15.2	15,7	855,6	10.7
1965	716,6	10.9	52,3	11.0	109,4	15.6	16,4	894,7	11.0
1966	743,3	11.4	54,2	11.3	113,2	15.9	17,4	928,1	11.5
1967	768,9	12.0	56,8	11.8	116,5	16.1	18,3	960,5	12.1
1968	784,2	12.3	57,0	12.1	121,0	16.9	19,4	981,6	12.4
1969	810,3	12.5	57,5	12.3	122,5	17.1	20,0	1,010,3	12.6
1970	851,5	12.7	58,2	12.6	125,0	17.3	20,6	1,055,3	12.8
1971	886,0	12.9	60,5	12.9	126,9	18.0	20,9	1,094,3	13.0
1972	915,1	13.1	61,0	13.0	129,8	18.2	21,2	1,127,1	13.2
1973	938,9	13.1	61,0	13.2	132,0	18.4	21,4	1,153,3	13.2
1974	962,7	13.0	61,4	13.0	134,7	18.7	24,4	1,183,2	13.2
1975	972,2	13.2	62,1	13.2	137,4	18.9	25,5	1,197,2	13.3
1976	976,8	13.2	62,4	13.2	144,0	17.9	26,6	1,209,8	13.3
1977	971,2	13.0	60,7	12.8	146,1	18.4	27,7	1,205,7	13.1
1978	968,9	12.5	60,2	12.5	148,9	18.6	4,8	1,182,8	12.6
1979	948,5	12.1	59,7	12.2	152,7	18.5	5,2	1,166,1	12.2
1980	953,8	12.1	59,5	12.0	154,0	18.8	6,1	1,173,4	12.2
1981	954,9	12.0	59,4	11.9	157,5	19.2	7,0	1,178,8	12.2
1982	957,6	12.2	59,8	11.9	158,3	19.5	9,6	1,185,3	12.4
1983	960,5	12.4	60,9	12.2	158,6	19.8	9,8	1,189,8	12.6
1984	965,2	12.6	61,5	12.4	158,9	20.0	10,2	1,195,8	12.8
1985	967,0	12.5	62,5	12.5	159,3	20.0	10,2	1,199,0	12.7

table: GE 4/1		density rates				GERMANY (-FRG)	
year	membership		dep.labour force		density rates		
	total	less pens.	total	employed only	gross	employed only	net
	1	2	3	4	1:3	1:4	2:3
1913	3,964,4	.	18,443	.	21.5	.	.
1914	3,195,5	.	18,716	.	17.1	.	.
1915	1,928,3	.	18,990	.	10.2	.	.
1916	1,678,7	.	19,263	.	8.7	.	.
1917	1,855,0	.	19,536	.	9.5	.	.
1918	3,055,3	.	19,810	.	15.4	.	.
1919	7,850,4	.	20,083	.	39.1	.	.
1920	10,684,6	.	20,357		52.5	.	.
1921	10,319,2	.	20,630	.	50.0	.	.
1922	10,720,0	.	20,904		51.3	.	.
1923	9,794,0	.	21,177	.	46.2	.	.
1924	6,596,1	.	21,451		30.8	.	.
1925	6,123,8	.	21,724	.	28.2	.	.
1926	5,882,7	.	21,750	19,377	27.0	30.4	.
1927	6,176,4	.	21,776	20,133	28.4	30.7	.
1928	6,808,5	.	21,801	20,415	31.2	33.3	.
1929	7,197,4	.	21,827	19,992	33.0	36.0	.
1930	7,150,3	.	21,853	19,067	32.7	37.5	.
1931	6,616,6	.	21,879	17,521	30.2	37.8	.
1932	.	.	21,950	16,211	.	.	.
.							

table: GE 4/2			density rates			GERMANY (-FRG)	
year	membership		dep.labour force		density rates		
	total	less pens.	total	employed only	gross	net	employed only
	1	2	3	4	1:3	2:3	2:4
1950	5,751,1	5,406,0	16,552	.	34.7	32.7	.
1951	6,540,8	6,144,4	17,052	.	38.4	36.0	.
1952	6,777,5	6,336,4	17,467	.	38.8	36.3	.
1953	6,958,4	6,473,5	17,912	.	38.8	36.1	.
1954	7,163,1	6,648,5	18,485	.	38.8	36.0	.
1955	7,147,3	6,609,6	19,037	18,103	37.5	34.7	36.5
1956	7,223,1	6,635,5	19,451	.	37.1	34.1	.
1957	7,409,4	6,787,0	19,828	.	37.4	34.2	.
1958	7,527,8	6,866,4	20,088	.	37.5	34.2	.
1959	7,634,8	6,948,3	20,104	.	38.0	34.6	.
1960	7,778,6	7,051,6	20,332	20,061	38.3	34.7	35.2
1961	7,834,2	7,078,5	20,632	.	38.0	34.3	.
1962	7,911,8	7,120,3	20,786	20,631	38.1	34.3	34.5
1963	7,937,9	7,116,4	21,022	20,836	37.8	33.9	34.2
1964	8,006,8	7,151,2	21,198	21,029	37.8	33.7	34.0
1965	8,098,4	7,203,7	21,436	21,289	37.8	33.6	33.8
1966	8,064,7	7,136,6	21,445	21,284	37.6	33.3	33.5
1967	7,946,9	6,986,4	21,024	20,565	37.8	33.2	34.0
1968	7,891,9	6,910,3	21,029	20,706	37.5	32.9	33.4
1969	7,999,8	6,989,5	21,446	21,267	37.3	32.6	32.9
1970	8,232,9	7,177,6	21,896	21,747	37.6	32.8	33.0
1971	8,387,5	7,293,2	22,291	22,106	37.6	32.7	33.0
1972	8,517,0	7,389,9	22,350	22,103	38.1	33.1	33.4
1973	8,709,6	7,556,3	22,668	22,395	38.4	33.3	33.7
1974	8,991,4	7,808,2	22,695	22,113	39.6	34.4	35.3
1975	8,970,4	7,773,2	22,563	21,489	39.8	34.5	36.2
1976	9,111,3	7,901,5	22,467	21,407	40.6	35.2	36.9
1977	9,196,1	7,990,4	22,562	21,532	40.8	35.4	37.1
1978	9,375,7	8,192,9	22,727	21,734	41.3	36.0	37.7
1979	9,519,4	8,353,3	23,003	22,127	41.4	36.3	37.8
1980	9,590,0	8,416,2	23,367	22,478	41.0	36.0	37.4
1981	9,679,3	8,500,5	23,606	22,334	41.0	36.0	38.1
1982	9,572,2	8,386,9	23,737	21,904	40.3	35.3	38.3
1983	9,458,9	8,269,1	23,785	21,527	39.8	34.8	38.4
1984	9,376,3	8,180,5	23,815	21,549	39.4	34.4	38.0
1985	9,443,4	8,244,4	24,011	21,707	39.3	34.3	38.0

Table GE 5/1 Union Membership by Sex, Industry and Status											GERMANY
year:1925		total		market			public			status	
isic	conf.	all	female	b-c	w-c	total	b-c	w-c	total	b-c	w-c
1	ADGB	195	.	195		195				195	
1	GCGD	81	.	81		81				81	
1	Gedag	14	.		14	14					14
		289	*.*	*276*	*14*	*289*				*276*	*14*
2-5	ADGB	3,223	.	3,223		3,223				3,223	
2-5	GCGD	422	.	422		422				422	
2-5	H-D	146	.	146		146				146	
2-5	Free	257	.		244	244		12	12		257
2-5	Gedag	164	.		163	163		2	2		164
2-5	Liber	93	.		93	93					93
		4,306	*.*	*3,792*	*500*	*4,291*		*14*	*14*	*3,792*	*514*
6+8	Free	92	.		92	92					92
6+8	Gedag	187	.		187	187					187
6+8	Liber	192	.		192	192					192
		470	*.*		*470*	*470*					*470*
7	ADGB	418	.	240		240	179		179	418	
7	GCGD	26	.	26		26				26	
7	H-D	2	.	2		2				2	
7	Free	77	.		8	8		69	69		77
7	Gedag	230	.		8	8		223	223		230
7	Liber	40	.					40	40		40
		793	*.*	*267*	*16*	*283*	*179*	*331*	*510*	*446*	*347*
9	ADGB	250	.	30	24	54	196		196	225	24
9	GCGD	40	.	27		27	13		13	40	
9	H-D	10	.	9		9	2		2	10	
9	Free	154	.		24	24		130	130		154
9	Gedag	103	.		2	2		101	101		103
9	Liber	84	.		30	30		54	54		84
		641	*.*	*66*	*80*	*146*	*210*	*285*	*495*	*276*	*365*
0	ADGB	11	.	11		11				11	
0	Free	14	.		14	14					14
		25	*.*	*11*	*14*	*25*				*11*	*14*
	ADGB	4,097	.	3,699	25	3,723	374		374	4,073	25
	GCGD	570	.	557		557	13		13	570	
	H-D	158	.	156		156	2		2	158	
	Free	594	.		383	383		211	211		594
	Gedag	698	.		372	372		325	325		698
	Liber	408	.		314	314		94	94		408
		6,524	*.*	*4,411*	*1,094*	*5,505*	*389*	*631*	*1,019*	*4,800*	*1,724*

Table GE 5/2 Union Membership by Sex, Industry and Status   GERMANY (FRG)

year:1951		total		market			public			status	
isic	conf.	all	female	b-c	w-c	total	b-c	w-c	total	b-c	w-c
1	DGB	101	.	81	1	83	16	2	18	97	
1	DBB	11	.					11	11		1
		112	*.*	*81*	*1*	*83*	*16*	*13*	*29*	*97*	*1*
2-4	DGB	3,640	.	3,375	219	3,594	34	11	45	3,409	23
2-4	DAG	94	.		94	94					9
		3,733	*.*	*3,375*	*313*	*3,688*	*34*	*11*	*45*	*3,409*	*32*
5	DGB	411	.	395	17	411				395	1
5	DAG	18	.		18	18					1.
		429	*.*	*395*	*35*	*429*				*395*	*3*
6+8	DGB	110	.	32	78	110				32	7
6+8	DAG	136	.		136	136					13
6+8	Other	6	.		6	6					
		252	*.*	*32*	*220*	*252*				*32*	*22*
7	DGB	729	.	76	8	84	401	245	646	477	25
7	DAG	7	.		7	7					
7	DBB	80	.				8	72	80	8	7
		817	*.*	*76*	*15*	*91*	*409*	*317*	*726*	*485*	*33*
9	DGB	566	.	21	38	58	198	310	508	218	34
9	DAG	68	.					68	68		6
9	DBB	122	.					122	122		12
9	Other	45	.					45	45		4
		801	*.*	*21*	*38*	*58*	*198*	*545*	*743*	*219*	*58*
	DGB	5,558	.	3,980	360	4,340	649	568	1,217	4,630	92
	DAG	323	.		255	255		68	68		32
	DBB	213	.				8	206	213	8	20
	Other	50	.		6	6		44	44		5
		6,144	*.*	*3,980*	*621*	*4,601*	*657*	*886*	*1,542*	*4,638*	*1,50*
incl. pens.:		=========	======	=====	====	=====	====	====	=====	=====	====
	DGB	5,912	1,011	4,191	373	4,564	733	614	1,348	4,924	98
	DAG	344	108		269	269		75	75		34
	DBB	234	.				9	226	234	9	23
	Other	50	.		6	6		44	44		5
		6,541	*.*	*4,191*	*648*	*4,839*	*742*	*959*	*1,701*	*4,933*	*1,60*

Table GE 5/3 Union Membership by Sex, Industry and Status GERMANY (FRG)

year:1961		total		market			public			status	
isic	conf.	all	female	b-c	w-c	total	b-c	w-c	total	b-c	w-c
1	DGB	67	.	47	1	47	16	3	19	63	4
1	DBB	12	.					12	12		12
		79	.	47	1	47	16	15	31	63	16
2-4	DGB	3,685	.	3,379	247	3,626	45	15	60	3,423	262
2-4	DAG	136	.		136	136					136
2-4	Other	6	.		6	6					6
		3,827	.	3,379	389	3,767	45	15	60	3,423	404
5	DGB	394	.	380	14	394				380	14
5	DAG	28	.		28	28					28
		422	.	380	42	422				380	42
6+8	DGB	160	.	38	122	160				38	122
6+8	DAG	162	.		162	162					162
		322	.	38	284	322				38	284
7	DGB	790	.	80	10	90	380	319	700	460	330
7	DAG	8	.		8	8					8
7	DBB	117	.				10	107	117	10	107
		914	.	80	18	98	390	426	816	470	444
9	DGB	682	.	25	28	53	262	367	629	287	394
9	DAG	85	.				.	85	85		85
9	DBB	434	.					434	434		434
9	Other	85	.					85	85		85
		1,286	.	25	28	53	262	971	1,233	287	998
0	CGB	230	35	100	60	160	20	50	70	120	110
		230	35	100	60	160	20	50	70	120	110
	DGB	5,777	.	3,948	422	4,370	703	704	1,408	4,651	1,126
	DAG	418	.		333	333		85	85		418
	DBB	563	.				10	553	562	10	553
	CGB	230	.	100	60	160	20	50	70	120	110
	Other	91	.		6	6		85	85		91
		7,079	.	4,048	821	4,869	733	1,477	2,210	4,781	2,298
incl. pens:											
	DGB	6,382	1,078	4,284	443	4,727	846	809	1,656	5,130	1,252
	DAG	462	157		364	364		97	97		462
	DBB	657	.				12	645	657	12	645
	CGB	230	35	100	60	160	20	50	70	120	110
	Other	104	.		6	6		98	98		104
		7,834	.	4,384	873	5,257	878	1,699	2,277	5,262	2,573

Table GE 5/4 Union Membership by Sex, Industry and Status   GERMANY (FRG)

year:1970		total		market			public			status	
isic	conf.	all	female	b-c	w-c	total	b-c	w-c	total	b-c	w-c
1	DGB	37	.	18	1	19	14	4	18	32	4
1	DBB	10	.					10	10		1(
		47	.	*18*	*1*	*19*	*14*	*13*	*27*	*32*	*1·*
2-4	DGB	3,721	.	3,260	387	3,647	49	26	75	3,308	41:
2-4	DAG	112	.		112	112					11:
2-4	Other	12	.		13	13					1:
		3,845	.	*3,260*	*511*	*3,771*	*49*	*26*	*75*	*3,308*	*53*
5	DGB	454	.	427	27	454				427	2'
5	DAG	29	.		29	29					2!
		483	.	*427*	*56*	*483*				*427*	*5·*
6+8	DGB	170	.	32	138	170				32	13#
6+8	DAG	169	.		169	169					16!
		340	.	*32*	*307*	*340*				*32*	*30*
7	DGB	736	.	53	13	66	310	361	670	362	37·
7	DAG	9	.		9	9					!
7	DBB	108	.				10	98	108	10	9#
		854	.	*53*	*23*	*75*	*320*	*459*	*779*	*373*	*48*
9	DGB	743	.	17	34	51	259	433	692	276	46'
9	DAG	84	.					84	84		8·
9	DBB	478	.					478	478		47#
9	Other	110	.					110	110		11#
		1,415	.	*17*	*34*	*51*	*259*	*1,105*	*1,364*	*276*	*1,13*
0	CGB	197	.	57	78	135	12	50	50	69	12#
		197	.	*57*	*78*	*135*	*12*	*50*	*50*	*69*	*12.*
	DGB	5,861	.	3,807	600	4,407	631	823	1,454	4,438	1,42
	DAG	403	.		319	319		84	84		40
	DBB	596	.				10	586	596	10	58
	CGB	197	.	57	78	135	12	50	62	69	12#
	Other	122	.		12	12		110	110		12:
		7,178	.	*3,864*	*1,009*	*4,873*	*653*	*1,653*	*2,306*	*4,516*	*2,66*
incl.	pens:	=========	=========	=========	=========	=========	=========	=========	=========	=========	=======
	DGB	6,712	1,027	4,294	651	4,945	795	973	1,768	5,089	1,62
	DAG	461	148		363	363		98	98		46
	DBB	721	120				14	707	721	14	70
	CGB	197	45	57	78	135	12	50	62	69	12
	Other	143	.		12	12		130	130		14
		8,234	*1,340*	*4,351*	*1,104*	*5,455*	*821*	*1,958*	*2,779*	*5,172*	*3,06*

```
Table GE 5/5 Union Membership by Sex, Industry and Status    GERMANY (FRG)
```

year:1979		total		market			public			status	
isic	conf.	all	female	b-c	w-c	total	b-c	w-c	total	b-c	w-c
1	DGB	34	.	15		15	14	5	18	28	5
1	DBB	7	.					7	7		7
1	Other	1			1	1					1
		41		*15*	*1*	*16*	*14*	*12*	*25*	*28*	*13*
2-4	DGB	4,166	.	3,482	614	4,095	45	26	70	3,526	640
2-4	DAG	93	.		93	93					93
2-4	Other	45	.		45	45					45
		4,303	.	*3,482*	*751*	*4,233*	*45*	*26*	*70*	*3,526*	*777*
5	DGB	472	.	431	42	472				431	42
5	DAG	26	.		26	26					26
5	Other	1	.		1	1					1
		499	.	*431*	*68*	*499*				*431*	*68*
6+8	DGB	339	.	48	291	339				48	291
6+8	DAG	196	.		196	196					196
6+8	Other	3	.		3	3					3
		537	.	*49*	*489*	*537*				*49*	*489*
7	DGB	803	.	69	18	86	313	404	717	381	421
7	DAG	7	.		7	7					7
7	DBB	102	.				11	91	102	11	91
		912	.	*69*	*25*	*93*	*324*	*495*	*818*	*392*	*519*
9	DGB	1,082	.	23	44	67	285	731	1,015	307	775
9	DAG	106	.					106	106		106
9	DBB	563	.					563	563		563
9	Other	44	.					44	44		44
		1,795	.	*23*	*44*	*67*	*285*	*1,444*	*1,728*	*307*	*1,488*
0	CGB	267	.	88	83	171	10	85	95	98	169
		267	.	*88*	*83*	*171*	*10*	*85*	*95*	*98*	*169*
	DGB	6,895	.	4,066	1,008	5,075	655	1,165	1,820	4,722	2,173
	DAG	428	.		322	322		106	106		428
	DBB	672	.				11	660	672	11	660
	CGB	267	.	88	83	171	10	85	95	98	169
	Other	92	.		48	48		44	44		92
		8,353	.	*4,154*	*1,461*	*5,615*	*676*	*2,060*	*2,736*	*4,831*	*3,522*
incl. pens:											
	DGB	7,844	1,541	4,576	1,082	5,658	811	1,374	2,185	5,388	2,456
	DAG	488	182		360	360		128	128		488
	DBB	824	206				15	809	824	15	809
	CGB	267	65	88	83	171	10	85	95	98	169
	Other	97	.		48	48		49	49		97
		9,519	*1,994*	*4,664*	*1,573*	*6,237*	*836*	*2,445*	*3,281*	*5,501*	*4,019*

101

Table GE 5/6 Union Membership by Sex, Industry and Status   GERMANY (FRG)

year:1985		total		market			public			status	
isic	conf.	all	female	b-c	w-c	total	b-c	w-c	total	b-c	w-c
1	DGB	36	.	17		17	15	5	19	31	
1	DBB	6	.					6	6		
1	Other	1	.		1	1					
		42	*.*	*17*		*17*	*15*	*10*	*25*	*31*	*1*
2-4	DGB	3,963	.	3,279	615	3,894	44	25	69	3,322	64
2-4	DAG	79	.		79	79					79
2-4	Other	52	.		52	52					52
		1,099	*.*	*3,279*	*716*	*1,001*	*44*	*25*	*69*	*3,322*	*77*
5	DGB	457	.	419	38	457				419	38
5	DAG	24	.		24	24					24
5	Other	1	.		1	1					
		482	*.*	*419*	*63*	*482*				*419*	*63*
6+8	DGB	370	.	46	324	370				46	324
6+8	DAG	208	.		208	208					208
6+8	Other	3	.		3	3					3
		580	*.*	*46*	*535*	*580*				*46*	*535*
7	DGB	791	.	69	21	90	302	399	701	371	420
7	DAG	6	.		6	6					6
7	DBB	90	.				14	77	90	14	77
		887	*.*	*69*	*27*	*96*	*315*	*476*	*791*	*385*	*502*
9	DGB	1,136	.	30	30	60	296	781	1,077	326	810
9	DAG	123	.					123	123		123
9	DBB	541	.					541	541		541
9	Other	53	.					53	53		53
		1,854	*.*	*30*	*30*	*60*	*296*	*1,499*	*1,794*	*326*	*1,528*
0	CGB	307	.	116	88	204	8	95	103	124	183
		307	*.*	*116*	*88*	*204*	*8*	*95*	*103*	*124*	*183*
	DGB	6,753	.	3,859	1,028	4,886	656	1,210	1,866	4,514	2,238
	DAG	438	.		316	316		123	123		438
	DBB	637	.				14	624	637	14	624
	CGB	307	.	116	88	204	8	95	103	124	183
	Other	109	.		56	56		53	53		109
		8,244	*.*	*3,975*	*1,488*	*5,463*	*678*	*2,105*	*2,783*	*4,652*	*3,592*
incl. pens:											
	DGB	7,720	1,705	4,371	1,114	5,485	813	1,424	2,237	5,184	2,537
	DAG	501	206		348	348		153	153		501
	DBB	796	200				20	777	796	20	777
	CGB	307	70	116	88	204	8	95	103	124	183
	Other	120	.		56	56		64	64		120
		9,444	*2,181*	*4,487*	*1,606*	*6.093*	*841*	*2,513*	*3,354*	*5,327*	*4,118*

Table GE 6/1 Dependent Labour Force by Sex, Industry and Status   GERMANY

1925	total		market			public			status	
isic	all	female	b-c	w-c	total	b-c	w-c	total	b-c	w-c
1	2,769	.	.	.	.	.	.	.	2,607	162
2-4	9,988	.	.	.	.	.	.	.	8,677	1,311
5	1,479	.	.	.	.	.	.	.	1,343	136
6+8	1,744	.	.	.	.	.	.	.	406	1,338
7	1,541	.	.	.	.	.	.	.	782	759
9	3,541	.	.	.	.	.	.	.	2,106	1,435
0	247	.	.	.	.	.	.	.	218	29
	21,309	6,443	.	.	.	.	1,392	.	16,139	5,170

Table GE 6/2 Dependent Labour Force by Sex, Industry and Status   GERMANY

1950	total		market			public			status	
isic	all	female	b-c	w-c	total	b-c	w-c	total	b-c	w-c
1	1,129	.	.	.	.	.	.	.	1,089	40
2-4	6,715	.	.	.	.	.	.	.	5,716	999
5	1,522	.	.	.	.	.	.	.	1,412	110
6+8	1,395	.	.	.	.	.	.	.	367	1,028
7	1,137	.	.	.	.	.	.	.	611	526
9	3,251	.	.	.	.	.	.	.	1,597	1,654
0	483	.	.	.	.	.	.	.	438	45
	15,631	4,801	10,389	2,896	13,285	840	1,506	2,346	11,229	4,402

Table GE 6/3 Dependent Labour Force by Sex, Industry and Status   GERMANY

1961	total		market			public			status	
isic	all	female	b-c	w-c	total	b-c	w-c	total	b-c	w-c
1	454	.	.	.	.	.	.	.	416	38
2-4	10,030	.	.	.	.	.	.	.	8,041	1,989
5	1,837	.	.	.	.	.	.	.	1,686	151
6+8	2,503	.	.	.	.	.	.	.	501	2,001
7	1,392	.	.	.	.	.	.	.	637	755
9	4,303	.	.	.	.	.	.	.	1,520	2,783
0	64	.	.	.	.	.	.	.	48	16
	20,582	6,997	11,850	5,667	17,517	1,000	2,065	3,065	12,850	7,732

Table GE 6/4 Dependent Labour Force by Sex, Industry and Status   GERMANY

1970	total		market			public			status	
isic	all	female	b-c	w-c	total	b-c	w-c	total	b-c	w-c
1	319	.	.	.	.	.	.	.	262	58
2-4	10,272	.	.	.	.	.	.	.	7,402	2,869
5	1,827	.	.	.	.	.	.	.	1,563	263
6+8	3,149	.	.	.	.	.	.	.	829	2,320
7	1,349	.	.	.	.	.	.	.	566	783
9	4,869	.	.	.	.	.	.	.	1,467	3,403
	21,784	7,606	11,059	7,063	18,121	1,030	2,633	3,663	12,089	9,695

Table GE 6/5 Dependent Labour Force by Sex, Industry and Status   GERMANY

1979	total		market			public			status	
isic	all	female	b-c	w-c	total	b-c	w-c	total	b-c	w-c
1	270	.	.	.	.	.	.	.	.	.
2-4	9,207	.	.	.	.	.	.	.	.	.
5	1,768	.	.	.	.	.	.	.	.	.
6+8	3,610	.	.	.	.	.	.	.	.	.
7	1,422	.	.	.	.	.	.	.	.	.
9	6,172	.	.	.	.	.	.	.	.	.
0	147	.	.	.	.	.	.	.	.	.
	22,596	8,645	10,210	7,940	18,150	1,078	3,368	4,446	11,288	11,308

Table GE 6/6 Dependent Labour Force by Sex, Industry and Status   GERMANY

1985	total		market			public			status	
isic	all	female	b-c	w-c	total	b-c	w-c	total	b-c	w-c
1	280	.	.	.	.	.	.	.	.	.
2-4	8,640	.	.	.	.	.	.	.	.	.
5	1,698	.	.	.	.	.	.	.	.	.
6+8	3,563	.	.	.	.	.	.	.	.	.
7	1,469	.	.	.	.	.	.	.	.	.
9	7,565	.	.	.	.	.	.	.	.	.
0	392	.	.	.	.	.	.	.	.	.
	23,607	9,377	10,179	8,821	19,000	1,075	3,532	4,607	11,254	12,353

Chapter 5: ITALY

LIST OF UNION CONFEDERATIONS: name, abbreviation and foundation year

1 *Confederazione Generale Italiana del Lavoro* (CGIL): 1944-
   General Confederation of Italian Labour

2 *Confederazione Italiana dei Sindacati Lavoratori* (CISL): 1950
   Italian Confederation of Labour Unions

3 *Unione Italiana del Lavoro* (UIL): 1950
   Italian Confederation of Labour

---

1. AGGREGATE MEMBERSHIP STATISTICS

1.1 General Series

Union membership statistics in Italy have improved enormously in the
past decade or so. Especially with the study of the regional membership
files of individual unions, undertaken by the Centre for Social and
Trade Union Studies (CESOS, Centro di Studi Sociali e Sindacali) in
Rome, it has become possible to arrive at a reliable time-series of
union membership for most of the post-war years. Unfortunately, the
CESOS study did not cover the UIL before 1977. This organization did
not keep its archives and until 1968 no reliable data as regards the
UIL membership exist. The only estimates of its membership in the 1950s
and 1960s which I have come across is from one of its former leaders,
Franco Simoncini, who attributes to the UIL 2.6% of all union members
in Italy in 1950, 6.1% in 1953, 15.6% in 1958 and about 16% in the
early 1960 (Simoncini, 1986: 76). I have included these estimates in my
tables on membership composition and shifts, but not in any of the
annual series before 1968.
       Unlike the other nine countries in this study, I have limited
myself to the postwar period in the case of Italy. Few reliable studies
and statistics are known about before the victory of fascism, in 1922,
and the subsequent repression of the democratic labour movement.
       The CESOS-studies provide the main source for my statistics on
postwar union membership in Italy. The first study (Romagnoli et.al.,
1980, vol.2: tables 1.1-4.4.7) reported the annual membership figures
between 1950 and 1977 in unions affiliated with the CGIL and the CISL.
It has been possible to extend this series to 1985 on the basis of
Romagnoli & Della Rocca (1982: 92, table 3.1) and the CESOS reports for
1981, 1982/3, 1983/4, 1984/5 and 1985/6 (CESOS, 1982, 1984, 1985, 1986
and 1987). The five annual CESOS-reports contain also membership
statistics of UIL-affiliates. A complete series of the membership in

each of its affiliates after 1977 was obtained directly from the UIL-secretariat in Rome (UIL-Report: 'Andamento generale per categorie e per settore'). With respect to the UIL before 1968, I have relied on the careful study by Sebastiano Coi. This author provides a wealth of information on membership, staff and finances of all three confederations, including a credible estimate of the 1968 and 1972-1978 aggregate membership of the UIL (Coi, 1979: 201, table 1). Romagnoli & Della Rocca (1982: 92, table 3.1) have extended this aggregate membership series of the UIL to the full 1970-1980 period, to which I have added the interpolated figure for 1969. Before 1968 the annual membership series does not include the UIL.

All membership figures refer to 31 December of each year. The general membership series does not include members organized in union organizations outside the three main Italian trade union confederations (see below).

1.2 Retired and Self-Employed Members

1.2.1 Pensioners

Each of the three Italian union confederations includes large numbers of retired workers and small tenant farmers in their reported membership. For the purpose of calculating comparable union density rates, I have excluded such members.

Retired workers and pensioners in the CGIL are organized in the *Sindacato Pensionati Italiani* (SPI), in the CISL in the *Federazione Nazionale dei Pensionati* (FNP), and in the UIL in the *Unione Italiana Lavoratori Pensionati* (UILP). The membership in the pensioners unions of the CGIL and CISL between 1950 and 1977 is reported in Romagnoli et.al. (1980, vol.2: table 1.2). It is probable that the figures they report between 1949 and 1954 also include the unemployed members which the CGIL and CISL until then organized via the local Labour Chambers. For the period after 1977, the membership data for these two pensioners unions, as well as the pensioner union affiliated with the UIL, is obtained from the CESOS reports and UIL-report. Unfortunately, Coi did not specify the 'passive' membership in the UIL, but from the sectoral data provided by Romagnoli & Della Rocca (1982) their number can be calculated for 1970 and 1975. On the basis of these figures I have interpolated the 'passive membership' in the UIL for the full 1968-1976 period.

1.2.2 Farmers

Self-employed farmers (and their families) are also organized in separate organizations: the *Federmezzadri* in the CGIL, the *Federcoltivatori* (SINADES, now UGE) in the CISL, and the *Unione Mezzadri e Coltivatori* (UIMEC) in the UIL. The *Federmezzadri* left in 1978 the CGIL in order to become part of the main farmers organization, the *Confederazione Italiana Coltivatori* (Biagioni, 1978; also: Romagnoli & Della Rocca, 1982: 91, note 6). The membership data of these organizations could be obtained indirectly by subtracting the members of the agricultural (wage earners) unions (the *Federbraccianti* in the CGIL and the *FISBA* in the CISL) from the total membership of these confederations in agriculture (Romagnoli et.al, 1980, vol 2.: tables 3.1 and 2.1). The

106

membership in the *Federbraccianti* is also reported in Amoretti (1974: 48, table 1; and 60: table 4) and for later years in Biagioni, Palmieri & Pipan (1980: 39, table 7). For the 1977-1985 the membership figures of the CISL- and UIL-unions of self-employed farmers are based on the five CESOS reports and the aforementioned internal UIL-report ('Andamento..'). For the years between 1968 and 1976 the number of self-employed farmers in the UIL has been estimated by the author. The reported membership of the UIL includes a small categories, called 'various members', including direct members to the confederation such as students, professionals and, possibly, also unemployed workers. I have counted such members as belonging to the 'active membership' of the UIL.

1.2.3 Unemployed workers

Reported membership in Italy includes unemployed workers, especially those unemployed workers who had been holding regular jobs in the official economy. In the Italian lay-off system (the so-called *Cassa Integrazione Guadagni*) the 'employment contract' with the former employer is retained, and so will probably his link with the union in case he was a member (Grais, 1982: Ch.7). Thus, all figures on 'active membership' given in the tables, with the exception perhaps of the years before 1954, include unemployed members. In 1980 the CGIL started to organize first-job seekers, an ever larger component of Italy's rising number of unemployed; in 1985 the CISL started to do likewise. Hitherto, rallying the unemployed in separate union structures has met with little success, and only small numbers have unionized (CESOS, 1987).

1.3. Female Membership

It is impossible to disaggregate union membership by gender. Italian unions do not register such data. Nor did they seem to apply special dues rates for women, which is often the administrate rationale why trade unions register such data in the first place. The only information derives from survey studies. A representative survey among CGIL members in 1977 showed that almost 30% of the overall CGIL membership were females (Biagioni, Palmieri & Pipan, 1980: 63-74). By the end of the decade this percentage appears to have increased to over 35% (CGIL, Rassegna Sindacale, 1979, no.5). I have not come across any figures relating to the female membership in the CISL or UIL.

1.4 Membership Outside The Main Confederations

A still unsolved problem is the compilation of any reliable series on membership outside the three main trade union confederations in Italy. Several so-called 'autonomous' unions and confederations exist, but little is known about their internal organization, functions, status and strength. Rarely, these organizations are involved in collective bargaining. The main area in which 'autonomous' union organizations are operating is the public sector, and it is here that they seem to have gained more weight in recent years - along with the newly emerging '*comitati di base*' (*COBAS*) or 'wild-cat organizations' of both union and non-union members. These organizations play an important role in Italian industrial relations insofar as they allow discontent union members to 'vote with their feet' in a collective way.

In 1950 the *Confederazione Italiana dei Sindacati Nazionale dei Lavoratori* (CISNAL) was founded. It used to be closely connected with the MSI, Italy's fascist party. The CISNAL is joined by over 60 small unions. Seven years later another confederations was founded, the *Confederazione Italiana dei Sindacati Autonomi Lavoratori* (CISAL). It represents the 'craft' tradition most strongly - or the tradition of sectional corporatism as they say in Italy - and now comprises some 60 small 'occupational' or 'company' unions. The most recent creation is the *Confederazione Sindacati Autonomi Lavoratori* (CONFSAL) which has its stronghold mainly in the public sector. Generally, these confederations claim a following which is wholly uncontrollable and most often quite incredible (see, for instance, the figures in the annual <u>1982 Europe Yearbook</u>, which uncritically reports a 1 million membership of the CISNAL and 300,000 members of the CISAL). Finally there exists still an Anarchist Union Federation - once a very important tradition in Italian labour. It now has only a minor regional influence in the North-Western part of Toscany.

In the 1970s the 'autonomous unions', affiliated to the CISNAL or CISAL, have been denied bargaining rights in the private sector by the employers' organizations and the three main confederations. Previously, they played at times an influential role - for instance, at FIAT in the late 1950s - alongside the non-communist unions. In the 1970s the phenomenon of 'autonomous' unions became with some notable exceptions (banking is the major one) confined to the (semi-)public service sector: railways, sea and air transport, public enterprises, central government (ministries and agencies), education and health services (see below).

Some research on the membership of the 'autonomous' unions, based on sectoral and regional surveys as well as on voting results for the administrative councils in the public service, has been carried out by the Research Department of the CGIL. The first survey, in 1975, suggested an overall membership of between 471,300 and 501,300 with less than 5% in industry and between 10% and 15% in banking and commerce. The remainder, including 150,000 pensioners, is in the (semi-)public sector. A second survey, in 1977, put the figure of 'employed' members in 'autonomous' unions near 350,000 (Biagioni, Palmieri & Pipan, 1980: 53-56). In the 1950s and 1960s the non-confederal unions attracted about one-fifth of the total union membership in the (semi-)public sector, in the late 1970s their share was estimated to lie between 12% and 15% of the total membership, perhaps with a slight tendency to increase in recent years (Biagioni, Palmieri & Pipan, 1980; Stefanelli, 1981: 26 and 40, table 2; CESOS, 1982 etc. These figures do not include the recently created organizations of supervisory and managerial staffs, or the members attracted by the recent (1986-1987) 'wild-cat' organization of the *COBAS*.

In recent years, the problem of measuring the weight of the 'autonomous unions' is compounded by the emergence of professional associations and unions of managers and supervisors. Interest organizations among these categories, surely not always to be counted as unions on my definition, seem to have proliferated after the so-called 'March of 40,000' (staff employees) in Turin in 1980 against a strike of the confederal unions of metalworkers at FIAT. This episode surprised and embarrassed the 'official' confederal unions, and had wide-ranging consequences. It marked the end of an era of wide support for and influence of the confederal unions, and seems to have sparked off a number of attempts to establish independent associations among white-collar staff (Baldissera, 1988).

The oldest association, so it seems, is the *Unione Italiana Quadri* (UNIONQUADRI), which was founded in 1975. It is currently joined by 11 professional and staff associations of employees with academic grades (in economics, law, engineering, architects, statisticians, medical staff, etc). One of its most important affiliates is the *Unione Sinda-cale dei Professionisti del Pubblico Impiego* (USPP) which recruits technical and professional staff in the public sector. The *Italquadri*, founded in 1983, is a federation of about 30 company-wise organized staff associations, mainly in industry and state enterprises. It has to compete with the *Associazione Nazionale dei Quadri del'Industria* (ANQUI), founded in late 1985, which claims the same domain and is the strongest organization at FIAT. This federation is also joined by company staff associations (nearly 20 in 1986). Yet another organi-zation of this kind exists in the form of the *Sindacato Nazionale Quadri Industria* (SINQUADRI), which is however a union rather than federation. The SINQUADRI is the strongest affiliate of the also recently founded *Confederazione dei Quadri*, which has in total 8 sectoral demarcated or 'industrial' affiliates. More than the others, the last mentioned organization claims to be a proper union, and wants to conquer a place at the bargaining table. It tries to deprive the CGIL, CISL and UIL unions of the prerogative to negotiate agreements, or express interests, on behalf of white-collar staffs. Hitherto, the *Confederazione dei Quadri* has failed to convince the relevant sectoral employers' associations. Finally, I should mention the *Confederazione Italiana Dirigenti d'Azienda* (CIDA). Founded in 1945, the CIDA unites 6 unions of higher and leading managerial staff in both private and state enterprises. This organization is best seen as a professional service organization (pensions, tax reclaims, etc.). It should be observed that nearly all these organizations are in some way tied into political parties or connected with party factions. Nearly all these organi-zations have overlapping domains and compete for membership and influ-ence with each other and with the three main confederations. Reliable figures on membership do not exist.

2.   MEMBERSHIP BY INDUSTRY AND STATUS

2.1. Classification by Industry

1   Agriculture:
- CGIL: *FEDERBRACCIANTI* (agricultural workers)
- CISL: *FISBA* (agricultural workers)
- UIL: *UISBA* (agricultural workers)

2-5   Mining, Manufacturing, Construction, and Gas, Water & Electricity:
- CGIL: *FILCEA* (oil refineries & chemical industry), *FILLEA* (con-struction, wood & furniture), *FIOM* (metal & engineering), *FILTEA* (textile & cloth), *FILZIAT* (food), *FIDAG* (printing), *FILPS* (paper & printing), *FILIS* (printing, paper & publishing), *FIDAG* (gas),

FILDA (water), *FIDAE* (electricity), *FNLE* (gas, water & electricity).
- CISL: *FULPIA* (food), *MONOPOLI DI STATO* (salt, tobacco, state monopolies), *FAT* (food & tobacco), *FEDERCHIMICI* (chemical & allied industry), *FEDERENERGIA* (energy production), *FLERICA* (gas, oil, chemical & allied industry), *FLAEI* (electricity), *FILCA* (construction), *FIM* (metal & engineering), *FEDERLIBRO* (printing & publishing), *FIS* (printing, publishing & entertainment), *FILTA* (textile & cloth).
- UIL: *UILIAS* (food), *UILTA* (textile, cloth and leather), *UILM* (metal and engineering), *UILPEM* (oil & gas), *UILCID* (chemical and allied industries), *UIL-MONOPOLI* (salt, tobacco etc., state monopolies), *FENEAL* (construction, wood & furniture), *UILSP* (public works), *UIL-RICERCA* (industry research), *FILSIC* (printing & publishing).

6+8 Commerce, Banking & Insurance:
- CGIL: *FILDA* (insurance), *SINAGI* (sales workers), *FIARVEP* (salesmen), *SNAV* (commercial travellers), *USPIE* (employees Bank of Italy), *FIDAC* (commercial banks), *FISAC* (banking, insurance & finance)
- CISL: *FILASCAT* (commerce), *FIB* (banking), *FILA* (insurance)
- UIL: *UILTUCS* (commerce, tourism and commercial services), *UIB* (banking & finance), *UILASS* (insurance), *FILE* (finance), *UILTCA* (municipal credit institutions).

7 Transport & Communication:
- CGIL: *FIAI* (car ferries), *FIFTA* (road transport), *SFI* (railways), *FIPAC* (air transport), *FILM* (sea transport), *FILP* (dockers), *FILT* (transport), *FIDAT* (telecommunication), *FIP* (post office), *FILPT* (post office & telecommunication)
- CISL: *FENLAI* (car ferries), *FILAC* (road transport), *FILM* (sea transport), *FILP* (dockers), *FILTAT* (air transport), *SAUFI* (railways), *FIT* (transport), *SILP, SILULAP, SILTS, SILTE* (all telephone), *FPT* (post office & telephone)
- UIL: *SIUF* (railways), *UILTATEP* (road transport), *FNAI* (car ferries), *UIGEA* (air transport), *UIM* (sea transport), *UIL-TRASPORTI* (transport), *UILPOST* (Post Office), *UILTES* (state telephone company), *UILTE* (telephone & communication)

9 Other Services:
- CGIL: *FILCAMS* (hotel & restaurants, partly in commerce), *FNELS* (local government & public services), *FIDEP* (bodies under public law), *SUNPU* (university non-teaching staff), *SNR* (research), *FNDS* (state employees), *FNLAV* (artists), *FILS* (entertainment), *SNS* (education), *FED-FUNZIONE PUBBLICA* (local & central government & health).
- CISL: *SINDACATO RICERCA* (research), *SINASCEL, SISM, UNIVERSITà* (higher education), *FEDERSCUOLA* (education), *MEDICI* (hospitals), *FISOS (health & hospitals)*, *FILS* (central government), *FIDEL* (local government), *FEDERPUBBLICI* (public bodies), *FP* (central and local government & public bodies), *VVFF* (fire guards), *FULS* (entertainment).
- UIL: *Federazione Sanità* (health services), *UILDEP* (public bodies), *UIL-SCUOLA* (education), *UIL-ORGANI COSTITUZIONALI*

110

(constitutional bodies), *UNDEL* (local government), *UILSTAT* (state employees), *UILEM* (public institutions and services Southern Italy).

In recent years union structures in all three confederations have been 'rationalized' along 'industrial lines' via amalgamations and by building federations between them. This process has been quite intense in printing, energy, commerce & banking, transport and in the public services. On the other hand, the list of unions and union names, given above, is still less than complete if we travel further back in history than 1970. The merger process has made it rather more difficult to classify the membership by industry. In some cases I have used the share of the membership before merging as the best estimate for sectoral shares (for instance, between commerce and other services, or between printing and entertainment).

2.2   Classification by Status

As to non-manual union membership, we have only the two ISTVET-surveys, of 1972 and 1982, among workers and employees in public and private industrial enterprises (excluding other sectors). From this surveys, I have compiled a summary table, with information on the membership composition of the three main confederation. The percentages shown in the table cannot easily the compared with those provided for the other countries, especially since they do not include the members working in the public and semi-public sector. The proportion of white-collar employees in the membership will probably be much larger than shown in these figures. A survey of the membership of the UIl, conducted in 1982, showed that of its total membership, including its members employed in the government sector, 30% belonged to the non-manual category: 6% of all members in agriculture, 9% in industry, 47% in transport, 60% in public services, and 68% in commerce, banking & insurance, and miscellaneous private services (CESOS, 1984: 241).

Membership Composition of Three Main Italian Confederations (in %) (excluding membership in agriculture, and government services)								
category	CGIL 1972	1982	CISL 1972	1982	UIL 1972	1982	total 1972	1982
workers -unskilled	35.4	35.7	33.0	30.3	27.8	25.4	33.2	29.7
-skilled	58.8	54.7	53.9	47.7	54.8	57.7	48.8	45.9
employees	5.8	9.6	13.1	21.0	17.5	16.9	18.0	24.4
total	100.0	100.0	100.0	100.0	100.0	100.0	100.0	100.0

2.3 Public sector unionism

In general, the classification of Italian trade union members according to private or public employment is rather simple - as there is virtually no cross-cutting membership in Italian unions, that is, if we exclude nationalized industries. I classified as belonging to the public sector the membership of all unions in public transport (rail, air & car ferries - the membership in recent years has been extrapolated on the basis of union membership figures before the amalgamations in these years), in the Post Office and in telecommunication, and in public services (central & local government or public bodies, education & health services). It is possible to make a further breakdown between the public and private sector in industry (gas, water & electricity, state monopoly), but for reasons of comparability with other countries I have not included such members in the public sector.
    As to the membership in the 'autonomous' unions, the following figures on their sectoral composition have been derived from various sources:

-- Railways and car ferries:
    Of the about 200,000 employees in this domain, the three confederal unions organized about 132,000 in the late 1970s, against 10,000 recruited by the *Federazione Italiana Sindacati Autonomi delle Ferrovie* (FISAF). The FISAF is a federation of occupational unions and is particular strong among train machinists, technical and station staff, and ferry pilots. A further group of occupational unions, some adhering to the CISNAL or the CISAL, recruited between 5,000 and 8,000 members (Stefanelli, 1981: 134-145). In 1985 the five FISAF-unions appeared to have increased their membership to 13,500, whereas 17 other small occupational unions had nearly 7,000 members, and 138,000 employees joined the confederal unions (CESOS, 1987: 212).

-- Air transport:
    The independent unions of aviation pilots, the *Associatione Nazionale Piloti Aviazione Commerciale* (ANPAC), organizes the majority of the 1,700 pilots in commercial air traffic (1,200 members against 250 in the confederal unions. The autonomous union of air traffic controllers, the *Associazione Tecnici di Volo*, is also the strongest in the field. It organizes 90 of the total of 160 employees, whereas the confederal unions attract another 60. With 900 members the confederal unions seem to be the main representatives of the 3,000 flight assistants, but the independent union, the *Associazione Nazionale Professionale Assistenti di Volo* (ANPAV), is also in a strong position (600 members). Only a small minority, about three to four hundred, of the 22,000 airport ground personnel is organized in the autonomous unions against almost 20,000 in the confederal unions (Stefanelli, 1981: 146--164). It is clear that the sector as a whole, like railways, is highly unionized. It should be observed that air transport in Italy is a publicly regulated service.

-- Sea transport (semi-public or nationalized):
    Here the autonomous unions of seamen and officers have become particularly strong after 1975 as a response to employment decline

and the reorganization of the sector, but no precise membership figures are available (see: Stefanelli, 1981: 164-167).

-- Banking & Finance:
In this domain there appears to exist an old 'corporatist' tradition based upon company unions. In addition to a small CISNAL union, this tradition has survived in the *Federazione Autonoma Bancari Italiani* (FABI), which was founded in 1948 as a federation of company unions. Already in the 1950s the FABI outnumbered the three confederal unions in commercial banks and financial institutions. In the early 1980s the FABI claimed 52,000 members. Various other independent unions - some regional, others restricted to one company, or a particular professional category - have emerged in the 1970s and 1980s, some affiliated to the CISAL. Many of these unions have acquired a place at the bargaining table and fiercely compete with the confederal unions (Stefanelli, 1981: 169-188; CESOS, 1985: 235; CESOS, 1987: 209-210).

-- Central Government:
The 'autonomous' unions attract one-fifth to one-fourth of all unionized employees in central state institutions. The most important independent organizations are the civil servant's association UNSA, the association of higher civil servants DIRSTAT, and the unions affiliated with the CISNAL, the CISAL and the CONFSAL. Most of these unions compete with one another. The most recent invention appears to be the *Unione Sindacale dei Professionalisti del Pubblico Impiego* (USPPI) which organizes professional and technical staff (Stefanelli, 1981: 62-68; CESOS, 1987: 213-4).

-- Local government & health:
In this domain the 'autonomous' unions represent between 6% and 10% of all unionized employees. In the health sector some 16 independent unions exist, the most important of which is the *Associazione Nazionale Aiuti e Assistenti Ospedalieri* (ANAAO) with 26,000 members in 1985. The CISAS has its own federation in the semi-public sector which takes part in bargaining (Stefanelli, 1981: 40; CESOS, 1987: 210-1).

-- Education:
The main 'autonomous' unions of teachers, schoolmasters and professionals in education originated, in 1948-1949, following the demise of the unitarian CGIL and the foundation of the CISL and UIL. Some of the teachers' unions broke away from the CGIL, passed over to the CISL or remained unaffiliated. Many of these organizations are tied to partisan politics and did not escape the logic of political factionalism. As unions they remained rather ineffective: with the reform of the legal status of state personnel in the mid-1950s, teachers did unlike others not acquire the status of civil servants, and education in Italy is still notorious for its many precarious, ill-qualified and badly paid jobs. With the expansion of the education sector in the 1970s unions of all kind increased in number and membership. In 1977-78 a number of these organizations merged into the *Sindacato Nazionale Autonomo dei Lavoratori della Scuola* (SNALS), which combined an estimated membership of 150,000 teachers and employees in eduction. This

figure compares with 160,000 in the CISL, 110,000 in the CGIL, 40,000 in the UIL, and perhaps a further 100,000 in other organizations (Stefanelli, 1981: 93-127; Biagioni, Palmieri & Pipan, 1980: 36-37). The SNALS is affiliated to the CONFSAL, and has grown to some 170,000 members in the mid-1980s (calculated from CESOS, 1987: 211), which is slightly less than the relevant CISL union and slightly more than the CGIL union in education.

3.   LABOUR FORCE STATISTICS

In principle, the official Italian Bureau of Statistics ISTAT, in Rome, offers a choice between three series of the dependent labour force. None of these series covers the full period. The 'old series', which has been in use until 1977, is believed to have severely underestimated people in marginal employment and the unemployed. The 'new series' is based upon the revised quarterly labour force sample surveys which appear to give a fuller picture of the labour market. In its present form the surveys exist since 1977, but the series has been revised backwards by the ISTAT till 1959. Finally, a 'new new series' exists since 1986, following the upward revision of the Italian GDP and labour force by about 15% on account of the 'submerged economy' and competition with the United Kingdom over its place in the League of Leading Economies. The last revision took into account the outcome of the most Population Census of 1981 which showed 1 to 1,5 million people more in (partly informal) employment than previously had been assumed. However, this latest revision covers only the most recent years, is still in elaboration and has not been officially published yet.

With respect to the period 1950-1959 I have used the 'old series' of the ISTAT: Occupati presenti in Italia, 1951-1973, Rome 1974, unpublished. The figure for 1950 is added on the basis of a backward interpolation (see: ISTAT, Sommario di Statistiche Storiche dell'Italia 1861-1965, Rome 1968: 127-128, tables 97-98: employed labour force less employers, self-employed and unpaid family workers). From 1960 to 1985 the 'new series' was used, in its most complete version, based on the quarterly labour force sample surveys and other sources, and published as part of the National Account Statistics: ISTAT, Annuario di Contabilità Nazionale, Rome 1986, vol.XIV, vol.1: 112-114, tables 3.3: 'Occupati presenti in Italia per ramo e branca; dipendenti'. The figure for 1985 was kindly provided by the ISTAT. These figures on the employed dependent labour force include the professional military, but not conscripts. The figures on employees in employment are annual averages, to which I have added the average number of unemployed. In their case, there is also a break in 1959/1960. For the first period I have not used the official ISTAT series, which suffers from severe understatement of unemployment, but registration data on unemployment ('class I+II' in the lists of the placement offices of the Ministry of Labour, excluding those unemployed which held no previous employment). In the years considered, the figures of the Ministry of Labour appear to reflect the development of unemployment in the 1950s better than the ISTAT data. For both series, and a comparison, see: Büchli, 1965: 49-50, tables 2-4; Ferri, 1971: 33. For the years 1959-85 I have used the 'new series' on unemployment of the ISTAT ('Persone in cerca di occupazione', including first-job seekers and re-entrants) based on the quarterly labour force sample surveys. Source: ISTAT, Annuario di Statistiche del Lavoro, Rome, annual, 'nuova serie 1959-'.

For the data on employment by industry I have used the same sources. It should be observed that these figures exclude the unemployed throughout. Classification of the unemployed by industrial sector was not possible. Comparison with the census data of 1951, 1961, 1971 and 1981 (for the first three census: Flora, Kraus and Pfenning, 1987: 558-560; ISTAT for the 1981 data), shows considerable differences, especially in recent years. The divergence is in part explained by the inclusion of the unemployed (those classifiable to their previous employment) in the census-data, and in part by the more extensive census-definition of employment to which I have referred earlier. For the classification by status, the censuses provide the only source. The data on employment in the public or private sector have been taken from the National Account Statistics, which derives from data of both the ISTAT and the Finance Ministry, but is published in the Italian Statistical Yearbook. It shows employment in central government (including ministries, education, Post Office and telecommunication, railways, but not state monopolies or other state enterprises) and local government (including regions, provinces and municipalities, health and social insurance, but not gas, water & electricity, or municipal enterprises).

4. TABLES

table: IT 1/2	Membership by Confederations				ITALY
year	CGIL	CISL	UIL	Other	total
	1	2	3		
1950	4,640,5	1,189,9	.	.	5,830,4
1951	4,490,8	1,337,8	.	.	5,828,6
1952	4,342,2	1,322,0	.	.	5,664,2
1953	4,074,6	1,305,4	.	.	5,380,0
1954	4,136,4	1,326,5	.	.	5,462,9
1955	4,194,2	1,342,2	.	.	5,536,4
1956	3,666,0	1,706,8	.	.	5,372,8
1957	3,137,8	1,261,8	.	.	4,399,6
1958	2,595,5	1,654,2	.	.	4,249,7
1959	2,600,7	1,283,9	.	.	3,884,6
1960	2,583,2	1,324,4	.	.	3,907,6
1961	2,531,3	1,398,9	.	.	3,930,2
1962	2,610,8	1,435,6	.	.	4,046,4
1963	2,625,6	1,503,6	.	.	4,129,2
1964	2,711,8	1,515,2	.	.	4,227,0
1965	2,542,9	1,468,0	.	.	4,010,9
1966	2,457,9	1,490,8	.	.	3,948,7
1967	2,423,5	1,522,9	.	.	3,946,4
1968	2,461,0	1,626,8	648,4	.	4,736,2
1969	2,626,4	1,641,3	714,2	.	4,981,9
1970	2,942,5	1,807,6	780,0	.	5,530,1
1971	3,138,4	1,973,3	825,0	.	5,936,7
1972	3,215,0	2,184,3	842,9	.	6,242,2
1973	3,435,6	2,214,1	901,9	.	6,551,6
1974	3,826,6	2,472,7	965,1	.	7,264,4
1975	4,081,4	2,593,5	1,032,6	.	7,707,5
1976	4,313,1	2,823,8	1,104,9	.	8,241,8
1977	4,475,4	2,809,8	1,160,1	.	8,445,3
1978	4,528,0	2,868,7	1,284,7	.	8,681,4
1979	4,583,5	2,906,2	1,326,8	.	8,816,5
1980	4,599,1	3,059,8	1,346,9	.	9,005,8
1981	4,595,0	2,988,8	1,357,3	.	8,941,1
1982	4,576,0	2,976,9	1,358,8	.	8,911,7
1983	4,556,1	2,953,4	1,351,5	.	8,861,0
1984	4,546,3	3,097,2	1,344,5	.	8,988,0
1985	4,592,0	2,953,1	1,306,3	.	8,851,4

table: IT 2	Confederal Membership Shares in per centage of total members			ITALY
year	CGIL	CISL	UIL	total
	1	2	3	
1950	79.6 (77.4)	20.4 (19.8)	(2.6)	100.0
1955	75.8 .	24.2 .	.	100.0
1960	66.1 (55.5)	33.9 (28.5)	(16.0)	100.0
1965	63.4 .	36.6 .	.	100.0
1970	(61.9) 53.2	(38.1) 32.7	14.1	100.0
1975	(61.1) 53.0	(38.9) 33.6	13.4	100.0
1980	(60.0) 51.1	(39.9) 34.0	15.0	100.0
1985	(60.9) 51.9	(39.1) 33.4	14.8	100.0

table: IT 3/1			Pensioners and self-employed members						ITALY
year	CGIL		CISL		UIL		total	
	pens	s-e	pens	s-e	pens	s-e	pens	s-e
1950	326,8	542,8	95,5	73,0	.	.	422,3	615,8
1951	352,8	534,9	133,0	111,4	.	.	485,8	646,3
1952	321,6	518,9	134,2	111,9	.	.	455,8	630,8
1953	329,5	513,3	121,2	114,2	.	.	450,7	627,5
1954	391,1	513,9	141,4	130,9	.	.	532,5	644,8
1955	452,9	514,4	176,1	118,3	.	.	629,0	632,7
1956	387,5	468,9	249,2	149,5	.	.	636,7	618,4
1957	322,1	423,3	139,5	116,7	.	.	461,6	540,0
1958	344,9	368,7	207,9	163,1	.	.	552,8	531,8
1959	344,7	368,6	162,0	129,9	.	.	506,7	498,5
1960	371,3	352,1	166,5	131,8	.	.	537,8	483,9
1961	355,5	326,6	151,8	115,1	.	.	507,3	441,7
1962	377,1	288,3	149,1	105,0	.	.	526,2	393,3
1963	357,1	245,8	134,1	98,6	.	.	491,2	344,4
1964	372,0	305,1	130,5	92,6	.	.	502,5	397,7
1965	385,4	289,0	149,9	90,4	.	.	535,3	379,4
1966	429,0	238,4	158,7	85,7	.	.	587,7	324,1
1967	398,6	225,0	147,3	81,2	.	.	545,9	306,2
1968	399,8	220,2	134,8	82,9	7,2	94,0	541,8	397,1
1969	424,0	198,6	142,8	62,8	11,1	92,0	577,9	353,4
1970	429,5	157,5	133,9	58,1	15,0	90,0	578,4	305,6
1971	436,0	133,8	137,8	62,3	18,9	88,0	592,7	284,1
1972	440,4	123,9	158,6	83,0	22,8	86,0	621,8	292,9
1973	470,8	107,0	148,2	84,7	26,7	84,0	645,7	275,7
1974	529,2	90,3	210,0	89,2	30,6	82,0	769,8	261,5
1975	676,0	79,0	252,4	66,4	34,5	80,0	962,9	225,4
1976	762,5	71,1	287,0	74,5	38,4	78,0	1,087,9	223,6
1977	872,7	62,7	320,3	70,5	42,3	76,3	1,235,3	209,5
1978	983,4	0	377,8	81,5	68,1	66,1	1,429,3	147,6
1979	1,056,2	0	396,0	92,5	66,3	57,4	1,518,5	149,9
1980	1,103,5	0	448,1	103,4	78,1	46,7	1,629,7	150,1
1981	1,186,2	0	509,5	106,3	87,5	45,7	1,783,2	152,0
1982	1,284,0	0	566,8	118,3	102,9	46,6	1,953,7	164,9
1983	1,398,8	0	595,8	131,6	118,8	43,9	2,113,4	175,5
1984	1,495,2	0	682,9	151,2	132,3	42,3	2,310,4	193,5
1985	1,619,1	0	744,0	147,2	146,7	38,6	2,509,8	185,8

table: IT 3/2	Pensioners and selfemployed in % of all members							ITALY
year	CGIL		CISL		UIL		total	
	% pens	% se	% pens	% se	% pens	% se	% pens	% se
1950	7.0	11.7	8.0	6.1	.	.	7.2	10.6
1951	7.9	11.9	9.9	8.3	.	.	8.3	11.1
1952	7.4	12.0	10.2	8.5	.	.	8.0	11.1
1953	8.1	12.6	9.3	8.7	.	.	8.4	11.7
1954	9.5	12.4	10.7	9.9	.	.	9.7	11.8
1955	10.8	12.3	13.1	8.8	.	.	11.4	11.4
1956	10.6	12.8	14.6	8.8	.	.	11.9	11.5
1957	10.3	13.5	11.1	9.2	.	.	10.5	12.3
1958	13.3	14.2	12.6	9.9	.	.	13.0	12.5
1959	13.3	14.2	12.6	10.1	.	.	13.0	12.8
1960	14.4	13.6	12.6	10.0	.	.	13.8	12.4
1961	14.0	12.9	10.9	8.2	.	.	12.9	11.2
1962	14.4	11.0	10.4	7.3	.	.	13.0	9.7
1963	13.6	9.4	8.9	6.6	.	.	11.9	8.3
1964	13.7	11.3	8.6	6.1	.	.	11.9	9.4
1965	15.2	11.4	10.2	6.2	.	.	13.3	9.5
1966	17.5	9.7	10.6	5.7	.	.	14.9	8.2
1967	16.4	9.3	9.7	5.3	.	.	13.8	7.8
1968	16.2	8.9	8.3	5.1	1.1	14.5	11.4	8.4
1969	16.1	7.6	8.7	3.8	1.6	12.9	11.6	7.1
1970	14.6	5.4	7.4	3.2	1.9	11.5	10.5	5.5
1971	13.9	4.3	7.0	3.2	2.3	10.7	10.0	4.8
1972	13.7	3.9	7.3	3.8	2.7	10.2	10.0	4.7
1973	13.7	3.1	6.7	3.8	3.0	9.3	9.9	4.2
1974	13.8	2.4	8.5	3.6	3.2	8.5	10.6	3.6
1975	16.6	1.9	9.7	2.6	3.3	7.7	12.5	2.9
1976	17.7	1.6	10.2	2.6	3.5	7.1	13.2	2.7
1977	19.5	1.4	11.4	2.5	3.6	6.6	14.6	2.5
1978	21.7		13.2	2.8	5.3	5.1	16.5	1.7
1979	23.0		13.6	3.2	5.0	4.3	17.2	1.7
1980	24.0		14.6	3.4	5.8	3.5	18.1	1.7
1981	25.8		17.0	3.6	6.4	3.4	19.9	1.7
1982	28.1		19.0	4.0	7.6	3.4	21.9	1.9
1983	30.7		20.2	4.5	8.8	3.2	23.9	2.0
1984	32.9		22.0	4.9	9.8	3.1	25.7	2.2
1985	35.3		25.2	5.0	11.2	3.0	28.4	2.1

table: IT 4/2			density rates				ITALY
year	membership		dep.labour force		density rates		
	total	less pens.	total	employed only	gross	net	employe only
	1	2	3	4	1:3	2:3	2:4
1950	5,830,4	4,792,3	11,900	10,300	49.0	40.3	46.5
1951	5,828,6	4,696,5	12,057	10,335	48.3	39.0	45.4
1952	5,664,2	4,577,6	12,341	10,491	45.9	37.1	43.6
1953	5,380,0	4,301,8	12,647	10,700	42.5	34.0	40.2
1954	5,402,9	4,205,0	12,833	10,898	42.5	33.3	39.3
1955	5,536.4	4,274,7	12,913	11,000	42.9	33.1	38.9
1956	5,372,8	4,117,7	13,042	11,105	41.2	31.6	37.1
1957	4,399,6	3,398,0	13,113	11,356	33.6	25.9	29.9
1958	4,249,7	3,165,1	13,247	11,488	32.1	23.9	27.6
1959	3,884,6	2,879,4	13,140	11,610	29.6	21.9	24.8
1960	3,907,6	2,885,9	13,203	11,988	29.6	21.9	24.1
1961	3,930,2	2,981,2	13,421	12,313	29.3	22.2	24.2
1962	4,046,4	3,126,9	13,598	12,629	29.8	23.0	24.8
1963	4,129,2	3,293,6	13,642	12,835	30.3	24.1	25.7
1964	4,227,0	3,326,8	13,714	12,810	30.8	24.3	26.0
1965	4,010,9	3,096,0	13,667	12,557	29.3	22.7	24.7
1966	3,948,7	3,036,9	13,632	12,440	29.0	22.3	24.4
1967	3,946,4	3,094,3	13,808	12,702	28.6	22.4	24.4
1968	4,736,2	3,797,3	14,014	12,842	33.8	27.1	29.6
1969	4,981,9	4,050,6	14,315	13,155	34.8	28.3	30.8
1970	5,530,1	4,646,1	14,450	13,339	38.3	32.2	34.8
1971	5,936,7	5,059,9	14,581	13,472	40.7	34.7	37.6
1972	6,242,2	5,327,5	14,861	13,565	42.0	35.8	39.3
1973	6,551,6	5,630,2	15,092	13,789	43.4	37.3	40.8
1974	7,264,4	6,233,1	15,205	14,094	47.8	41.0	44.2
1975	7,707,5	6,519,2	15,398	14,172	50.1	42.3	46.0
1976	8,241,8	6,930,3	15,725	14,305	52.4	44.1	48.4
1977	8,445,3	7,000,5	15,952	14,414	52.9	43.9	48.6
1978	8,681,4	7,104,5	16,053	14,493	54.1	44.3	49.0
1979	8,816,5	7,148,1	16,406	14,720	53.7	43.6	48.6
1980	9,005,8	7,226,0	16,540	14,856	54.4	43.7	48.6
1981	8,941,1	7,005,9	16,819	14,924	53.2	41.7	46.9
1982	8,910,9	6,792,3	16,964	14,912	52.5	40.0	45.5
1983	8,861,0	6,572,1	17,075	14,811	51.9	38.5	44.4
1984	8,988,0	6,484,1	17,125	14,734	52.5	37.9	44.0
1985	8,851,4	6,155,8	17,351	14,880	51.0	35.5	41.4

isic	conf.	all	female	b-c	w-c	total	b-c	w-c	total	b-c	w-c

Table IT 5/1 Union Membership by Sex, Industry and Status ITALY

year:1951		total		market			public			status	
isic	conf.	all	female	b-c	w-c	total	b-c	w-c	total	b-c	w-c
1	CGIL	1,008	.	.	.	1,008				.	.
1	CISL	241	.	.	.	241				.	.
		1,250	.	.	.	1,250				.	.
2-5	CGIL	1,820	.	.	.	1,820				.	.
2-5	CISL	459	.	.	.	459				.	.
		2,279	.	.	.	2,279				.	.
6+8	CGIL	83	.	.	.	83				.	.
6+8	CISL	29	.	.	.	29				.	.
		112	.	.	.	112				.	.
7	CGIL	321	.	.	.	150	.	.	170	.	.
7	CISL	166	.	.	.	66	.	.	100	.	.
		487	.	.	.	217	.	.	270	.	.
9	CGIL	371	.	.	.	146	.	.	225	.	.
9	CISL	199	.	.	.	34	.	.	164	.	.
		570	.	.	.	180	.	.	389	.	.
	CGIL	3,603	.	.	.	3,207	.	.	396	.	.
	CISL	1,094	.	.	.	830	.	.	264	.	.
		(4,697)	.	.	.	(4,037)	.	.	(660)	.	.
+	UIL	300	.	.	.	250	.	.	50	.	.
		4,997	.	.	.	4,287	.	.	710	.	.

Table IT 5/2 Union Membership by Sex, Industry and Status											
year:1961		total		market			public			status	
isic	conf.	all	female	b-c	w-c	total	b-c	w-c	total	b-c	w-c
1	CGIL	519	.	.	.	519				.	.
1	CISL	205	.	.	.	205				.	.
		724	.	.	.	724				.	.
2-5	CGIL	846	.	.	.	846				.	.
2-5	CISL	383	.	.	.	383				.	.
		1,229	.	.	.	1,229				.	.
6+8	CGIL	60	.	.	.	60				.	.
6+8	CISL	50	.	.	.	50				.	.
		110	.	.	.	110				.	.
7	CGIL	229	.	.	.	114	.	.	115	.	.
7	CISL	185	.	.	.	68	.	.	116	.	.
		414	.	.	.	183	.	.	231	.	.
9	CGIL	195	.	.	.	71	.	.	124	.	.
9	CISL	310	.	.	.	22	.	.	287	.	.
		505	.	.	.	93	.	.	411	.	.
	CGIL	1,849	.	.	.	1,610	.	.	239	.	.
	CISL	1,132	.	.	.	728	.	.	404	.	.
		(2,981)	.	.	.	(2,338)	.	.	(643)	.	.
+	UIL	520	.	.	.	400	.	.	120	.	.
		3,501	.	.	.	2,738	.	.	763	.	.

year:1971		total		market			public			status	
isic	conf.	all	female	b-c	w-c	total	b-c	w-c	total	b-c	w-c
1	CGIL	379	.	.	.	379				.	.
1	CISL	194	.	.	.	194				.	.
1	UIL	72	.	.	.	72				.	.
		645	.	.	.	645				.	.
2-5	CGIL	1,481	.	.	.	1,481				.	.
2-5	CISL	799	.	.	.	799				.	.
2-5	UIL	312	.	.	.	312				.	.
		2,592	.	.	.	2,592				.	.
6+8	CGIL	94	.	.	.	94				.	.
6+8	CISL	71	.	.	.	71				.	.
6+8	UIL	39	.	.	.	39				.	.
		203	.	.	.	203				.	.
7	CGIL	274	.	.	.	153	.	.	120	.	.
7	CISL	236	.	.	.	97	.	.	140	.	.
7	UIL	104	.	.	.	52	.	.	52	.	.
		614	.	.	.	302	.	.	312	.	.
9	CGIL	342	.	.	.	80	.	.	262	.	.
9	CISL	474	.	.	.	33	.	.	441	.	.
9	UIL	173	.	.	.	18	.	.	155	.	.
		988	.	.	.	131	.	.	858	.	.
0	UIL	18	.	.	.	18				.	.
		18	.	.	.	18				.	.
	CGIL	2,569	.	.	.	2,186	.	.	382	.	.
	CISL	1,773	.	.	.	1,192	.	.	581	.	.
	UIL	718	.	.	.	512	.	.	206	.	.
		5,060	.	.	.	3,890	.	.	1,169	.	.

Table IT 5/3 Union Membership by Sex, Industry and Status   ITALY

Table IT 5/4 Union Membership by Sex, Industry and Status										ITALY
year:1981		total		market			public			status
isic	conf.	all	female	b-c	w-c	total	b-c	w-c	total	b-c	w-c
1	CGIL	519	.	.	.	519				.	.
1	CISL	379	.	.	.	379				.	.
1	UIL	121	.	.	.	121				.	.
		1,019	.	.	.	*1,019*				.	.
2-5	CGIL	1,774	.	.	.	1,774				.	.
2-5	CISL	961	.	.	.	961				.	.
2-5	UIL	484	.	.	,	484				.	.
		3,218	.	.	.	*3,218*				.	.
6+8	CGIL	168	.	.	.	168				.	.
6+8	CISL	111	.	.	.	111				.	.
6+8	UIL	71	.	.	.	71				.	.
		350	.	.	.	*350*				.	.
7	CGIL	288	.	.	.	155	.	.	133	.	.
7	CISL	289	.	.	.	123	.	.	166	.	.
7	UIL	156	.	.	.	89	.	.	66	.	.
		732	.	.	.	*367*	.	.	*365*	.	.
9	CGIL	650	.	.	.	123	.	.	527	.	.
9	CISL	634	.	.	.	51	.	.	583	.	.
9	UIL	312	.	.	.	36	.	.	276	.	.
		1,595	.	.	.	*210*	.	.	*1,386*	.	.
0	CGIL	10	.	.	.	10				.	.
0	UIL	81	.	.	.	81				.	.
		91	.	.	.	*91*				.	.
	CGIL	3,409	.	.	.	2,749	.	.	660	.	.
	CISL	2,373	.	.	.	1,624	.	.	749	.	.
	UIL	1,224	.	.	.	882	.	.	342	.	.
		7,006	.	.	.	*5,255*	.	.	*1,751*	.	.

Table IT 5/5 Union Membership by Sex, Industry and Status										ITALY
year:1985		total		market			public			status	
isic	conf.	all	female	b-c	w-c	total	b-c	w-c	total	b-c	w-c
1	CGIL	411	.	.	.	411				.	.
1	CISL	301	.	.	.	301				.	.
1	UIL	114	.	.	.	114				.	.
		826	.	.	.	*826*				.	.
2-5	CGIL	1,464	.	.	.	1,464				.	.
2-5	CISL	731	.	.	.	731				.	.
2-5	UIL	408	.	.	.	408				.	.
		2,603	.	.	.	*2,603*				.	.
6+8	CGIL	167	.	.	.	167				.	.
6+8	CISL	105	.	.	.	105				.	.
6+8	UIL	70	.	.	.	70				.	.
		341	.	.	.	*341*				.	.
7	CGIL	274	.	.	.	143	.	.	131	.	.
7	CISL	286	.	.	.	110	.	.	176	.	.
7	UIL	158	.	.	.	98	.	.	60	.	.
		718	.	.	.	*351*	.	.	*368*	.	.
9	CGIL	636	.	.	.	94	.	.	542	.	.
9	CISL	634	.	.	.	53	.	.	581	.	.
9	UIL	314	.	.	.	33	.	.	281	.	.
		1,584	.	.	.	*181*	.	.	*1,403*	.	.
0	CGIL	22	.	.	.	22				.	.
0	CISL	5	.	.	.	5				.	.
0	UIL	57	.	.	.	57				.	.
		84	.	.	.	*84*				.	.
	CGIL	2,973	.	.	.	2,300	.	.	673	.	.
	CISL	2,062	.	.	.	1,304	.	.	758	.	.
	UIL	1,121	.	.	.	780	.	.	341	.	.
		6,156	.	.	.	*4,384*	.	.	*1,772*	.	.

Table IT 6/1 Dependent Labour Force by Sex, Industry and Status   ITALY

1921	total		market			public			status	
isic	all	female	b-c	w-c	total	b-c	w-c	total	b-c	w-c
1	4,420	.	.	.	.	.	.	.	4,386	34
2-5	3,474	.	.	.	.	.	.	.	3,443	31
6+8	262	.	.	.	.	.	.	.	45	217
7	651	.	.	.	.	.	.	.	530	121
9	1,794	.	.	.	.	.	.	.	1,001	793
	10,601	2,976	.	.	.	.	.	.	9,406	1,195

Table IT 6/2 Dependent Labour Force by Sex, Industry and Status   ITALY

1951	total		market			public			status	
isic	all	female	b-c	w-c	total	b-c	w-c	total	b-c	w-c
1	2,687	.	.	.	.	.	.	.	2,660	27
2-5	5,331	.	.	.	.	.	.	.	4,940	391
6+8	565	.	.	.	.	.	.	.	308	258
7	649	.	.	.	.	.	.	.	481	168
9	2,333	.	.	.	.	.	.	.	1,319	1,014
0	1,095	.	.	.	.	.	.	.	1,095	.
	12,660	3,414	.	.	.	.	.	.	10,802	1,858

Table IT 6/3 Dependent Labour Force by Sex, Industry and Status   ITALY

1961	total		market			public			status	
isic	all	female	b-c	w-c	total	b-c	w-c	total	b-c	w-c
1	2,107	.	.	.	.	.	.	.	2,075	33
2-5	6,977	.	.	.	.	.	.	.	6,408	568
6+8	741	.	.	.	.	.	.	.	353	388
7	822	.	.	.	.	.	.	.	632	190
9	2,589	.	.	.	.	.	.	.	1,451	1,137
0	581	.	.	.	.	.	.	.	581	.
	13,816	3,526	.	.	.	.	.	.	11,500	2,316

126

Table IT 6/4 Dependent Labour Force by Sex, Industry and Status   ITALY

1971	total		market			public			status	
isic	all	female	b-c	w-c	total	b-c	w-c	total	b-c	w-c
1	1,351	.	.	.	.	.	.	.	1,309	42
2-5	7,199	.	.	.	.	.	.	.	6,135	1,064
6+8	1,082	.	.	.	.	.	.	.	506	576
7	859	.	.	.	.	.	.	.	549	310
9	3,367	.	.	.	.	.	.	.	1,505	1,862
0	975	.	.	.	.	.	.	.	975	.
	14,833	4,073	.	.	.	.	.	.	10,980	3,853

Table IT 6/5 Dependent Labour Force by Sex, Industry and Status   ITALY

1981	total		market			public			status	
isic	all	female	b-c	w-c	total	b-c	w-c	total	b-c	w-c
1	1,124	.	.	.	.	.	.	.	.	.
2-5	6,947	.	.	.	.	.	.	.	.	.
6+8	1,617	.	.	.	.	.	.	.	.	.
7	1,091	.	.	.	.	.	.	.	.	.
9	4,799	.	.	.	.	.	.	.	.	.
0	1,696	.	.	.	.	.	.	.	.	.
	17,274	6,343	.	.	.	.	.	.	.	.

Table IT 6/6 Employees in employment by Sex, Industry and Status   ITALY

1951 isic	total all	female	market b-c	w-c	total	public b-c	w-c	total	status b-c	w-c
1	2,251	.	.	.	2,251	.	.	.	.	.
2-5	4,556	.	.	.	4,556	.	.	.	.	.
6+8	678	.	.	.	678	.	.	.	.	.
7	513	.	.	.	244	.	.	269	.	.
9	2,337	.	.	.	1,143	.	.	1,194	.	.
	10,335	.	.	.	8,871	.	.	1,463		

Table IT 6/7 Employees in employment by Sex, Industry and Status   ITALY

1961 isic	total all	female	market b-c	w-c	total	public b-c	w-c	total	status b-c	w-c
1	1,665	.	.	.	1,665	.	.	.	.	.
2-5	5,881	.	.	.	5,881	.	.	.	.	.
6+8	1,061	.	.	.	1,061	.	.	.	.	.
7	642	.	.	.	367	.	.	275	.	.
9	3,064	.	.	.	1,440	.	.	1,624	.	.
	12,313	.	.	.	10,414	.	.	1,899	.	.

Table IT 6/8 Employees in employment by Sex, Industry and Status   ITALY

1971 isic	total all	female	market b-c	w-c	total	public b-c	w-c	total	status b-c	w-c
1	1,219	.	.	.	1,219	.	.	.	.	.
2-5	6,554	.	.	.	6,553	.	.	.	.	.
6+8	1,260	.	.	.	1,260	.	.	.	.	.
7	767	.	.	.	390	.	.	377	.	.
9	3,672	.	.	.	1,436	.	.	2,236	.	.
	13,472	.	.	.	10,859	.	.	2,613	.	.

```
Table IT 6/9 Employees in employment by Sex, Industry and Status    ITALY
```

1981	total		market			public			status	
isic	all	female	b-c	w-c	total	b-c	w-c	total	b-c	w-c
1	1,035	.	.	.	1,035	.	.	.	.	.
2-5	6,470	.	.	.	6,470	.	.	.	.	.
6+8	1,653	.	.	.	1,653	.	.	.	.	.
7	921	.	.	.	456	.	.	465	.	.
9	4,845	.	.	.	1,832	.	.	3,013	.	.
	14,924	.	.	.	11,446	.	.	3,478	.	.

```
Table IT 6/10 Employees in employment by Sex, Industry and Status    ITALY
```

1985	total		market			public			status	
isic	all	female	b-c	w-c	total	b-c	w-c	total	b-c	w-c
1	908	.	.	.	908	.	.	.	.	.
2-5	5,771	.	.	.	5,771	.	.	.	.	.
6+8	1,856	.	.	.	1,856	.	.	.	.	.
7	945	.	.	.	472	.	.	472	.	.
9	5,401	.	.	.	2,281	.	.	3,120	.	.
	14,880	.	.	.	11,288	.	.	3,592	.	.

Chapter 6: NETHERLANDS

LIST OF UNION CONFEDERATIONS: name, abbreviation and foundation year

1 *Nationaal Arbeids-Secretariaat* (NAS): 1893-1940
   National Labour Secretariat

2 *Nederlands Verbond van Vakverenigingen* (NVV): 1905-1981
   Dutch Confederation of Trade Unions (merger with NKV to form FNV)

3 *Nederlands Katholieke Vakbeweging* (NKV): 1909-1981
   Dutch Catholic Trade Union Confederation (merger with NVV to FNV)

4 *Federatie Nederlandse Vakbeweging* (FNV): 1981-
   Confederation of Dutch Trade Unions (federation from 1-1-1976)

5 *Christelijk Nationaal Vakverbond* (CNV): 1909-
   Protestant National Trade Union Confederation

6 *Algemeen Nederlands Vakverbond* (ANV): 1912-1929
   Liberal Federation of Dutch Trade Unions (merged with 7)

7 *Verbond van Vakorganisaties van Hoofdarbeiders* (VVH): 1923-1929
   Federation of Salaried Employee Organizations (merged with 6)

8 *Nederlandse Vakcentrale* (NVC): 1929-1940, and 1947-1963
   Liberal Dutch Trade Union Centre (formed by 6 and 7 in 1929;
   joined NVV in 1940; refounded in 1947)

9 *Nederlands Syndicalistisch Vakverbond* (NSV): 1923-1940
   Dutch Syndicalist Trade Union Federation (break-away from 1)

10 *Eenheids Vakcentrale* (EVC): 1945-1964
    United Centre of Trade Unions

11 *Centrale van Middelbare en Hogere Ambtenaren* (CMHA): 1917-
    Centre for Higher Civil Servants (affil. with 13 from 1974)

12 *Nederlandse Centrale voor Hoger Personeel* (NCHP): 1966-
    Dutch Federation of Staff Associations (affil. with 13 from 1974)

13 *Vakcentrale voor Middelbaar en Hoger Personeel* (MHP): 1974-
    Federation of White-Collar Employee Organizations

14 *Centrale van Rijkspersoneel* (CRP): 1916- Central Government
    Employee Organization (1920-1922 affil. with 6; from 1946 with 15

15 *Ambtenaren-Centrale* (AC): 1946- Civil Cervant's Centre

1. AGGREGATE MEMBERSHIP STATISTICS

1.1 General Series

The main source for data on trade union membership is the Central Bureau of Statistics (CBS) in The Hague. Already before WO I the CBS started with an annual survey of union organizations and union membership. With the exception of some years during the German occupation in World War II, this annual series continues till 1964 (CBS, 1909-1942; CBS, 1946-1964). The publication was resumed in 1967 as a biennial survey of trade unions. However, between 1971 and 1985 the CBS did publish only the summary tables on union membership and not the data referring to individual unions as it had done previously (CBS, 1967-1985). Of the unions affiliated to the NVV, NKV, FNV, CNV, and later also of the member federations of the MHP the Bureau published quarterly membership statistics twice a year in the Sociaal-Economische Maandstatistiek (Monthly Bulletin of Social-Economic Statistics, The Hague). The second main source, especially for the years after 1967, are the Jaarverslagen (Annual Reports) of the (Con)federations listed above and most larger unions. They are essential for the purpose of separating the retired membership, and for disaggregating the membership by gender, industry, and status. I have also been able to consult the filled-out questionnaires which NVV, NKV, FNV and most CNV unions returned to the CBS. The Annual Reports can generally be consulted at Confederal and Union Headquarters, the International Institute of Social History (IISG) in Amsterdam or the Catholic Documentation Centre in Nijmegen, or -in the case of Civil Servant organizations- through the library of the Ministry of Home Affairs. Direct information was obtained from the AC, the CRP and the CMHA. In the case of unaffiliated unions (mainly teachers, nurses, artists and entertainment, and military personnel) some information was obtained via their federations. The remaining membership in independent unions was estimated on the basis of the CBS series (CBS, 1967-1985).

The table on trade membership by confederation does not provide a full list of all union confederations which have existed during this period. The membership of some very small confederations, most often break-away organizations, is included in the statistic on independent unions. Such is the case with the membership of the *Syndicalistisch Verbond van Bedrijfsorganisaties* (1927-1929, a small break-away from the syndicalist federation NSV), the *Oud-Katholiek Verbond van Bedrijfsorganisaties* (a split within the Catholic camp which lasted from 1936 till 1941), the *Christelijk Nationale Vakcentrale* (this a Protestant split existing from 1938 till 1941), the *Algemeen Vrijzinnig Vakverbond* (a Liberal Union Federation founded after WO II which joined the NVC in 1950), the *Centrale voor Hogere Gemeente Ambtenaren* (a Central Organization for Higher Municipal Employees, which was founded in 1921 and joined the Centre for Higher Civil Servants CMHA in 1958), and the *Federatie van Werknemersorganisaties* (1964-1974), which tried to continue the liberal heritage of the NVC but ceased to operate in 1974). No membership data on the communist *Eenheids Vakcentrale* (EVC) is available after 1951, although the organization officially ceased to operate in 1958. Its membership is believed to have been dwindling after the early 1950s. The still existing syndicalist federation, the *Onafhankelijk Verbond van Bedrijfsorganisaties* (OVB, 1948-), which is a break-away from the EVC, never published or reported any membership figure. Its importance is mainly local, in particular among dockers in Rotterdam.

Union membership statistics in the Netherlands are quite extensive, especially from the end of the First World War when the CBS started to include union organizations and professional associations in education, public administration, health and entertainment. On the basis of data for 1919 and 1920 the Bureau made an upward revision of the 1910-1920 membership series as well (CBS, Omvang van de vakbeweging in 1920, The Hague 1921). Moreover, the membership of independent locals is included in the series from 1910. Finally, it should be observed that the membership of unions recruiting police and military officers, is included, with the exception of the years between 1933 and 1950 when members of the armed forces could not legally join trade unions.

Until 1972, the CBS used 1 January as reporting date. For mysterious reasons this was changed after 1973 to 31 March. I have readjusted all figures to 31 December of each year (as a matter of fact most federations and unions use end-of-year data in their own reports; otherwise I have redefined 1 January to 31 December of the previous year, and in a few cases I have made seasonal adjustments). Another source of difference between my series and the series published by the Central Bureau of Statistics (CBS, 1909-1942; CBS, 1946-1964; CBS, 1967-1985) is that I have included apprentices among the membership throughout, whereas the CBS excludes such members in the pre-war period (although very inconsistently), and includes them after 1945. Apprentices accounted for almost 4% of total membership in 1920, declining to less than 1.5% in 1939.

1.2   Retired Members and Conscripts

On the basis of the sources mentioned above, in particular the Jaarverslagen, the questionnaires returned to the Central Bureau of Statistics and our own survey conducted among FNV-unions in November 1985 (Visser & Veltman, 1986), I have been able to identify the non-active membership for the full post-war period. This category comprises pensioners, conscripts, disabled members who have withdrawn from the labour market, and members living on pre-retirement pensions. The latter two categories and the ageing process in many Dutch unions account for the conspicuous rise in recent years. In contrast to the CBS, which assumed a constant 5% share of non-active members for the period 1945-1967 in its retrospective series (CBS, 1967-1985), the annual data on the basis of individual union reports show much greater variation and a rising proportion of non-active membership over the full post-war period. Comparison with the data for 1920, 1930 and 1939 shows that before the war their number (and that of self-employed members) was negligible - less than 1%. For the period after 1967 the CBS has equated 'pensioners' and 'members older than 65 years'. This proofs to be a reasonable approximation of 'inactive' membership until the mid-1970s, but in recent years the two figures do compare less well: members on pension schemes clearly exceed those in the 65+ age bracket (see Visser, 1986). Another contrast with the CBS series is that I have included the unemployed among the active membership. Also unlike the CBS I have excluded, in calculating density rates, the membership of the two unions of military conscripts, the Vereniging van

Dienstplichtige Militairen (VVDM) and the *Algemene Vereniging van Nederlandse Militairen* (AVNM), and - in earlier years - the membership of some NKV- or CNV-unions catering for (ex-)employees in the Dutch colonies or among repatriates. Nor are included the members of the Women's Leagues of FNV or CNV, or of the *Bond Bijzondere Leden* which was affiliated with the NKV.

1.3. Female membership

The CBS series on union membership reported membership by gender between 1920 and 1964 annually and per union or confederation (CBS, 1909-1942; CBS, 1946-1964). From 1973 it resumed reporting female membership, in an aggregated fashion, on the basis of its biennial reports (CBS, 1967-1985). Most Annual Reports of the larger unions - together representing 80% or more of total membership- report membership by gender. Female membership in the smaller, non-reporting unions has been estimated on the basis of the CBS surveys, or from confederal data.

2. CLASSIFICATION BY INDUSTRY AND STATUS:

2.1. Classification by industry

1 Agriculture & Fishing: *Kathol. Bond Werknemers Agrarische Bedrijfstakken; Algem. Nederl. Agrarische Bedrijfsbond; Christ. Agrarische Bedrijfsbond; Fed Land-, Tuin- en Veenarbeiders; Friese Bond Prot-Christ. Land-, Tuin- en Zuivelarbeiders; Bond Bloembinderijpersoneel; Bond Land-, Tuin-, en Veenarbeiders; Christ. Nation. Ver. Werklieden Land- en Tuinbouw, Zuivel en Veen; Fed Land-, Tuin-, Veen-, Zuivelbewerkers; Algem. Bedrijfsbond Land-, Tuin-,Veen-, en Zuivelarbeiders; Bond Arbeiders Land-,Tuinbouw- en Zuivelbedrijf; Christ. Bond Werknemers Argarische en Tabakindustrie; Bond Christ. Noordzeeschippers; Christ. Zeeliedenbond*

2-4 Mining & Industry, Gas, Water & Electricity: *Ver. Glas- en Aardewerkers; Bond RK Glas- en Aarde werkers; RK Steenfabrieksarbeidersbond; Algem. Nederl. Diamantbewerkersbond; Algem. Nederl. Grafische Bond; Kathol. Grafische Bond; Grafische Bond CNV; Lito--,Foto- en Chemigrafenbond; RK Lito-, Foto- en Chemigrafenbond; Ver. Chefs Grafisch Bedrijf; Grafische Bond NVC; Nieuwe Nederl. Typografenbond; Bond Werknemers Grafische en Papierverwerkende Bedrijven; Druk en Papier FNV; VHP Van Gelder Concern; Nederl. Journalisten Kring; RK Journalistenvereniging; Ver. Journalisten Sociaal-Democratische Bladen; Nederl. Ver. Fotojournalisten; Verbond Nederl. Journalisten; Nederl. Journalisten Kring '45; Kathol. Journalisten Kring; Prot-Christ. Journalisten Kring; Nederl. Ver.Journalisten; Onafhankelijke Ver.Journalisten; VHP Uitgeverijen en Nieuwsvoorziening; Bond Scheikundig Personeel; Bedrijfsgroep Chemische Nijverheid; VHP Rayonindustrie; VHP Chemie Zuid; VHP AKZO; VHP Shell; VHP Chemie; Algem. Bedrijfsbond Meubilerings- en Houtbedrijven; Christ. Bond Werknemers Houtindustrie; Borstelmakersbond; Fed Meubelmakers en Houtbewerkers; Kathol. Bond*

134

Werknemers Meubel en Hout; RK Bond Kuipers-en Kistenmakersbedrijf;
Fed Meubelmakers; Bond Werkers Hout- en Meubileringsindustrie;
Christ.Textielarbeidersbond; Algem. Bedrijfsbond Textiel en
Kleding; Fed Textielarbeiders; RK Textielbond; Bond Bazen Textiel-
industrie; Politiek Onafhankelijke Textielarbeidersbond; Fed Bond
Arbeiders Textielindustrie; Ver. RK Meesterknechts en Textiel-
bazen; Syndikale Fed Textielarbeiders; Bond Textielarbeiders; Bond
Werkers Textiel- en Kledingindustrie; Christ. Bond Werknemers
Textiel- en Kledingbedrijf; Kathol. Bond Werknemers Kleding- en
Textielbedrijf; VHP Textiel; VHP Textielindustrie; Eerste Algem.
Nederl.Coupeursbond; Nederl.Bond Mnl/Vrl Arbeiders
Kledingindustrie; RK Naaister- en Kleermakersbond; Fed Arbeiders
Kledingindustrie; Bond Christ. Arbeiders/-sters Kledingindustrie;
Centr Bond Coupeurs en Kleermakers; Nieuwe Nederl.Coupeursbond; RK
Coupeursbond; Nederl. Coupeursbond; RK Schoen en Lederbewerkers-
bond; Neutrale Schoen- en Lederbewerkersbond; Nederl. Bond Schoen-
makersgezellen; Kathol. Mijnwerkersbond; Algem. Nederl. Bedrijfs-
bond Mijnindustrie; Ver. Staatsmijnbeambten Limburg; Prot-Christ.
Mijnwerkersbond; Fed Werkers Mijn- en Bruinkoolbedrijf; Neutrale
Mijnwerkersbond; Christ. Ver. Mijnbouwkundige Ambtenaren; Onafhan-
kelijke Fed Mijnwerkers; Fed Arbeiders Mijnindustrie; Limburgse
RK Ver. Mijntechnici; Syndikale Fed Mijnwerkers; Ver. Technische
Mijnbeambten Limburg; Limburgse Mijnwerkersbond; Centrale Bond
Werknemers Mijnbedrijf; RK Ver. Adm Mijnbeambten; Prot-Christ.
Ver. Beambten Mijnbedrijf; Ver. Leidinggevend Personeel Mijn-
streek; Christ. Ver. Mijnbeambten; Algem. Industriebond Nederland;
Bond Mijntechnici Limburg; Kathol. VHP Mijnbedrijf; VHP Mijn-
bedrijf; Werkliedenver "Eendracht"; Bond Veenpolderambtenaren
Friesland; Ver. Academici Stoomwezen; VHP Gasunie; Algem. Nederl.
Bedrijfsbond Metaalnijverheid en Electrotechnische Industrie;
Christ. Bedrijfsbond Metaalnijverheid en Electrotechnische Indu-
strie; Kathol. Bond Werknemers Metaal en Electrotechniek; Fed
Metaalbewerkers; Neutrale Bond Metaalbewerkers; Bond Metaal-
Technici; Ver. Nederl. Werktuigkundigen; Bond Werkmeesters en
Bazen Metaal; Bond Carosserie-,Rijtuig- en Wagenmakersgezellen;
Syndicale Fed Metaalbewerkers; Onafhankelijk Bedrijfsfed Werkers
Metaalindustrie; Centr Bond Werknemers Metaalindustrie; Centr Bond
Metaalbewerkers; Bond Oud-Kathol. Metaalbewerkers; Nat Metaal-
bewerkersbond; Bond Werkers Metaalnijverheid; Politiek Onafhanke-
lijke Metaalbewerkersbond Groot- en Kleinbedrijf; VHP Verblifa;
VHP RSV; VHP Holec; VHP VMF; MHP Metaalelectro; Fed Hoger Philips
Personeel; Bond Personeel Muziekinstrumentbedrijven; Uurwerk-
makersbond; Bond Arbeiders Zeilmakerijen; Ver. Werknemers
Opticiensbedrijf; Kathol. Personeel Tandtechnici en Opticiens;
Banketbakkersbediendenvereniging; Algem. Nederl. Bond Arbeiders/-
sters Bakkers, Chocolade en Suiker; RK Bond Bakkers, Cacao, Chocolade en Suiker; VHP Avebe; VHP Meneba; Algem. Nederl. Bedrijfsbond
Tabakverwerkende Industrie; RK Tabaksbewerkersbond; Christ. Bond
Sigarenmakers en Tabakbewerkers; Fed Sigarenmakers en Tabakbewerkers; Bond Sigarenmakers en Tabakbewerkers; Fed Bond
Arbeiders/sters Tabakindustrie; Bond Werkers Tabakbe- en
verwerkende Industrie; Nederl. Bond Arb-ers/-sters in Slagers-
bedrijf; RK Slagersgezellenbond; RK Zuivel-en Margarinebewerkers-
bond; Zuivelbewerkersbond; VHP Zuivel; VHP Melkunie; Bedrijfsorg
Brouwerijarbeiders; VHP Heineken; Bond Christ. Arbeiders/-sters

135

Voeding- en Genotmiddelen; Neutrale Bond Personeel Voedings-
bedrijven; Bedrijfsgroep Voeding- en Genotmiddelen; Kathol. Bond
Arbeiders/sters Voeding- en Genotmiddelen; Algem. Nederl.
Bedrijfsbond Voedings- en Genotmiddelen; Kathol. Bond Personeel
Agrarische, Voedings- en Genotmiddelen, Tabakverwerkende en
Horecabedrijven; VHP Unilever; Agrarische en Voedingsbond NVV;
Voedingsbond CNV; Voedingsbond FNV; Fed Hoger Personeel Voeding,
Genotmiddelen en Agrarische Sector; Algem.emene Bedrijfsgroepen
Centrale; Christ. Bedrijfsgroepen Centrale; Fed Fabrieksarbeiders-
/sters; Kathol. Bond Werknemers/sters Industriële Bedrijven;
Syndikale Fed Fabrieksarbeiders; Neutrale Fabrieksarbeidersbond;
Ver. Industriearbeiders; Noord-Brabantse Bond RK Fabrieks-
arbeiders; Fed Bond Arbeiders Fabriekmatige Bedrijven; Syndicalis-
tisch Verbond van Bedrijfsorganisaties; Gemengde Syndicalistische
Ver.; Nationale Werknemers Ver.; Bond Oud-Kathol. Fabrieks- en
Transportarbeiders; Bond Fabrieks- en Transportarbeiders; Algem.
Bond Fabrieks- en Transportarbeiders; Bedrijfsgroep Fabriekmatige
Industrie; Nederl. Organisatie van Werkers; Bedrijfsgroep
Chemische en Fabriekmatige Industrie; Algem.emeen Vrijzinnig Vak-
verbond; Ver. Vrije Werknemers; Onafhankelijk Verbond Bedrijfs-
organisaties; GSW-Groep; Industriebond NVV; Industriebond NKV;
Christ. Bedrijfsgroepen Centrale Unitas; Industriebond CNV;
Industriebond FNV; Industrie- en Voedingsbond CNV; Bond van
Technici; Kathol. Bond Leidinggevend en Toezichthoudend Personeel;
Ver. Christ. Technici; Centr Bond Werkmeesters en Opzichthoudend
Personeel; Kathol. Bond Hogere Middelbare en Lagere Technici en
Chemici; Christ. Werkmeestersbond; Bond Middelbaar en Hoger
Personeel; Algem. Bond Technici, Werkmeester en Opzichthoudend
Personeel; Bond Werkmeesters, Technici en Opzichthoudend
Personeel; Centr Bond Werkmeesters, Toezichthoudend Personeel en
Technici; Bond Middelbare en Hogere Technici; Christ. Ver. Hoger
Personeel; Kathol. Ver. Hoger Personeel; Ver. Hoger Personeel;
Christ. Beambtenbond; Kathol. Bond Administratief en Commerciëel
Personeel Industrie; VHP Diverse Branches; Unie Beambten en Hoger
Personeel; Unie Beambten, Leidinggevend en Hoger Personeel

5 Construction: Schildersgezellenbond; Stucadoorsbond; Christ. Bouw-
arbeiders bond; Opzichters en Tekenaarsbond; Fed Bouwvakarbeiders;
Kathol. Bond Werknemers Bouwnijverheid; Bond Arbeiders Straten- en
Wegenbouw; Grondwerkersbond; Christ. Nat Bouwvakarbeidersbond;
Ver. Bouwvakarbeiders; Bond Uitvoerders en Bazen; Algem. Nederl.
Bond Bouwnijverheid; Fed Hei- en Funderingswerkers; Syndikale Fed
Bouwvakarbeiders; Ver. Bouwvakarbeiders; Bond Oud-Kathol. Bouwvak-
arbeiders; Algem. Bond Werkers Bouwnijverheid; Fed Werkers Bouw-
nijverheid; Het Zwarte Korps; Hout- en Bouwbond CNV; Algem.
Nederl. Bond Bouw- en Houtnijverheid; Kathol. Bond Bouw- en Hout-
nijverheid; VHP Bouw; Bouw- en Houtbond FNV

6+8 Commerce, Banking & Insurances: Algem. Apothekers Assistentenbond;
Nederl. Handelsreizigersver.; Handelsreizigers-Ver.; Bond Boek-
verkopersbedienden; Ver. Christ. Kantoor- en Handelsbedienden;
Bond Personeel Kleding- en Modebedrijven; Algem. Nederl. Bond
Handels- en Kantoorbedienden; Nationale Bond Handels- en Kantoor-
bedienden; Nederl. Kathol. Bond Administratief, Verkopend en
Verzekeringspersoneel; Nederl. Ver. Reizigers Bewerkte Tabak; RK

Ver. Handelsreizigers; Ver. Vertegenwoordigers Lak-, Vernis- en
Verffabrieken; Ver. Reizigers Ruwe Tabak; Kathol. Apothekers
Assistenbond; Christ. Apothekers Assistentenbond; Fed Handels-,
Kantoor-, Winkel- en Magazijnpersoneel; Neutrale Bond Personeel
Winkel- en Grossiersbedrijf; Algem. Nederl. Bond Incasseerders en
Kantoorlopers; Nederl. Bond Kantoormachine Mecaniciens; Bond
Confectiebedienden; Ver. Christ. Handelsreizigers en -agenten;
Bond Veilingpersoneel; Nederl. Ver.Singerreizigers; Bond Oud-
-Kathol. Handels-, Kantoor- en Winkelbedienden; Ver. Reizigers,
Inkopers en Administratief Pers Bloembollenbedredrijf;
Dienstenbond NVV; Algem. Bond Werknemers Handel-Bank-Verzekering;
Nederl. Filiaalhoudersbond; Ver. Standard Buitendienst; Nederl.
Handelsreizigers en Handelsagenten Ver.; Nederl. Ver. Admini-
stratief Personeel; Ver. Vertegenwoordigers van Handelaren en
Industrielen; Bedrijfsorganisatie Handel en Geld; Nederl. Christ.
Ver. Apothekers Assistenten; Nederl. Bond Werknemers Boekhandel en
Uitgeverijen; Dienstenbond NKV; Dienstenbond CNV; VHP Grootwinkel-
bedrijven; Handelsagenten en Vertegenwoordigersver.; VHP Handel;
Dienstenbond FNV; Nederl. Verzekeringsbond; Ver. Ambtenaren Wis-
kundige Bureaux Verzekeringsinstellingen; Bond van Verenigingen
van Vertegenwoordigers van Verzekeringsmaatschappijen en Zieken-
fondsen; Nederl.Bond Inspecteurs Verzekeringsbedrijf;RK Bond
Verzekeringspersoneel; Nederl. Bond Verzekeringsagenten, Zieken-
fondsboden en Incasseeerders; Ver. Buitendienstambtenaren
Verzekeringsbedrijf; Landelijk Verband Agentenverenigingen
"Utrecht"; Christ. Bond Verzekeringsagenten en Ziekenfondsboden;
Nederl. Bond Assurantie-Agenten; Bond Ziekenfondsboden; Ver. Werk-
nemers Bank- en Verzekeringsbedrijf en Administratieve Kantoren;
VHP Bankwezen; VHP Verzekeringswezen; Ver. Kaderpersoneel Bank- en
Verzekeringswezen; Ver. Personeel Nederlandse Bank

7 Transport & Communication: Ver. Technici Scheepvaart; Fed
Transportarbeiders; Ver. Nederl. Gezagvoerders en Stuurlieden
Koopvaardij; Ver. Scheepswerktuigbouwkundigen; Ver.Gezagvoerders
Binnenvaart; Bond Particuliere Chauffeurs; Centrale Bond Tran-
sportarbeiders; Kathol. Bond Werknemers Transportbedrijf; Ver.
Radio-Telegrafisten Koopvaardij en Luchtvaart; Ver. Jacht-
schippers; Christendemocratische Bond Zeelieden, Haven- en
Transportarbeiders; Bond Opzichthouders Transportbedrijf; RK Bond
Directeuren en Hoger Personeel VGL; Bond Werknemers Automobiel-
bedrijf; Syndikale Fed Transportarbeiders; Ver. Kapiteins en
Stuurlieden Rijn- en Binnenvaart; Ver. Officieren Koopvaardij;
Bond Bezorgers/-sters Krantenbedrijf; Ver. Nederl. Verkeers-
vliegers; Ver. Personeel Groninger- en Lemmer-Stoomboot; Ver.
Boordwerktuigkundigen KLM; Ver. Kapiteins Grote Vaart; Landelijke
Bedrijfsgroep Transport; Ver. KLM-Radiotelegrafisten; Ver. KLM
Pursers en Hofmeesters; Centr Kapiteins en Officieren Koopvaardij;
Nederl. Bond Zeevarenden; Bond Melkrijders; Ver. KLM Stewardessen;
Algem. Bond Luchtvaartpersoneel; Vervoersbond NVV; Centrale Zee-
varenden Koopvaardij en Visserij; Ver. Operations-Officers KLM;
Ver. Technical Officers KLM; Ver. Nederl. Koopvaardijofficieren;
VHP KLM-Personeel; Fed Haven Vakvereniging; Ver. KLM-Cabine-
personeel; Algem. Ver. Zeevarenden; Centr Kapiteins en Offieren
Koopvaardij; Ver. Werknemers Personen- en Beroepsgoederenvervoer;
Ver. Kapiteins en Officieren Koopvaart; Fed Werknemersorganisaties

Zeevaart; Ver. Nederl. Helikopter Verkeersvlieger; VHP Wegtransport; Ver. Personeel Luchthaven Schiphol; Vervoersbond FNV; VHP Haven en Transport; Nederl. Ver. Spoor- en Tramwegpersoneel; Bond Orde van Personeel HIJSM; Kathol. Bond Vervoerspersoneel; Vervoersbond CNV; Bond Ambtenaren NS; Nederl. Stationskruiersbond; Neutrale Bond Spoorwegpersoneel; Onafh Bond Spoorwegpersoneel; Ver. Beambten Rotterdamse Tramwegmaatschappij; Syndikale Fed Spoorwegpersoneel; Bond Locomotiefpersoneel; Centr Bond Spoorwegpersoneel; Algem. Bond Spoor- en Tramwegpersoneel; Landelijke Bedrijfsgroep Spoor-, Tram- en ATO-personeel; Ver. Hoger Spoorwegpersonee; Vakver Rijdend Personeel NS; Vakver Administratief Personeel NS; Vakver Technisch Personeel NS; Vakver Stationspersoneel NS; Fed Spoorweg Vakvereniging; Broederschap Commiezen Posterijen; Ver. Directeuren PTT; Bond Kantoorhouders PTT; Nederl. Post- en Telegraafbond; Ver. Technisch Hoger Personeel PTT; Bond Rijkstelefonisten; Bond Technisch Personeel PTT; Ver. Hogere Ambtenaren PTT; Ver. Bureel-Ambtenaren PTT; RK-Bond PTT-Personeel; Christ. Bond PTT-Personeel; Nederl. Bond Schrijvers PTT; Bond Lager Personeel PTT; Centr Bond Nederl. PTT-Personeel; Genootschap Ingenieurs PTT; VHP PTT-dienst; Ver. Kantoorpersoneel Staatsbedr PTT; Algem. Bond PTT-Personeel; Ver. Pers Gelddiensten PTT; Bond RK PTT-Personeel; Landelijke Bedrijfsgroep Nederl. PTT-Personeel; Centr Bond Nederl. PTT-Personeel; Centrale Bond PTT-Ambtenaren; Algem. Bond Werkers PTT-bedrijf; Bond Technisch Personeel PTT; Associatie Hogere Functionarissen Staatsbedrijf PTT; Ver. Postpersoneel; Ver. Ingenieurs Rijkstoezicht Spoorwegdiensten; Bond Lager Loodspersoneel; Ver. Ambtenaren Nederl. Loodswezen; Bond Personeel Rijksbetonning en -verlichting; Ver. Rijksbakenmeesters Rijkswaterstaat; Loodsenvereniging "Nederland"; Ver. lager Machinepers Rijksloodswezen; Ver. Werktuigbouwkundigen Betonning en Verlichting Loodswezen; Ver. Personeel Rijksluchtvaartdienst; Scheldeloodsen-Ver.; Ver. Leidinggevende Nautische Functionarissen Loodswezen; Ver. "De Nederlandse Loods"; Ver. Ambtenaren Radardienst; Ver. Administratieve Ambtenaren Loodswezen; Ver. Radar- en Radiocommunicatiepersoneel Rijksloodsen; Luchtverkeersleidersgilde

9 Other Services: Nederl. Bond Gemeente-Ambtenaren; Ver. Hogere Ambtenaren Departementen en Hoge Colleges van Staat; Departementsbond; Nat Verbond Gemeente-Ambtenaren; Fed Bond Personeel Openbare Dienst; Bond Gemeenteboden en Concierges; Christ. Bond Personeel Publieke Dienst; RK Bond Overheidspersoneel; Fed Personeel Rijksdienst; Ver. Ambtenaren Gemeentefinanciën; Christ. Ambtenaarsbond; Algem. RK Ambtenaarsvereniging; Centr Nederl. Ambtenaarsbond; Bond Technische Ambtenaren; Bond Ambtenaren Waterschappen; Bond Machinisten en Stokers Watergemalen Friesland; Bond Ambtenaren Zeewerende Waterschappen; Fed Bond Ambtenaren Openbare Dienst; Algem. Bond Overheidspersoneel; Algem. Bond Provinciaal Personeel; Algem. Ver. Gemeenteambtenaren; Ver. Ambtenaren Provincie Gelderland; Ver. Ambtenaren Rijksinstellingen; Ver. Directeuren Gemeentewerken; Bond Personeel Overheidsdienst; Nederl. Instituut Directeuren en Ingenieurs Gemeentewerken; Gelders-Overijsselse Bond Gemeenteboden en Concierges; Syndikale Fed Overheidspersoneel; Algem. Bond Overheids- en Semi-overheidspersoneel; RK Ver. Technische Ambtenaren Overheidsdienst; Bond Rijkspersoneel Buitendiensten; Fed Bond Personeel Openbare Dienst; Bond

138

Overheids- en Semi-overheidspersoneel; Bedrijfsgroep Overheid; Algem. Bond Arbeidscontractanten Overheidsdienst; Algemene Bond van Ambtenaren; Christ. Bond Overheidspersoneel; Bond Nederl. Overheidspersoneel; Kathol. Bond Overheidspersoneel; Bond Hoofden Gemeentewerken Provicie Noord-Holland; Algem. Bond Gemeentepersoneel; Belangenvereniging Provinciaal Personeel Gelderland; Broederschap Beroeps-Brandweerofficieren; Ver. Middelbare en Hogere Ambtenaren Lagere Overheden; Ver. Bevordering Belangen Burgemeesters; CNV-bond Overheid, Gezondheid, Welzijn en Sociale Werkvoorziening; ABVA-KABO; Kon Broederschap Ontvangers Rijksbelast; Deurwaarders Belastingen; Ver. Inspecteurs Rijksbelastingen; Ver. Surnumerairs Belastingen; Ver. Controleurs Grondbelasting; Bond Personee Financiën; Bond Visiterende Ambtenaren Rijksbelastingen; Bond Hoofdkommiezen Belastingen; Bond Belastingambtenaren Christ. Grondslag; Ver. Boekhouders Rijks Schatkist; Ver. Hulpkommiezen Belastingen; Bond Assistenten Rijksbelastingen; Bond Verificateurs en Adjunct-Verificateurs; Bond Kommiezen te Water Rijksbelastingen; Ver. Verificateurs Rijksbelastingen; Ver. Accountants Belastingen; Ver. Accountants Rijksdienst; Ver. Overheidsaccountants; Neutr Bond Ambtenaren Belastingen; Bond Ambtenaren Rijksbelastingen; Ver. Ontvangers, Hoofdkommiezen en Kommiezen Rijksbelastingen; Ver. Ontvangers Belastingen; Ver. Adjunct-Inspecteurs Rijksbelastingen; Ver. Kommiezen Aanslagregeling en Controle; Ver. Dienstgeleiders Douane Nederland; Ver. Ambtenaren Registratie en Domeinen; Ver. Kadaster en Landmeetkunde; Ver. Beëdigde Klerken Hypotheken, Kadaster en Scheepsbewijzen; Bond Personeel Registratie, Domeinen, Hypotheken en Kadaster; Ver. Hoofdambtenaren Kadaster; Ver. Technische Ambtenaren Kadaster; Ver. Inspecteurs Registratie en Domeinen; Bond Tijdelijke Ambtenaren Registratie en Domeinen; Ver. Boekhouders Hypotheken Kadaster en Scheepsbewijzen; Ver. Meetarbeiders Kadaster; Ver. Administratieve Ambtenaren Registratie en Domeinen; Ver. Technici en Landmeetassistenten Kadaste; Ver. Inspecteurs Registratie en Domeinen; Ver. Hypotheekbewaarders; Bond Personeel Domeinen; Ver. Gemeente- en Waterschapsarchivarissen; Ver. Rijksarchiefambtenaren; Ver. Archivarissen; Broederschap Essayeurs; Ver. Ambtenaren Industriëel Eigendom; Ver. Hogere Ambtenaren Ijkwezen; Ver. Bedienden Ijkwezen; Ver. Directeuren-Veilingmeesters; Ver. Hoofdambtenaren Marktwezen Nederland; Ver. Assistenten Rijkswaarborg Platina, Goud en Zilver; Ver. Personeel Dienst Ijkwezen; Ver. Lagere Ambtenaren Ijkwezen; Ver. Waterstaatkundige Ambtenarn Rijkswaterstaat; Ver. Administratief Personeel Rijkswaterstaat; Ver. Personeel Rijkswaterstaat; Bond Machinepersoneel Rijkswaterstaat; Ver. Ambtenaren Scheepvaartinspectie; Ver. Techn Ambtenaren Provinciale Waterstaat; Ver. Ingenieurs Rijkswaterstaat; Bond Buiteng Opz en Techn Pers Rijkswaterstaat; Ver. Ingenieurs Zuiderzeewerken; Ver. Personeel Zuiderzeewerken; Ver. Waterstaatambtenaren Limburg; Ver. Hoger Ambtenaren Rijks- -Verkeersinspectie; Ver. Personeel Rijksdienst Ijselmeerpolders; Ver. Hogere Functionarissen Rijkswaterstaat; Ver. Hogere Noodwachtambtenaren; Bond KNMI-Ambtenaren; Ver. Hoger Technisch Personeel Rijksgebouwendienst; Bond Personeel Schade-Enquete- -Commissies; Unie Employees Nederl. Beheersinstituut; Bond Klerken Rechterlijke Macht; Bond Personeel Strafinrichtingen; Ver. Secretarissen Voogdijraden; Ver. Directieambtenaren Penitentaire

*Inrichtingen; Ver. Ambtenaren Kinderbescherming, Reclassering en
Sociale Dienst Gevangenissen; Ver. Geneeskundigen Justitie;
Neutrale Bond Gevangenispersoneel; Bond Administratieve Ambtenaren
Rechtelijke Macht; Bond Keurmeesters Vee en Vlees; Ver. Opzichters
Veeartsenij Veterinaire Inspectie Volksgezondheid; Ver. Rijkskeur-
meesters Algem.emene Dienst; Ver. Personeel Plantenziektekundige
Dienst; Ver. Rijksconsulenten Landbouw; Ver. Lagere Ambtenaren
Staatsbosbeheer; Ver. Technische Ambtenaren Visserijinspectie;
Ver. Analytisch Personeel Rijksdienst; Ver. Ambtelijk Rijkstoe-
zicht Visserij; Bond Administratief Personeel Rijkslandbouw Proef-
stations; Ver. Middelbare en Hogere Ambtenaren Rijksdiensten en
Wetenschappelijke Instellingen; Ver. Controle Opsporing Vervalsing
Rijkslandbouwproefstations; Ver. Hogere Ambtenaren Staatsbos-
beheer; Ver. Bezoldigde Rijkszuivelvisiteurs; Ver. Inspecteurs
Veeartsenijdienst; Ver. Assistenten Voorlichtingsdienst Landbouw;
Bond Inspectie-Ambtenaren Landbouw; Bond Ambtenaren Landbouw-
ordening; Ver. Behartiging Belangen Personeel Controledienst; Ver.
Landbouwvoorlichting; Ver. Ambtenaren Directies Landbouw &
Visserij; Ver. Pluimveekeurmeesters; Personeelsbelangenvereniging
Muskusrattenbestrijding; Belangenvereniging Bedrijfsleiders
Staatslandbouwpolders; Ver. Middelbaar en Hoger TNO-Personeel;
Ver. Nijverheidsconsulenten; Ver. Leden Rijksschooltoezicht; Ver.
Inspecteurs Gymnasia en MO; Ver. Controleurs Leerlingstelsels
Nijverheidsonderwijs; Ver. Ambtelijk Rijkstoezicht Lichamelijke
Opvoeding; Ver. Rijksinspecteurs Onderwijs; Ver. Staf-
functionarissen Museumwezen; Ver. Personeel Openbare Biblotheken;
Ver. Secretarissen Armenraden; Algem. Bond Ambt Raden van Arbeid;
Ver. Adm Pers Directie van den Arbeid; Ver. Hogere Technici
Arbeidsinspectie; Ver. Controlerende Ambtenare Sociale Zaken; Ver.
Administratief Personeel Arbeidsinspectie; Ver. Medische Staven
Raden van Arbeid; Ver. Hoger Pers Arbeidsinspectie; Genootschap
Agenten Rijksverzekeringsbank, Ver. Inspecteurs Raden van Arbeid;
Ver. Geneeskundige Ambtenaren Rijksverzekeringsbank; Ver. Ambte-
naren Organen Sociale Verzekering; Onderling Belang; Ver.
Werktuigkundigen Artillerie; Bond Technisch Personeel Luchtvaart-
afdeling; Ver. Administratieve Ambtenaren Rijkswerven; Ver.
Technisch en Toezichthoudend Personeel Rijkswerven; Vakorganisatie
Hoofdwerktuigbouwkundigen Luchtvaartafdeling; Bond Algem.emeen
Rijkspersoneel; Nederl. Ver. Personeel Defensie; Ver. Ambtenaren
Grensbewaking; Ver. Ingenieurs Defensie; Ver. Hoger Technisch
Personeel Defensie; Algem. Nederl. Politiebond; Broederschap
Commissarissen Politie; Rijkspolitie Ver.; Ver. Hoger Politie
Ambtenaren; Algem. Bond Politiepersoneel; Centrale Bond Gemeente-
veldwachters; Kathol. Politiebond; Bond Christ. Politieambtenaren;
Ver. RK Hoger Politiepersoneel; Bond Beambten Politie Rijkswerven;
Ver. Districtscommandanten Rijksveldwacht; Ver. Gemeenteveld-
wachters Provicie Groningen; Nederl. Politiebond; Bond Personeel
Politieke Recherche; Algem. Nederl. Politie Ver.; Algem. Christ.
Politiebond; Ver. Officieren Marinestoomvaartdienst; Kon Ver.
Militairen; Algem. Bond Minder Marinepersoneel; Bond Marine-Onder-
officieren; Ver. Beroepsschepelingen Zeemacht; Torpedomakers-
vereniging; Bond Onderofficieren-machinisten en -stoker Marine;
Ver. Officieren Kon Landmacht en Luchtmacht; Marechaussee Ver.;
Ver. Geweermaker en Zwaardveger Nederl. Landmacht; Ver. Militaire
Kleermakers; Ver. Militaire Zadelmakers; Bond Korporaals Kon*

*Marine; Ver. Militaire Apothekersbedienden; Bond Monteurs Kon
Marine; Nederl. RK Onderofficieren Bond; Ver. Militaire Hoef-
smeden; Bond Nederl. Militaire Musici; Ver. Nederl. Reserve-
officieren; Ver. Militaire Schoenmakers; Bond Militair Personeel
Geneeskundige Dienst Landmacht; Algem. Ver. Marine-Officieren; Nat
Christen Onderofficieren Ver.; RK Ver. Marinepersoneel; Algem. RK
Officieren Ver.; Ver. Smeden-Bankwerkers Landmacht; Bond Christ.
Marinepersoneel beneden rang Officier; Bond Vrijwillig Dienende
Militairen; Bond Korporaals Vestingsartillerie; Bond Mindere
Militairen Nederl. Landmacht; Nat Christ. Officieren Ver.; Ver.
Technici Marine; Ver. Onderofficieren Genie; Ver. Lichamelijke Op-
voeding Militairen; Bond Marine Schepelingen; Neutrale Onder-
officieren Ver. Democr Grondslag; Ver. Officieren Militaire
Administratie; Ver. Militair Technisch Beroepspersoneel; Onder-
officieren Ver.; Kathol. Ver. Militaire Ambtenaren tot 2e Lt, Land
& Luchtmacht; Algem. Christ. Officieren Ver.; Christ. Ver. Mili-
tairen; Land Korporaals Ver.; Militaire Advies, Belangen, Rechts-
bijstand Organisatie; Kon Nederl. Officieren Ver.; Algem. Christ.
Organisatie Militairen; Nederl. Onderwijzers Genootschap; Ver.
Christ. Onderwijzers; Bond Nederl. Onderwijzers; RK Diocesane
Onderwijsbonden; Unie Christ. Onderwijzers/-essen; Ver. RK Onder-
wijzeressen Bisdom Den Bosch; Bond RK Openbaar Onderwijs; Ver.
Hoofden RK Bijzondere Scholen Bisdom Haarlem; Ver. Hoofden RK
Scholen; Ver. Hoofden Scholen in Ned; Bond Nederl. Schoolhoofden;
Nederl. Onderwijzers Ver.; Ver. Gereformeerde Onderwijzers en
Leraren; Prot-Christ. Bond Onderwijzen Pers; Ver. Christ. Onder-
wijzers; Ver. Hoofden Scholen; Vrije Ver. Nederl. Onderwijzers;
Algem. Nederl. Leerkrachten Organisatie; Algem. Bond Onderwijzend
Personeel; Algem. Ver. Leerkrachten; Prot-Christ. Vakorganisaties
Onderwijs; Kathol. Onderwijzers Ver.; Kathol. Onderwijs Vak-
organisatie; Nederl. Ver. Kleuterleidsters; Ver. Leraressen
Christ. Kleuteronderwijs; Ver. Christ. Opleiders/sters Onder-
wijzeressen Christ. Bewaarscholen; Diocesane Bonden
Onderwijzeressen RK Kleuteronderwijs; Unie Othopedagogen; Unie
Christ. Buitengewoon Onderwijs; Ver. Onderwijzend Personeel
Christ. Philantropische Opvoedingsgestichten; Ver. Docenten
Christ. Opleidingsinstituten Onderwijsgevenden; Ver. Onderwijzers-
/essen Inrichtingen Opleiding Onderwijzers/essen VO; Ver. Direc-
teuren/icen, Onderwijzers/-essen Rijkskweekscholen; Kathol. Ver.
Docenten Pedagogische Academies; Ver. Docenten Opleidings-
instituten Onderwijsgevenden; Ver. Docenten Lerarenopleidingen;
Ver. Christ. AVO; Ver. MULO; Genootschap Leraren Nederl. Gymnasia
en Lycea; Algem. Ver. Leraren VHMO; Ver. Rectoren en Conrectoren;
Ver. Directeuren HBS; Nederl. Lectorenvereniging; Ver. Leraren
Rijks HBS; Ver. Docenten Christ. VWO; Kathol. Leraren Ver.; Ver.
Academisch gevormde Leraren MO; Bond Leraren; Ver. Rectoren
Nederl. Lycea; Ver. Rectoren en Directeuren Scholen VO en MO;
Kathol. Rectorenver; Ver. Rijksleraren MO; Ver. Rectoren en
Directeuren Scholen Christ. VHMO; Ver. Academici VHMO; Ver.
Directrices Scholen VHMO Meisjes; Algem. Ver. Rectoren en
Directeuren Scholen VHMO; Ver. Schoolleiders Openbaar VHMO;
Nederl. Genootschap Leraren; Ver. Rectoren en Docenten Avondlycea;
Algem. Ver. Schoolleiders VWO en AVO; Ver. Hoogleraren; Ver.
Assistenten, Conservatoren en Lectoren Rijksuniversiteiten; Ver.
Interacademiaal Overleg Universiteiten; Ver. Academici Wetenschap-*

pelijk Onderwijs; Ver. Directies Nijverheidsscholen; Ver. Directeuren en Onderwijzers Rijks-dagnormaallessen; Nederl. Bond Leraren/-essen Nijverheidsonderwijs; Ver. Onderwijzers Rijksdagnormaallessen; Organisatie Theorieleraren Ambachtscholen; Verbond Leraarsverenigingen; Bond Ver. Leraren Middelbare Nijverheidscholen; Ver. Nijverheidsonderwijs Meisjes; Bond Leraren Nijverheidsavondonderwijs; Ver. Christ. Leerkrachten LTO; Kathol. Ver. Directeuren, Docenten en Consulenten Beroepsonderwijs; RK Ver. Leraressen Nijverheidsonderwijs; Bond Leerkrachten Nijverheidsonderwijs Meisjes; Ver. Christ. Leraren Beroepsonderwijs; Ver. Directies Beroepsonderwijs; Bond Leerkrachten Nijverheidsonderwijs; Ver. Directeuren HBO; Algem. Ver. Leraren en Directeuren UTO; Ver. Prot-Christ. Leraren en Directeuren UTO; Ver. RK Leraren en Directeuren UTO; Ver. Doc Laboratoriumscholen; Nederl. Ver. Land & Tuinbouwonderwijzers; Ver. Tuinbouwvakonderwijzers; Ver. Directeuren en Leraren Middelbaar Land & Tuinbouwonderwijs; Ver. Leerkrachten Huishoudonderwijs; RK Ver. Leerkrachten Huishoudonderwijs; Christ. Ver. Leerkrachten Huishoudonderwijs; Ver. Directeuren en Leraren Middelbaar Handelsavondonderwijs; Ver. Leraren Hogere Handelsavondonderwijs; Ver. Leraren Stenografie en Machineschrijven; Ver. Leraren Lit--economisch MO; Bond Directeuren Handelscholen; Bond Directeuren en Leraren Handelsavondonderwijs; Ver. Directeuren en Leraren Algem.emeen Vormend Avondonderwijs; Ver. Leraren Christ. HAO; Ver. Leraren Schoonschrijven; Ver. IMO Leraren; Bond Leraren Tertiair Onderwijs; Unie MTO-verenigingen; Federatie Middelbaar Econ-Adm Onderwijs; Ver. Docenten MO-opleidingen; Ver. Onderwijzers Gevangeniswezen; Ver. Personeel Onderwijs Schipperskinderen; Ver. Gediplomeerde Onderwijzers Lichaamsoef Nederl. Landmacht; Ver. Leraren Luchtvaart en Nautisch Onderwijs; Nederl. Ver. Tekenonderwijzers; Bond Leraressen Huishoudscholen; Ver. Onderwijzeressen Handwerken; Ver. Docenten Kunstonderwijs; Ver. Leraren Handvaardigheid; Nederl. Ver. Leraren en Onderwijzers Lichamelijke Opvoeding; Kon Nederl. Ver. Leraren en Onderwijzers Lichamelijke Opvoeding; Ver. Leraren Gymnastiek; Ver. RK Leiders/sters Lichaamsbeoefening; Christ. Ver. Leraren Lichamelijke Opvoeding; Nat RK Ver. Leraren en Onderwijzers Gymnastiekonderwijs; Nederl. Ver. Logopedisten Onderwijs; Ver. Technici, Amanuensis en Concierges Onderwijs; Bond Hoger Onderwijspersoneel; Bond Niet--Onderwijzen Schoolpersoneel; Bond Administratief Personeel Nijverheidsonderwijs; Ver. Administratief Personeel VHMO en Kweekschoolonderwijs; RK Bond Administratief Personeel Nijverheidsonderwijs; Ver. Christ. Administratief en Bedienend Personeel Nijverheidsond; Bond Medewerkers Onderwijs; Federatie Niet-onderwijs Personeel Onderwijs; Ver. Bevordering Belangen Verpleegsters/-ers; RK Bond Ziekenverplegers; Nat Vakbond Verplegenden; Nederl. Tandtechnische Ver.; Nederl. Bond Tuberculose-Huisbezoeksters; Zeeuwse Bond Tuberculose-Huisbezoeksters; Ver. Wijkverplegenden; Bond Christ. Verplegers/sters; Ver. Gestichtsartsen; Bond Wijkverplegenden; Nat Bond Verplegenden; Ver. Controlerend Geneesheren; Vakbond Tandtechnici; Ver. Docenten Verpleegkunde; Ver. Tandheelkundigen; Nederl. Mij Bevord Tandheelkunde; Ver. Verplegenden; Bedrijfsgroep Ziekenhuis en Verplegenden; Christ. Ver. Verplegenden en Verzorgenden; Ver. Medische Analysten; Ver. Radiologische Laboranten; Christ. Bond Tandtechnici; Algem. Bond Zieken-

verzorgsters/ers; Nederl. Bond Ziekenverpleging; Ver. Verpleeg-
kundigen; Bond Maatschappelijk Werkers; Ver. Werkers Kinderbe-
scherming; VHP Welzijn; Genootschap Fysiotherapie; Landelijke Bond
Werkers Gezondheidszorg; Kathol. Unie Verpleegkundigen en
Verzorgenden; Het Beterschap; Nederl.Inst Psychologen; Landelijke
Ver. Artsen in Dienstverband; Ver. Logopedisten; Landelijke Ver.
Psychotherapeuten in dienstverband; Ver. Bewegingsleer Cesar; Ver.
Geestelijke Verzorgers Ziekenhuis; Ver. Diëtisten; Mensendieck
Bond; Ver. Orthopedisten; Ver. Apothekersassistenten Ziekenhuisen;
Kon Nederl. Mij Bevordering Diergeneeskunde; VHP Gezondheids- en
Bejaardenzorg; Ver. Psychomotorische Therapie; Bond Israelitische
Godsdienstonderwijzers; Ver. Kosters Prot Kerkgenootschappen; Bond
Nederl. Predikanten; Ver. Vrijzinnige Godsdienstonderwijzers en
Voorgangers; Bond Godsdienstonderwijzers; RK Diocesane Kosters-
bonden; Christ. Kostersvereniging; Prot-Christ. Ver. Kosters;
Kathol. Bond Kosters; Kon Nederl. Toonkunstenaars Ver.; Orga-
nistenvereniging; Toneelkunstenaarsver.; Nederl. Bond Geemploy-
eerden Kunst- en Amusementsbedrijf; Kathol. Dirigenten- en
Organistenvereniging; Toonkunstenaarsbond; Artistenbond; Bond
Correctoren; Artistenorganisatie; Bond Orkestdirigenten; Bond
Personeel Theater- en Bioscoopbedrijf; Nederl. Ver. Concert-
zangeressen en -zangers; RK Ver. Toonkunstenaars; Algem. Nederl.
Bond Musici: Bond Commercieel-Geempl Filmverhuurbedrijf; Ver.
Personeel Kermisbedrijf; Personeelsbond Film- en Theaterbedrijven;
Beroepsver Beeldende Kunstenaars; Bond Artisten en Musici; Ver.
Toneelkunstenaars; Artisten Organisatie Nederland; Organisatie
Kleinkunst Artisten; Ver. Geengageerden Nederl. Opera; Verbond
Nederl. Artisten; Ver. Voetbaloefenmeesters; Algem. Nederl. Bond
Bioscoop- en Theaterpersoneel; Organisatie Musici en Artisten;
Kathol. Bond Musici en Artisten; Fed Musici en Artisten; Algem.
Bedrijfsbond Kunst, Film, Theater en Amusementsbedrijf; Bond
Christ. Kunstenaars; Dirigentenorganisatie; Ver. Administratief en
Technisch Personeel Toneelbedrijf; Unie Werknemers Film en TV Ver.
Geëngageerden Operagezelschap Forum; Ver. Contractspelers; Algem.
Nederl. Organisatie Uitvoerende Kunstenaars; Orkestenverbond;
Beroepsver Mimebeoefenaars; BBK '69; Beroepsver Theatertechnici;
Ver. Hoger Omroeppersoneel; Kunstenbond FNV; Bond Omroepmusici;
Bond Ensemblespelers; Kring Nederl. Filmjournalisten; Bond
Werknemers Sport; Nederl. Instituut van Accountants; Bond Perso-
neel Rechtspractijk en Cand-Deurwaarders; Ver. Cand-Deurwaarders;
Bond Medewerkers Notariaat; Bond Onbezoldigde Opsporingsambtenaren
en Bewakingspersoneel; Ver. Beheerders Landgoederen en Landelijke
Bezittingen; Ver. Bibliothecaressen; Ver. Woningopzichteressen;
Geneefse Bond Hotel-, Café- en Restaurantpersoneel; Kathol. Bond
Hotel-, Café- en Restaurantpersoneel; Neutrale Vakbond Hotel, Bond
Café en Restaurant Geëmployeerden; Bond Hotel-, Café- en
Restaurantpersoneel; Algem. Nederl. Bond Hotel-, Café- en
Restaurantpersoneel; Nederl. Koksorganisatie; Fed Verband Hotel-
personeel; Horecabond; Bond Werknemers Hotel-, Café-, Luchroom- en
Restaurantpersoneel; Genfer Bond Bedienend Personeel Horeca-
bedrijf; Bond Hoger Hotel-, Rest- en Cafepersoneel; Bond Kappers-
en Barbiersbedienden; RK Kappers- en Barbiersbediendenbond;
Neutrale Bond Personeel Wasindustrie; Ver. Barbiers- en Kappers-
bedienden; Bond Kapperspersoneel; Kappersbond FNV; Centr Bond
Kapperspersoneel; Bedrijfsgroep Bijzondere Bedrijven; Algem.

Personeelsbond Bad- en Zweminrichtingen; Bond Personeel Sociaal-Hygiënische Instellingen; Algem. Bedrijfsbond Sociaal-Hygiënische Instellingen en Huishoudelijke Dienst; Christ. Bond Kapperspersoneel; Algem. Nederl. Bond Huispersoneel; Christ. Bond Huispersoneel; Ver. Behartiging Belangen Personeel Koninklijke Hofhouding

This list contains all national unions which existed one year or longer between 1920 and 1986, but does not include independent local organizations. In the tables their membership is included, though. The large majority of the unions listed above recruits membership in one sector (defined at the 1-digit ISIC level), in one status category, and in either the public or private sector. However, as a consequence of the merger processes, especially in recent decades, the membership of the larger (multi-industrial) unions now straddles across the economy. For instance, the unions in agriculture also have members in the dairy industry, in quarrying and ore mining, the unions in construction recruit also wood and furniture workers, the unions in transport organize also in agriculture (fishery), etc. On the basis of <u>Annual Reports</u>, and - before 1967 - the CBS files, it has been possible to disaggregate the membership union by union. With the help, in some cases, of internal reports which could be consulted by (and can be obtained from) the author, the membership of the large multi-industrial unions has also been divided-up by industrial sector. The *Industriebonden* (general industry unions), which were founded in the early 1970s, have members in mining, manufacturing industries, construction as well as in services (e.g., leasing activities, hairdressers, cleaners and domestic servants). In the course of their history the *Dienstenbonden* (general service unions), or their predecessors, have absorbed many smaller unions and now have members in publishing, commerce and retail, banking & insurance and business services, some transport related activities, and other services (social insurance, art and entertainment, communication, etc.). Similarly, the *Ambtenarenbonden* (general unions of public employees), which originated in the late 1940s, organize members in agriculture (public gardening), in industry (gas, water & electricity, social workshops), in commerce and banking (municipal distribution centres, Central Bank) in transport (bus & tram, port and inland water services, sea pilots, air traffic controllers, and of course in public administration, education, health and welfare activities. The membership of the MHP-federations, and of its union of white-collar employees (*Unie van Beambten, Leidinggevend en Hoger Personeel*), also needed further disaggregation by industrial sector (see also: Van Diest, 1987).

2.2 Classification by Status

Classification by status poses similar problems. Again, the fast majority of unions organizes either manual or non-manual employees. However, following the application of the principle of 'industrial unionism', the color-line gradually blurred (Harmsen & Reinalda, 1975; Reinalda, 1981; 1985). Until 1967, the CBS-files distinguished three categories: *handarbeiders* or manual workers in the private sector, *beambten* or white-collar employees in the private sector, and *ambtenaren* or public employees. After 1969 the CBS retained only the

144

distinction private-public. Until the 1970s most unions distinguished between manual and non-manual membership. Some unions still do, apparently for the purpose of separate collective agreements (but this is less and less the case) or for the purpose of balanced representation at delegate conferences or in executive councils. My figures on membership by status are based on Annual Reports or internal documents made available, in addition to the CBS-files. On the basis of the Jaarverslagen of the three (now two) major Ambtenarenbonden (ABVA, KABO, and NCBO) I have also distinguished between manual and non-manual membership in the public sector. Most members in railways, tram & bus, public works, garbage collecting, public gardening, gas-, water & electricity, and polder boards are classified as manual. These figures are however only a crude approximation, and would need further refinement.

2.3   Public Sector Unionism

The classification of members by employment in the private or public sector is relatively uncomplicated. The unions which organize across this line are few. The most important exceptions are the general transport unions (railways and public road transport) and service unions (social insurance). The (semi-)public sector includes central and local government (state, provinces, municipalities, polder boards), education and health services, social insurance, bodies under public law, welfare and social care activities, gas, water and electricity production (provincial, municipal or semi-public), and social workshops (employment relief programmes for the handicapped). Included are the police and the armed forces (only the professional military, not the unions of conscripts). Not included in the (semi-)public sector are nationalized mining and nationalized industries (coal mining before 1966) or state participations.

3.   LABOUR FORCE STATISTICS

No continuous series for the dependent labour force is available for the full period 1913-1985, The Central Bureau of Statistics provides only a continuous series for the total labour force, measured in man--hours (CBS 1985). However, on the basis of the results of the Population Censuses of 1909, 1920, 1930, 1947, 1960 and 1971, it is possible to calculate and interpolate the dependent labour force. Additionally, I checked the interpolated figures against those reported in Oomens & Van der Kolk (1949) for the years between 1921 and 1942, in CBS (1967) for the period 1947-1966, and in the National Account Statistics for later years, as published in the official Statistical Yearbook of the Netherlands, The Hague or in the Annual Reports on the Dutch economy by the Central Planning Bureau, also in The Hague.

Regarding unemployed workers, I have used the time-series published by the CBS (CBS, 1985, and earlier editions), as well as the series of Oomens & Van der Kolk (1949) for the earlier years. The unemployment figures include: the registered male and female unemployed, those in public relief or pubic employment programmes, and an estimated number of non-insured unemployed, given the incomplete coverage of the pre-war union-related unemployment insurance schemes (see: Kloosterman, 1984). Before 1971 the unemployment statistics did not include part-time unemployed people.

All figures until 1970 relate to man-hours, that is, to the dependent labour force recalculated on the basis of the annual average number of hours worked by full-time employees. As part-time labour was of little importance (see Population Censuses of 1960 and 1971) and many workers worked longer rather than fewer hours, this tends to overstate the size of the employed dependent labour force, but the difference - with the number of persons in employment reported in the censuses - is slight. After 1971, the picture is different as a consequence of the rapid diffusion of part-time labour and, also, the changes in working-time hours and patterns of full-time employees (Visser, 1989). Thus, for the period 1970-1985 I have used the adjusted series of the CBS, based on the biennial labour force sample surveys ('Arbeidskrachtentellingen'). The figures relate to the number of persons in employment and working 20 or more hours (Department of Social Affairs and Employment, Rapportage Arbeidsmarkt: 'Zelfstandige en afhankelijke beroepsbevolking naar geslacht, per 1 januari'). Hence, a small break in the series - in 1970 - cannot be avoided. Another difference is that the pre-1970 data refer to annual averages, while the figures for later years are to end-of-year data (actually the CBS uses 1 January as reporting data, which I have taken as the end-of-year value of the previous year). The unemployment statistics after 1971 also refers to persons, until 1979 on the basis of those looking for work of 25 and more hours, after 1979 on the basis of 20 or more hours. Other discontinuities are due to the fact that after 1979 those aged 65 years and over were excluded; and in 1984 those unemployed aged 57,5 years and over did not need to register. Conscripts, whose numbers was known from the biennial labour force sample surveys and easy to interpolate every second year, are not included in the series.

The classification of the dependent labour force by sex, industry and status was made on the basis of the Population Censuses 1920, 1930, 1947, 1961 and 1971 and the labour force sample surveys of 1979 and 1985. My calculation from the censuses yield some differences in comparison with the data reported in Flora, Kraus and Pfenning (1987: 562-570): I have excluded military conscripts in both the pre- and post-war period, and classified the unemployed by occupational category on the basis of registration data of the labour exchange offices (published in the Monthly Bulletin of the CBS). The (semi-)public sector has been defined as including public administration (including police, armed forces and social insurance), bodies under public law, education and health services, social care and welfare activities, public gardening & public works, social workshops, gas, water & electricity production, railways and other public transport, and the Post Office (including financial services, but not the Central Bank). Employment figures are based on the biennial Labour Force Sample Surveys (Arbeidskrachtentellingen) of 1973-1985, or on the Population Censuses in earlier years.

4. TABLES

table: NE 1/1			Membership by Confederation							NETHERLANDS	
year	NAS	NVV	NKV	CNV	ANV	VVH	NSV	CHA	CRP	Other	Total
	1	2	3	5	6	7	9	11	14		
1913	9,7	86,1	29,4	11,1	3,9					128,1	268,3
1914	9,2	89,3	35,3	12,4	4,7					124,4	275,3
1915	10,5	103,2	42,1	15,2	5,0					128,8	304,8
1916	14,4	133,8	58,8	20,9	5,6				4,0	124,7	362,2
1917	23,7	166,3	73,7	28,8	7,8				4,7	129,2	434,2
1918	34,0	200,0	98,2	47,9	10,6				6,8	135,8	533,3
1919	52,6	259,7	151,0	70,4	40,3			2,5	9,9	124,3	710,7
1920	37,4	224,7	158,6	76,3	52,7			2,7	11,6	111,9	674,9
1921	31,6	223,8	150,9	73,4	50,1			3,7	20,8	125,1	658,6
1922	23,7	201,1	122,8	62,6	47,8			3,9	8,6	123,8	585,7
1923	13,9	183,3	101,2	54,0	32,5		7,8	3,7	7,9	129,0	525,4
1924	14,0	187,0	94,4	50,7	24,0	16,6	7,4	3,5	6,4	99,9	503,9
1925	13,8	193,2	93,0	49,0	13,3	16,3	6,2	3,2	6,9	105,3	500,2
1926	14,0	199,1	99,6	52,0	11,7	15,7	5,0	3,2	7,2	104,0	511,5
1927	14,5	205,9	104,8	53,6	12,4	15,7	4,8	3,4	7,2	105,7	528,0
1928	16,3	220,8	114,9	58,6	12,7	15,9	2,1	3,5	7,6	110,9	563,3
					└─NVC (8)┘						
1929	17,5	255,6	136,6	72,9	36,7		2,8	3,7	7,7	104,1	637,6
1930	17,5	276,2	152,9	82,1	40,8		2,3	3,8	8,0	107,7	691,3
1931	20,7	320,3	183,1	103,3	46,1		2,7	3,9	8,4	106,6	795,1
1932	23,0	340,1	198,1	116,9	49,3		2,8	3,8	8,2	99,6	841,8
1933	19,6	324,9	194,6	116,8	47,2		2,4	3,8	7,7	88,6	805,6
1934	13,0	300,3	182,7	114,0	46,7		2,0	3,7	7,7	88,9	759,0
1935	12,0	287,4	175,9	109,3	44,7		2,0	3,7	8,0	90,6	733,6
1936	11,4	285,3	171,0	109,1	44,7		1,9	3,6	8,4	94,2	729,6
1937	11,2	296,0	173,3	111,5	45,6		2,0	3,6	9,0	97,9	750,1
1938	10,8	309,0	182,0	115,1	46,4		1,6	3,6	9,7	100,4	778,6
1939	10,5	322,3	191,7	120,3	50,9		1,6	3,6	10,6	97,5	809,0
1940		333,7	177,6	113,9				3,6	10,1	92,8	731,7
1941		323,8						3,5	9,5	38,4	375,2

table: NE 1/2			Membership by Confederation							NETHERLANDS
year	NVV	NKV	CNV	NVC	EVC	CHA	NCHP	AC	Other	Total
	2	3	5	8	10	11	12	15		
1945	237,8	182,8	94,0		162,3	3,2		(6,1)	76,3	763
1946	301,6	224,9	119,1		169,4	3,5		17,9	124,9	961
1947	331,7	251,5	131,6	2,0	176,9	7,4		18,8	133,2	1,053
1948	368,1	269,5	147,5	2,1	163,4	7,2		20,4	130,3	1,109
1949	381,6	296,4	155,6	2,8	163,2	8,1		21,8	129,9	1,160
1950	405,8	311,4	166,5	18,0	163,8	9,9		22,9	115,2	1,214
1951	420,7	320,8	174,8	16,8	164,4	10,4		23,1	125,4	1,257
1952	435,6	334,7	182,0	17,5		10,3		24,3	131,0	1,137
1953	453,9	347,3	191,1	19,6	.	10,9		25,7	134,6	1,184
1954	463,3	361,0	201,4	14,8	.	12,0		27,7	141,4	1,223
1955	468,4	381,7	204,5	10,7	.	12,7		29,1	147,5	1,256
1956	500,3	412,0	216,0	12,5	.	14,3		29,3	148,6	1,334
1957	486,2	405,0	218,5	12,0	.	8,2		29,0	183,1	1,342
1958	476,7	395,9	217,6	11,8	.	8,0		30,3	191,5	1,331
1959	486,7	400,4	217,0	11,7	.	8,1		30,1	198,1	1,352
1960	507,0	411,8	223,8	10,7	.	8,3		30,7	206,5	1,398
1961	507,2	417,8	224,9	10,0	.	8,2		31,5	219,5	1,419
1962	512,2	418,5	227,5	9,6	.	8,5		31,8	227,0	1,435
1963	528,6	418,9	229,8	10,1	.	8,7		33,1	240,3	1,469
1964	527,2	407,7	229,2		.	8,6		33,9	257,5	1,464
1965	535,7	412,0	234,6			9,0		35,7	261,3	1,488
1966	556,3	425,3	241,0			9,7	5,4	36,5	262,1	1,536
1967	558,2	428,4	241,0			10,2	5,6	36,8	263,9	1,544
1968	557,6	409,4	240,3			17,1	5,9	37,5	263,1	1,530
1969	562,4	400,2	237,4			19,0	8,0	38,9	257,3	1,523
1970	611,4	404,0	237,7			22,5	9,6	40,9	249,5	1,575
1971	623,8	399,7	239,1			31,4	11,3	45,2	266,1	1,616
1972	633,1	395,4	235,9			33,3	14,6	48,1	267,9	1,628
1973	664,1	397,9	231,8			35,1	29,2	69,4	246,6	1,674
						└MHP (13)┘				
1974	677,1	355,2	227,9			109,5		70,4	239,9	1,680
	└FNV (4) ┘									
1975	1,058,6		230,1			106,0		89,4	235,1	1,719
1976	1,052,1		258,5			111,9		100,6	228,4	1,751
1977	1,072,0		295,9			113,2		102,9	203,3	1,787
1978	1,080,8		301,1			117,4		105,4	186,6	1,791
1979	1,076,8		303,9			118,5		112,3	147,1	1,758
1980	1,054,1		302,4			113,2		110,2	142,4	1,722
1981	1,008,0		346,2			113,4		112,8	134,1	1,714
1982	998,8		335,3			112,6		115,2	111,7	1,673
1983	956,2		317,0			111,2		112,1	115,7	1,612
1984	918,5		302,5			109,4		102,7	130,3	1,563
1985	903,5		296,4			106,9		100,7	130,6	1,538

table: NE 2		Membership Shares by Confederation in per centage of total members							NETHERLANDS
year	NAS	NVV	NVV	FNV	CNV	NVC	EVC	MHP	total
	1	2	3	4	5	8	10	13	
1915	3.4	33.9	13.8		5.0				100.0
1920	5.5	33.3	23.5		11.3				100.0
1925	2.8	38.6	18.6		9.8				100.0
1930	2.5	40.0	22.1		11.9	5.9			100.0
1935	1.6	39.2	24.0		14.9	6.1			100.0
1940		45.6	24.3		15.6				100.0
1945		31.2	24.0		12.3		21.3		100.0
1950		33.4	25.6		13.7	1.5	13.5		100.0
1955		37.2	30.3		16.3	0.9	.		100.0
1960		36.2	29.4		16.0	0.8	.		100.0
1965		36.0	27.7		15.8				100.0
1970		38.8	25.6		15.1				100.0
1975		(40.6)	(20.7)	61.6	13.4			6.2	100.0
1980		(42.8)	(18.0)	61.2	17.6			6.6	100.0
1985				58.7	19.3			7.0	100.0

year	NVV		NKV		CNV		MHP		other	total	
	abs	%	abs	%	abs	%	abs	%	abs	abs	%
1945	2,4	1.0	4,1	2.2	1,2	1.3			1,0	8,7	1.˙
1946	4,4	1.5	5,0	2.2	1.6	1.3			1,7	12,7	1.˙
1947	6,2	1.9	5,9	2.3	1,8	1.4			2,8	16,7	1.(
1948	6,9	1.9	6,8	2.5	1,8	1.2			3,0	18,5	1.˙
1949	7,9	2.1	7,6	2.6	2,2	1.4			3,2	20,9	1.(
1950	8,8	2.2	8,3	2.7	3,0	1.8			3,0	23,1	1.(
1951	10,2	2.4	9,9	3.1	3,8	2.2			3,3	27,2	2.2
1952	11,7	2.7	10,9	3.3	5,0	2.7			4,1	31,7	2.8
1953	13,6	3.0	12,2	3.5	6,1	3.2			4,3	36,2	3.˙
1954	15,1	3.3	13,3	3.7	6,8	3.4			5,0	40,2	3.?
1955	16,6	3.5	14,8	3.9	6,7	3.3			5,6	43,7	3.!
1956	20,1	4.0	17,3	4.2	7,5	3.5			6,2	51,1	3.8
1957	21,0	4.3	20,0	4.9	8,0	3.7			8,3	57,3	4.3
1958	23,2	4.9	21,8	5.5	9,8	4.5			9,1	63,9	4.8
1959	24,8	5.1	23,7	5.9	10,7	4.9			9,8	69,0	5.˙
1960	27,7	5.5	25,1	6.1	12,0	5.4			10,5	75,3	5.4
1961	30,2	6.0	27,6	6.6	13,2	5.9			11,1	82,1	5.8
1962	32,0	6.2	28,4	6.8	13,9	6.1			12,4	86,7	6.C
1963	34,1	6.5	29,8	7.1	14,5	6.3			13,3	91,7	6.2
1964	34,8	6.6	30,6	7.5	15,7	6.8			14,3	95,4	6.!
1965	37,1	6.9	31,8	7.7	16,9	7.2			15,2	101,0	6.8
1966	43,9	7.9	34,3	8.1	18,6	7.7			17,7	114,5	7.5
1967	46,8	8.4	34,4	8.0	18,7	7.8			23,4	123,3	8.0
1968	49,3	8.8	33,3	8.1	18,6	7.7			26,8	128,0	8.4
1969	51,5	9.2	39,1	9.8	18,6	7.8			28,7	137,9	9.1
1970	53,9	8.8	42,4	10.5	19,8	8.3			30,0	146,1	9.3
1971	65,0	10.4	43,4	10.9	21,2	8.9			32,7	162,3	10.0
1972	68,6	10.8	45,2	11.4	20,1	8.5			34,6	168,5	10.3
1973	74,1	11.2	46,3	11.6	20,4	8.8			35,8	176,6	10.5
1974	78,9	11.7	44,7	12.6	21,3	9.3	5,5	5.0	37,4	187,8	11.2
	└── FNV ──┘										
1975		127,7 12.1			25,1	10.9	5,6	5.3	37,9	196,3	11.4
1976		136,2 12.9			29,7	11.5	6,1	5.5	35,2	207,2	11.8
1977		138,2 12.9			34,5	11.7	6,6	5.8	31,1	210,4	11.8
1978		141,1 13.1			35,2	11.7	7,9	6.7	32,3	216,5	12.1
1979		142,3 13.2			35,8	11.8	9,0	7.6	34,5	221,6	12.6
1980		141,7 13.4			39,1	12.9	10,5	9.3	34,6	225,9	13.1
1981		150,9 15.0			47,4	13.7	11,5	10.1	34,1	243,9	14.2
1982		153,8 15.4			50,7	15.1	12,4	11.0	33,5	250,4	15.0
1983		157,4 16.5			51,4	16.2	13,6	12.2	32,9	255,3	15.8
1984		161,1 17.5			52,4	17.3	14,8	13.5	33,6	261,9	16.8
1985		163,5 18.1			53,7	18.1	15,5	14.5	34,5	267,2	17.4

table: NE 4/1	density rates				NETHERLANDS		
year	membership		dep.labour force		density rates		
	total	less pens.	total	employed only	gross	net	employed only
	1	2	3	4	1:3	2:3	2:4
1913	268,3	268,3	1,590	1,530	16.9	16.9	17.5
1914	275,3	275,3	1,620	1,460	17.0	17.0	18.9
1915	304,8	304,9	1,650	1,520	18.5	18.5	20.1
1916	362,2	362,2	1,690	1,630	21.4	21.4	22.2
1917	434,2	434,3	1,730	1,650	25.1	25.1	26.3
1918	533,3	533,2	1,780	1,690	30.0	30.0	31.6
1919	710,7	710,7	1,840	1,750	38.6	38.6	40.6
1920	675,9	675,9	1,890	1,820	35.8	35.8	37.1
1921	658,6	658,7	1,940	1,860	33.9	34.0	35.4
1922	585,7	585,5	1,980	1,870	29.6	29.6	31.3
1923	525,4	525,5	1,950	1,830	26.9	26.9	28.7
1924	503,9	503,8	1,980	1,880	25.4	25.4	26.8
1925	500,2	500,2	2,020	1,920	24.8	24.8	26.1
1926	511,5	511,4	2,060	1,970	24.8	24.8	26.0
1927	528,0	528,0	2,100	2,010	25.1	25.1	26.3
1928	563,3	562,3	2,170	2,090	26.0	25.9	26.9
1929	637,6	637,6	2,240	2,160	28.5	28.5	29.5
1930	691,3	691,2	2,300	2,200	30.1	30.1	31.4
1931	795,1	795,0	2,320	2,130	34.3	34.3	37.3
1932	841,8	841,9	2,270	1,960	37.1	37.1	43.0
1933	805,6	805,5	2,300	1,950	35.0	35.0	41.3
1934	759,0	759,1	2,340	1,960	32.4	32.4	38.7
1935	733,6	733,7	2,370	1,940	31.0	31.0	37.8
1936	729,6	729,6	2,440	1,960	29.9	29.9	37.2
1937	750,1	750,0	2,470	2,060	30.4	30.4	36.4
1938	778,6	778,5	2,500	2,130	31.1	31.1	36.5
1939	809,0	808,9	2,490	2,190	32.5	32.5	36.9
1940	731,7	731,6	2,490	2,210	29.4	29.4	33.1
1941	375,2	375,2	.	.	.	.	.
.							
.							
1945	763,0	754,3	.	.	.	.	.
1946	961,9	949,2	2,339	2,249	41.1	40.6	42.2
1947	1053,8	1,037,1	2,609	2,509	40.4	39.8	41.3
1948	1109,6	1,091,1	2,729	2,659	40.7	40.0	41.0
1949	1160,3	1,139,4	2,782	2,719	41.7	41.0	41.9

table: NE 4/2		density rates			NETHERLANDS		
year	membership		dep.labour force		density rates		
	total	less pens.	total	employed only	gross	net	employee only
	1	2	3	4	1:3	2:3	2:4
1950	1,214,6	1,191,5	2,827	2,747	43.0	42.1	43.4
1951	1,257,6	1,230,4	2,864	2,771	43.9	43.0	44.4
1952	1,137,4	1,105,7	2,906	2,767	39.1	38.0	40.0
1953	1,184,6	1,148,4	2,956	2,849	40.1	38.8	40.3
1954	1,223,3	1,183,1	3,040	2,964	40.2	38.9	39.9
1955	1,256,4	1,212,7	3,103	3,050	40.5	39.1	39.8
1956	1,334,6	1,283,5	3,165	3,125	42.2	40.6	41.1
1957	1,342,0	1,284,7	3,219	3,167	41.7	39.9	40.6
1958	1,331,8	1,267,9	3,243	3,145	41.1	39.1	40.3
1959	1,352,1	1,283,1	3,276	3,199	41.3	39.2	40.1
1960	1,398,8	1,323,5	3,345	3,296	41.8	39.6	40.2
1961	1,419,1	1,337,0	3,404	3,369	41.7	39.3	39.7
1962	1,435,1	1,348,4	3,500	3,467	41.0	38.5	38.9
1963	1,469,5	1,377,8	3,571	3,537	41.2	38.6	39.0
1964	1,464,1	1,368,7	3,642	3,612	40.2	37.6	37.9
1965	1,488,3	1,387,3	3,715	3,680	40.1	37.3	37.7
1966	1,536,3	1,421,8	3,768	3,723	40.8	37.7	38.2
1967	1,544,1	1,420,8	3,808	3,722	40.5	37.3	38.2
1968	1,530,9	1,402,9	3,858	3,777	39.7	36.4	37.1
1969	1,523,2	1,385,3	3,914	3,852	38.9	35.4	36.0
1970	1,575,8	1,429,7	3,971	3,917	39.7	36.0	36.5
1971	1,616,6	1,454,3	4,041	3,972	40.0	36.0	36.6
1972	1,628,3	1,459,8	4,112	3,951	39.6	35.5	36.9
1973	1,674,1	1,497,5	4,266	4,102	39.2	35.1	36.5
1974	1,680,0	1,492,2	4,334	4,141	38.8	34.4	36.0
1975	1,719,2	1,522,9	4,396	4,137	39.1	34.6	36.8
1976	1,751,5	1,544,3	4,469	4,191	39.2	34.6	36.8
1977	1,787,3	1,576,9	4,520	4,249	39.5	34.9	37.1
1978	1,791,3	1,574,8	4,581	4,308	39.1	34.4	36.6
1979	1,758,6	1,537,0	4,728	4,447	37.2	32.5	34.6
1980	1,722,3	1,496,4	4,879	4,554	35.3	30.7	32.9
1981	1,714,5	1,470,6	5,016	4,536	34.2	29.3	32.4
1982	1,673,6	1,423,2	5,151	4,496	32.5	27.6	31.7
1983	1,612,2	1,356,9	5,195	4,394	31.0	26.1	30.9
1984	1,563,4	1,301,5	5,294	4,472	29.5	24.6	29.1
1985	1,538,1	1,270,9	5,387	4,626	28.6	23.6	27.5

```
Table NE 5/1  Union Membership by Sex, Industry and Status    NETHERLANDS
```

year:1920		total		market			public			status	
isic	conf.	all	female	b-c	w-c	total	b-c	w-c	total	b-c	w-c
1	NAS	1	.	1		1				1	
1	NVV	10	.	10		10				10	
1	NKV	10	.	10		10				10	
1	CNV	11	.	11		11				11	
1	Other	2	.	2		2				2	
		34	*.*	*34*		*34*				*34*	
2-4	NAS	14	.	14		14				14	
2-4	NVV	107	.	107		107				107	
2-4	NKV	90	.	88	2	90				88	2
2-4	CNV	33	.	33		33				33	
2-4	Other	14	.	11	4	14				11	4
		259	*.*	*253*	*6*	*259*				*253*	*6*
5	NAS	9	.	9		9				9	
5	NVV	30	.	29	1	30				29	1
5	NKV	28	.	27		28				27	
5	CNV	11	.	11		11				11	
5	Other	2	.	1	1	2				1	1
		80	*.*	*78*	*2*	*80*				*78*	*2*
6+8	NAS	1	.	1		1				1	
6+8	NVV	8	.	2	6	8				2	6
6+8	NKV	9	.	2	7	9				2	7
6+8	CNV	4	.		4	4					4
6+8	Other	21	.	1	20	21				1	20
		43	*.*	*6*	*37*	*43*				*5*	*37*
7	NAS	8	.	8		8			1	8	
7	NVV	41	.	18		18	20	3	23	38	3
7	NKV	15	.	2		2	13	1	14	15	1
7	CNV	9	.	3		3	4	2	6	7	2
7	Other	39	.	4	6	9	4	26	29	8	31
		112	*.*	*33*	*6*	*40*	*41*	*32*	*73*	*75*	*38*
9	NAS	5	.				5		5	5	
9	NVV	28	.	5	1	5	15	8	23	20	8
9	NKV	7	.	1		1	5	1	6	6	1
9	CNV	10	.				4	6	9	4	6
9	Other	100	.	1	6	7	7	85	93	9	91
		149	*.*	*7*	*7*	*14*	*36*	*99*	*135*	*44*	*106*
	NAS	37	1	32		33	5		5	37	
	NVV	225	15	172	7	179	35	11	46	207	18
	NKV	159	12	130	9	139	18	2	20	148	11
	CNV	76	5	56	5	61	8	7	15	65	12
	Other	179	23	21	34	56	11	111	122	31	147
		676	*56*	*411*	*58*	*467*	*77*	*131*	*208*	*488*	*188*

year:1930		total		market			public			status	
isic	conf.	all	female	b-c	w-c	total	b-c	w-c	total	b-c	w-c
1	NVV	14	.	14		14				14	
1	NKV	10	.	10		10				10	
1	CNV	10	.	10		10				10	
1	Other	1	.	1		1				1	
		35	.	*35*		*35*				*35*	
2-4	NAS/NSV	5	.	5		5				5	
2-4	NVV	124	.	123	1	124				123	
2-4	NKV	89	.	88	1	89				88	
2-4	CNV	34	.	33		34				33	
2-4	Other	13	.	8	5	13				8	
		264	.	*257*	*7*	*264*				*257*	
5	NAS/NSV	5	.	5		5				5	
5	NVV	36	.	36		36				36	
5	NKV	27	.	26	1	27				26	
5	CNV	12	.	11		12				11	
5	Other	3	.	2	1	3				2	
		82	.	*81*	*2*	*82*				*81*	
6+8	NAS/NSV	1	.	1		1				1	
6+8	NVV	15	.	2	13	15				2	1
6+8	NKV	6	.	1	5	6				1	
6+8	CNV	5	.		5	5					
6+8	Other	16	.	1	15	16				1	1
		42	.	*4*	*38*	*42*				*4*	*3*
7	NAS/NSV	4	.	3		3		1	1	3	
7	NVV	50	.	27		27	19	4	23	46	
7	NKV	15	.	2		2	12	1	13	14	
7	CNV	11	.	4		4	5	2	6	9	
7	Other	34	.	1	6	7	8	19	27	9	2
		113	.	*37*	*6*	*43*	*45*	*26*	*71*	*82*	*3*
9	NAS/NSV	5	.				5		5	5	
9	NVV	37	.	2		2	17	18	35	19	1
9	NKV	7	.				6	1	7	6	
9	CNV	11	.				4	7	11	4	
9	Other	95	.	2	6	8	4	83	87	6	8
		156		*4*	*6*	*10*	*37*	*109*	*146*	*41*	*11*
	NAS/NSV	20		14		14	5	1	6	19	
	NVV	276	8	204	14	218	36	22	58	240	3
	NKV	153	6	127	7	133	18	2	20	144	
	CNV	82	4	59	6	65	9	8	18	68	1
	Other	161	20	14	32	46	12	102	114	27	13
		691	*49*	*418*	*58*	*476*	*81*	*134*	*215*	*498*	*19*

Table NE 5/3 Union Membership by Sex, Industry and Status									NETHERLANDS	

year:1939		total		market			public			status	
isic	conf.	all	female	b-c	w-c	total	b-c	w-c	total	b-c	w-c
1	NVV	28	.	28		28				28	
1	NKV	16	.	16		16				16	
1	CNV	24	.	24		24				24	
1	Other	2	.	2		2				2	
		70	*.*	*70*		*70*				*70*	
2-4	NAS/NSV	5	.	5		5				5	
2-4	NVV	146	.	144	2	146				144	2
2-4	NKV	102	.	101	1	102				101	1
2-4	CNV	44	.	43	1	43				43	1
2-4	Other	12	.	4	7	12				4	7
		309	*.*	*298*	*11*	*309*				*298*	*11*
5	NAS/NSV	4	.	4		4				4	
5	NVV	42	.	42	1	42				42	1
5	NKV	31	.	31	1	31				31	1
5	CNV	17	.	16	1	17				16	1
5	Other	5	.	3	2	5				3	2
		99	*.*	*96*	*4*	*99*				*96*	*4*
6+8	NVV	21	.	2	19	21				2	19
6+8	NKV	12	.	1	11	12				1	11
6+8	CNV	8	.		8	8					8
6+8	Other	15	.	1	15	15				1	15
		57	*.*	*4*	*53*	*57*				*4*	*53*
7	NAS/NSV	3	.	3		3				3	
7	NVV	51	.	34		34	13	3	17	47	4
7	NKV	21	.	8		8	8	5	13	16	5
7	CNV	15	.	8		8	4	3	6	12	3
7	Other	27	.	1	6	7	8	13	21	7	19
		116	*.*	*54*	*6*	*60*	*32*	*24*	*56*	*85*	*31*
9	NVV	34	.	4		5	15	15	29	19	15
9	NKV	8	.	1		1	6	1	7	8	1
9	CNV	14	.				5	8	14	5	8
9	Other	102	.	2	5	6	7	88	95	8	93
		158	*.*	*7*	*5*	*12*	*33*	*`112*	*146*	*40*	*118*
	NAS/NSV	12		12		12				12	
	NVV	322	16	254	23	276	28	18	46	281	41
	NKV	192	6	159	13	172	14	6	20	173	19
	CNV	120	3	91	10	100	9	11	20	100	21
	Other	163	27	13	32	47	15	102	116	28	135
		810	*52*	*529*	*78*	*607*	*66*	*137*	*203*	*595*	*215*

Table NE 5/4 Union Membership by Sex, Industry and Status   NETHERLANDS

isic	conf.	total		market			public			status	
year:1947		all	female	b-c	w-c	total	b-c	w-c	total	b-c	w-c
1	NVV	26	.	26		26	1		1	26	
1	NKV	20	.	20		20				20	
1	CNV	23	.	23		23				23	
1	EVC	7	.	7		7				7	
1	Other	1	.	1		1				1	
		78	.	77		77	1		1	78	
2-4	NVV	151	.	134	10	144	5	3	8	138	1
2-4	NKV	131	.	118	9	127	3	1	4	121	1
2-4	CNV	48	.	43	5	48	1		1	44	
2-4	EVC	82	.	82		82				82	
2-4	Other	22	.	15	6	21		1	1	15	
		432	.	390	30	420	9	5	14	399	3
5	NVV	38	.	38	1	39				38	
5	NKV	40	.	39	1	40				39	
5	CNV	15	.	14	1	15				15	
5	EVC	37	.	37		37				37	
5	Other	5	.	5	1	5				5	
		134	.	131	3	134				132	
6+8	NVV	13	.	1	12	13				1	1
6+8	NKV	11	.	3	9	11				3	
6+8	CNV	6	.	1	5	6				1	
6+8	EVC	3	.		3	3					
6+8	Other	5	.	2	3	5				2	
		38	.	6	32	38				6	3
7	NVV	62	.	25	7	32	18	12	31	43	1
7	NKV	30	.	11		11	11	8	19	22	
7	CNV	14	.	4		4	5	5	10	9	
7	EVC	29	.	21		21	3	5	8	25	
7	Other	4	.	2		2		2	2	2	
		139	.	62	7	69	38	32	70	100	3
9	NVV	35	.	5	1	6	5	24	28	10	2
9	NKV	14	.	4		4	5	6	11	8	
9	CNV	23	.	1	1	1	7	15	22	7	1
9	EVC	20	.	4	1	6	10	5	15	14	
9	Other	123	.		9	9	3	112	114	3	12
		216	.	14	12	26	28	161	189	42	17
	NVV	326	10	229	30	259	28	39	67	257	6
	NKV	246	6	193	19	212	19	15	34	212	3
	CNV	130	3	83	15	97	13	21	34	96	3
	EVC	177	.	151	4	154	13	10	24	164	1
	Other	159	30	24	19	42	3	115	117	27	13
		1,037	50	659	85	764	77	200	277	756	28

156

Table NE 5/5 Union Membership by Sex, Industry and Status   NETHERLANDS

year:1960		total		market			public			status	
isic	conf.	all	female	b-c	w-c	total	b-c	w-c	total	b-c	w-c
1	NVV	29	.	27	1	28	2		2	29	1
1	NKV	22	.	21		21	1		1	22	
1	CNV	23	.	23		23				23	
		75	.	71	1	72	3		3	73	1
2-4	NVV	230	.	200	18	218	7	6	12	207	23
2-4	NKV	219	.	194	18	211	5	2	7	199	20
2-4	CNV	86	.	73	10	83	2	1	3	75	11
2-4	Other	23	.	6	14	21		2	2	6	16
		557	.	473	59	533	14	10	24	487	70
5	NVV	64	.	63	1	64				63	1
5	NKV	61	.	60	1	61				61	1
5	CNV	29	.	28	1	29				28	1
5	Other	3	.	3		3				3	
		156	.	153	3	156				155	3
6+8	NVV	24	.		24	24					24
6+8	NKV	19	.	3	16	19				3	16
6+8	CNV	8	.		8	8					8
6+8	Other	4	.		4	4					4
		54	.	3	51	54		1	1	3	51
7	NVV	70	.	26	6	32	21	17	38	47	23
7	NKV	36	.	13	1	14	12	10	22	25	11
7	CNV	20	.	6	1	6	6	8	14	12	8
7	Other	9	.		5	5		4	4		9
		135	.	45	12	57	39	39	78	84	51
9	NVV	63	.	10	2	12	9	42	51	19	44
9	NKV	30	.	5	1	6	5	19	24	10	20
9	CNV	46	.	2	2	4	8	34	42	11	36
9	Other	208	.		8	9	2	197	199	3	205
		346	.	18	13	31	24	292	316	42	306
	NVV	479	27	326	51	377	37	65	103	364	116
	NKV	387	20	296	36	332	23	32	55	320	68
	CNV	212	8	133	21	153	17	42	59	149	63
	Other	246	62	9	31	41	2	203	205	12	234
		1,324	116	765	139	903	79	342	421	845	480

Table NE 5/6 Union Membership by Sex, Industry and Status											NETHERLANDS
year:1971		total		market			public			status	
isic	conf.	all	female	b-c	w-c	total	b-c	w-c	total	b-c	w-c
1	NVV	17	.	15		15	2		2	17	
1	NKV	13	.	11		11	1		1	13	
1	CNV	10	.	9		9				9	
		39	*.*	*35*	*1*	*36*	*3*		*3*	*39*	
2-4	NVV	228	.	183	28	210	10	8	18	193	36
2-4	NKV	184	.	152	24	175	5	3	9	157	27
2-4	CNV	81	.	68	9	77	4	1	5	77	0
2-4	Other	21	.	7	12	19		2	2	7	14
		514	*.*	*409*	*73*	*481*	*19*	*13*	*33*	*428*	*86*
5	NVV	80	.	78	2	80				78	2
5	NKV	79	.	77	2	79				77	2
5	CNV	38	.	37	1	38				37	1
5	Other	7	.	6	1	7				6	1
		204	*.*	*198*	*6*	*204*				*198*	*6*
6+8	NVV	29	.		39	29					29
6+8	NKV	17	.		17	17					17
6+8	CNV	9	.		9	9					9
6+8	Other	8	.		8	8					8
		63	*.*		*73*	*63*		*1*	*1*		*63*
7	NVV	73	.	29	4	33	15	25	40	44	29
7	NKV	35	.	13		13	9	13	22	23	13
7	CNV	19	.	5		5	5	9	14	10	9
7	Other	15	.	4	3	7	2	6	8	6	9
		143	*.*	*51*	*8*	*58*	*32*	*53*	*85*	*83*	*60*
9	NVV	131	.	9	14	23	14	95	108	22	109
9	NKV	30	.	5	1	6	5	19	24	11	20
9	CNV	61	.	2	3	5	10	47	57	12	50
9	Other	268	.		15	15	3	251	253	3	266
		490	*.*	*16*	*33*	*49*	*31*	*411*	*442*	*47*	*443*
	NVV	559	51	313	88	391	41	127	168	354	205
	NKV	356	18	259	44	302	21	35	57	280	78
	CNV	218	16	121	22	142	19	57	76	139	79
	Other	319	57	17	39	56	5	259	263	21	298
		1,454	*142*	*709*	*193*	*891*	*85*	*477*	*564*	*796*	*659*

Table NE 5/7 Union Membership by Sex, Industry and Status NETHERLANDS

isic	conf.	total		market			public			status	
year:1979		all	female	b-c	w-c	total	b-c	w-c	total	b-c	w-c
1	FNV	17	.	13		13	4		4	17	
1	CNV	9	.	9		9				9	
1	MHP	1	.		1	1					1
1	Other	1	.	1	1	1				1	1
		28	.	23	2	24	4		4	27	2
2-4	FNV	366	.	305	35	340	15	11	27	320	47
2-4	CNV	65	.	50	8	58	4	3	7	54	11
2-4	MHP	47	.		47	47		1	1		47
2-4	Other	6	.	4	1	5		1	1	4	2
		484	.	358	91	449	20	16	35	378	107
5	FNV	133	.	129	4	133				129	4
5	CNV	34	.	33	1	34				33	1
5	MHP	3	.		3	3					3
5	Other	7	.	5	2	7				5	2
		177	.	167	10	177				167	10
6+8	FNV	51	.		50	50		1	1		51
6+8	CNV	8	.		8	8					8
6+8	MHP	21	.		21	21					21
6+8	Other	5	.		5	5					5
		85	.		84	84		1	1		85
7	FNV	110	.	49	4	53	22	35	57	71	39
7	CNV	19	.	6		6	5	9	14	11	9
7	MHP	4	.		2	2		2	2		4
7	Other	11	.	1	2	3	2	6	8	3	9
		145	.	55	9	64	29	52	81	84	61
9	FNV	259	.	19	25	44	20	195	215	39	220
9	CNV	133	.	2	3	4	8	121	129	10	123
9	MHP	34	.		8	8		26	26		34
9	Other	195	.		9	9	4	182	186	4	191
		618	.	20	44	65	32	522	556	53	568
	FNV	935	123	514	119	632	62	242	304	575	361
	CNV	268	41	98	20	119	18	132	149	116	152
	MHP	110	9		82	82		29	29		110
	Other	225	74	10	20	30	6	189	195	16	208
		1,537	247	622	240	862	85	591	676	707	831

isic	conf.	total all	female	market b-c	w-c	total	public b-c	w-c	total	status b-c	w-c
1	FNV	14	.	9		9	4		4	13	
1	CNV	4	.	4		4				4	
1	Other	1	.		1	1					1
		19	*.*	*13*	*1*	*15*	*5*		*5*	*18*	*1*
2-4	FNV	259	.	209	30	238	11	9	20	220	39
2-4	CNV	47	.	33	7	40	4	2	7	38	9
2-4	MHP	39	.		35	35		4	4		39
2-4	Other	4	.	2	1	3		1	1	2	2
		348	*.*	*244*	*72*	*316*	*15*	*16*	*32*	*260*	*88*
5	FNV	97	.	93	4	97				93	4
5	CNV	25	.	24	1	25				25	1
5	MHP	1	.		1	1					1
5	Other	7	.	5	3	7				5	3
		129	*.*	*121*	*8*	*129*				*122*	*8*
6+8	FNV	41	.		41	41					41
6+8	CNV	7	.		7	7					7
6+8	MHP	15	.		15	15					15
6+8	Other	5	.		5	5					5
		68	*.*		*68*	*68*					*68*
7	FNV	89	.	35	3	38	17	33	51	52	37
7	CNV	16	.	5		5	4	7	11	9	7
7	MHP	4	.		2	2		2	2		4
7	Other	11	.		2	2	2	7	9	2	9
		119	*.*	*40*	*7*	*47*	*23*	*49*	*73*	*63*	*57*
9	FNV	239	.	15	21	38	12	193	205	27	215
9	CNV	144	.	2	3	4	5	135	140	6	138
9	MHP	33	.		9	9		25	25		33
9	Other	169	.		14	14	5	150	155	5	164
		586	*.*	*17*	*47*	*64*	*22*	*504*	*525*	*38*	*551*
	FNV	740	130	361	99	460	45	236	281	405	335
	CNV	243	53	67	18	85	13	145	158	81	162
	MHP	91	7		61	61		30	30		91
	Other	197	46	7	25	32	7	158	165	14	183
		1,271	*236*	*435*	*203*	*639*	*64*	*569*	*633*	*500*	*772*

Table NE 5/8 Union Membership by Sex, Industry and Status   NETHERLANDS

year: 1985

| Table NE 6/1 | Dep. | Labour Force by Sex, Industry and Status | | | | | | | NETHERLANDS | |

1920	total		market			public			status	
isic	all	female	b-c	w-c	total	b-c	w-c	total	b-c	w-c
1	420	.	.	.	.	.	.	.	413	7
2-4	659	.	.	.	.	.	.	.	606	54
5	153	.	.	.	.	.	.	.	143	10
6+8	224	.	.	.	.	.	.	.	74	150
7	196	.	.	.	.	.	.	.	160	36
9	493	.	.	.	.	.	.	.	320	174
0	31	.	.	.	.	.	.	.	30	1
	2,177	545	.	.	.	.	.	.	1,746	431

| Table NE 6/2 | Dep. | Labour Force by Sex, Industry and Status | | | | | | | NETHERLANDS | |

1930	total		market			public			status	
isic	all	female	b-c	w-c	total	b-c	w-c	total	b-c	w-c
1	389	.	.	.	.	.	.	.	385	4
2-4	772	.	.	.	.	.	.	.	695	77
5	215	.	.	.	.	.	.	.	203	12
6+8	294	.	.	.	.	.	.	.	107	187
7	213	.	.	.	.	.	.	.	171	42
9	583	.	.	.	.	.	.	.	376	206
0	33	.	.	.	.	.	.	.	33	.
	2,498	640	.	.	.	.	.	.	1,970	528

| Table NE 6/3 | Dep. | Labour Force by Sex, Industry and Status | | | | | | | NETHERLANDS | |

1947	total		market			public			status	
isic	all	female	b-c	w-c	total	b-c	w-c	total	b-c	w-c
1	241	.	233	8	241	.	.	.	233	8
2-4	925	.	769	127	896	19	10	30	788	137
5	195	.	184	10	195	.	.	.	184	10
6+8	291	.	87	204	291	.	.	.	87	204
7	236	.	120	21	141	52	42	95	173	64
9	600	.	187	59	246	55	298	353	243	357
0	67	.	61	6	67	.	.	.	61	6
	2,554	619	1,642	434	2,076	127	351	478	1,769	785

Table NE 6/4   Dep. Labour Force by Sex, Industry and Status   NETHERLANDS

1960	total		market			public			status	
isic	all	female	b-c	w-c	total	b-c	w-c	total	b-c	w-c
1	127	.	121	6	127	.	.	.	121	6
2-4	1,250	.	925	280	1,205	30	15	45	955	295
5	344	.	312	32	344	.	.	.	312	32
6+8	434	.	100	334	434	.	.	.	100	334
7	254	.	111	42	153	52	49	101	163	91
9	770	.	220	81	301	99	369	469	319	451
0	26	.	22	4	26	.	.	.	22	4
	3,204	781	1,812	779	2,590	181	433	614	1,992	1,212

Table NE 6/5   Dep. Labour Force by Sex, Industry and Status   NETHERLANDS

1971	total		market			public			status	
isic	all	female	b-c	w-c	total	b-c	w-c	total	b-c	w-c
1	79	.	72	7	79	.	.	.	72	7
2-4	1,339	.	924	363	1,287	30	21	51	954	384
5	473	.	391	82	473	.	.	.	391	82
6+8	593	.	136	457	593	.	.	.	136	457
7	258	.	86	66	152	42	64	106	128	129
9	1,084	.	173	142	315	132	637	769	305	779
0	202	.	136	66	202	.	.	.	136	66
	4,027	1,086	1,918	1,183	3,101	204	722	926	2,122	1,905

ble NE 6/6   Dep. Labour Force by Sex, Industry and Status   NETHERLANDS

'79 ic	total all	total female	market b-c	market w-c	market total	public b-c	public w-c	public total	status b-c	status w-c
1	92	.	81	12	92	.	.	.	81	12
4	1,142	.	692	405	1,097	19	25	44	712	430
5	465	.	364	101	465	.	.	.	364	101
8	710	.	138	572	710	.	.	.	138	572
7	304	.	99	66	165	46	93	139	145	159
9	1,550	.	170	286	456	230	865	1,094	400	1,151
0	343	160	230	112	343	.	.	.	230	112
	4,606	1,513	1,775	1,554	3,328	295	983	1,278	2,069	2,537

ble NE 6/7   Dep. Labour Force by Sex, Industry and Status   NETHERLANDS

85 ic	total all	total female	market b-c	market w-c	market total	public b-c	public w-c	public total	status b-c	status w-c
1	85	.	74	10	84	.	.	.	74	10
4	1,059	.	636	381	1,017	17	25	42	653	406
5	355	.	273	82	355	.	.	.	273	82
3	786	.	119	666	786	.	.	.	119	666
7	311	.	89	89	179	41	91	132	131	180
9	1,885	.	231	468	699	214	973	1,187	444	1,441
0	789	335	488	300	789	.	.	.	488	300
	5,269	1,871	1,911	1,997	3,908	272	1,088	1,361	2,183	3,086

163

Chapter 7: NORWAY

---

1. AGGREGATE MEMBERSHIP STATISTICS

1.1 General Series

All membership data have been taken from the Statistisk Årbok i Norge, the Norwegian Yearbook of Statistics, published by the Bureau of Statistics in Oslo. Unfortunately, the Bureau reported the membership of federations and unions outside the LO only from 1956. I do not know of any source from which the membership outside the LO in earlier years could be ascertained. Hence, there is a major break in the aggregate membership series in 1956 (idem: Bain & Price, 1980: 156-).

The membership figures for all peak associations and those of independent unions differ from those published in the Statistisk Årbok as I have recalculated the membership of LO, EL, SF, FSO, YH, AF, YS and independent unions on the basis of the entries for individual union, as given in the Yearbook, thus adjusting for double membership, and disaffiliations.

Membership reported at 1 January has been redefined to 31 December of the previous year. All membership figures are therefore end-of-year data.

1.2 Retired Members

Reported union membership in Norway, in particular of the Norwegian Confederation of Trade Unions, the LO, includes retired members. Only for some recent years their number could be identified (see: Kjellberg, 1983: 286-7). It appears that in 1980 pensioners made up almost 16% of the total LO membership. Total reported union membership in Norway is therefore overstated by about 10% and the overall rate of unionization by about 6% in comparison with other countries. Information about earlier years is not available.

Another element causing distortions is due to the inclusion of self-employed members in a number of professional associations. Their number is quite large in the *Akademikernes Fellesorganisasjon*, which was constituted from a merger between the Federation of Civil Servants, the *Embetsmennenes Landsforbundet* (EL) and a number of professional associations co-operating in the *Norsk Akademikersamband*. The EL actually included members having civil servant status within the other associations organizing the academic professions. My estimates of the self-employed members in professional associations is therefore based on a comparison with the original EL figures. Some of these professional associations do not represent employees vis-à-vis employers or the government as independent organizations other than through lobbying or providing educational and legal services to members. Thus I have excluded all or part of the membership of the *Advokatforening, Arkitektenes Fagforbund, Apothekerforening, Lægeforening, Tannlægeforening, Veterinærforening, Farmaceutiske Forening, Juristforbund, Økonomforbund, Foskerforbund, Fysiokjemikerforbund, Landbrukakademiker, Psykologforbund, Sivilingeniørs Forening, Siviløkonomers Forening, Sivilagronomslag*, and their predecessors.

1 January 1977 a Confederation of Occupational Unions, the *Yrkesorganisasjonnenes Sentralforbund* (YS) was founded by two federations in the public sector, the Federation of Public Employee Unions YH, which mainly recruited miliary officers cooperating in the *Befalets Fellesorganisasjon* (BF), and the Federation of State Employees (ST). BF and SF continue to exist as separate federations within the YS, which was furthermore joined by a number of independent occupational unions in the private sector.

1.3 Female Membership

Male and female membership could only be separated for the unions affiliated with the Norwegian Confederation of Trade Unions (LO). The source is the LO, <u>Beretning</u> (Annual Report), Oslo. The same source has been used for calculating the membership by industry and status for the LO-unions.

2. MEMBERSHIP BY INDUSTRY AND STATUS

2.1 Membership by Industry

1   Agriculture, Forestry & Fishing: *Fangst- og Fiskerforbund; Skog- og Landarbeiderforbund; Skogteknikerforbund*

2-4   Mining, Manufacturing, and Gas, water & Electricity: *Arbeidsmandsforbund; Arbeidslederforbund; Forbund for Arbeidsledere og Tekniske Funksj.; Baker- og Konditorforbund; Bekledningsarbeiderforbund; Bokbinderforbund; Bokbinder- og Kartonasjearbeiderforbund; Centralforbund for Boktrykkers; Elektrikerforbund; Elektriker- og Kraftstasjonsforbund; Typografforbund; Farmaceutiske Forening; Formerforbund; Fysiokjemikerforb; Grafisk Forbund; Gulsmedarbeiderforbund; Hovlerarbeiderforbund; Hydros Merk. Sentralforening; Ingeniør og Teknikerorg. NITO; Jern- og Metallarbeiderforbund; Kjemisk Industriarbeiderforbund; Kjottindustriarbeiderforbund; Litografiskforbund; Litograf- og Kjemigrafforbund; Meierifolks Landsforening; Møbelindustriarbeiderforbund; Nærings- og Nytelsesmiddelarbeiderforbund; økonomforbund; Olje- og Energimeddarbeiders Fellesorg.; Olje- og Petrokjemikerforbund; Papirindustriarbeiderforbund; Sallmaker- og Tapetseverforbund; Sivilingeniørers Forening; Siviløkonomers Forening; Skinn- og Lærarbeiderforbund; Skibsrbygerienens Tekniske Funktionærers Landsforbund; Skotøarbeiderforbund; Skredderforbund; Stenhuggerforbund; Steinindustriarbeidersforbund; Stoperiarbeiderforbund; Tekstilarbeiderforbund; Tobakkarbeiderforbund; Treindustriarbeiderforbund; Urmaker Svenneforbund*

5   Building and Construction: *Bygningsindustriarbeiderforbund; Malerforbund; Murerforbund; Sag- Tomt- og Høvleriarbeiderforbund*

6+8   Commerce, banking & Insurance: *Bokhandler-Medhjelper Forening; Handel og Kantor i Norge; Handelsbestyrerforbundet; Handels-økonomers Forening; Handelsreisendes Landsforband; Innkjøpssjef og Materialforv. Forbund; Overordnede Funksjonærers Forening ved A/S Vinmonopolet; Tekniske Apotekerpersonales Forening; Assuranddørers Forbund; Bankfunksjonærforbund; Banks Funktionærers Forbund; Forsikringsfunksjonærenes Landsforbund*

7   Transport & Communication: *Flygferforbund; Funksjonærersforbund ved NSB; Jernbaneforbund; Helikopteransattes Forbund; Kvinnelige Telegraf- og Telefonfunksjonær Landsforening; Lokomotivmannsforbund; Losforbund; Luftrafikkledelsens Forening; Maskinistforbund; Matros- og Fyrbøterunionen; Postforbund; Postfolkenes Fellesforbund; Postorganisasjon; Rutebilarbeiderforbund; Ruteflygerer Forening; Sikringstekn. Forening NSB; Sjømannsforbund; Skipsførerforbund; Styrmandsforening; Teletjenesteforbund; Telefonbund; Teleorganisasjon; Transportarbeiderforbund*

9   Other Services: *Arbeiderpartiet Presseforbund; Arkitektenes Fagforbund; Befalslag; Barnehagelærerinners Landsforbund; Barnevernpedagogforbund; Barber- og Frisørsvennenes; Brandfunksjonær Forbund; Biblitekarlag; Diakeners Broderforbund; Embetskontorfunksjonær Landsforbund; Fengselstjenestemannsforbund; Forsvarets*

Sivile Tjenestemenns landsforening; Funksjonærforbund; Fysiotera-
peuterforbund; Hotell- og Restaurantarbeiderforbund; Helsetjene-
stemens Adm.Forbund; Herredskogmesterlag; Hjelpepleierforbund;
Husdyrkontrollens Regnskapfører lag; Jordmoreforening; Journalist-
lag; Kommunearbeiderforbund; Kommunenstjenestemanns Landsforbund;
Kommuneforbund; Kommunale Funksjonær Landsforbund; Kringkastings-
forening; Lærerlag; Lærinneforbund; Landsforbund for Universi-
tets-, Høgeskole- og Forskningspersonell; Lensmannslag; Lensmanns-
etatens Landslag; Musikerforbund; Organistforbund; Oslo Lærerlag;
Oversetterforening; Politiforbund; Privatansattes Fellesorgani-
sasjon; Riksrevisjonens Tjenestemannslag; Rikskringskastings
Funksj. lag; Skatterevisorenes Forening; Skolenes Landsforbund;
Skuespillerforbund; Sosionomforbund; Spesialskolers Lærerlag;
Sufflørforbund; Sykehusadministrasjons Landsforbund; Sykehus-
forvalteres Landslag; Sykepleierforbund; Tjenestemannslags;
Tollerforbund; Tolltjenestemannforbund; Barnepleierforbund;
additionally all BF-, YH- and EL-affiliates, and all AF- and
ST-affiliates not specified elsewhere.

2.2 Classification by Status

The membership of the LO has been classified as manual, except for
journalists, musicians, commercial and office employees, supervisors
and foremen, pilots, Post Office employees, police, military officers,
nurses, schoolteachers, social workers, prompters, government employees
and a part of the membership of the *Kommunearbeiderforbund* (local
government) workers. The non-manual membership in the latter union was
estimated on the basis of the LO-figures for the 'cartel' of state
functionaries within the LO (existing since 1933). Until the 1970s a
form of co-operation between white-collar members from various unions
in the LO existed as well. The membership of EL, SF, YH and AF has been
classified as non-manual. The membership of YS has been classified as
non-manual, except for those in the oil- and gas-industry and those
among coach drivers. Except for one union in the dairy industry and the
union of coach drivers before it joined the YS, the membership of all
independent unions has been classified in the non-manual category.

2.3 Public Sector Unionism

The public sector includes central and local government, military, education, religion, social welfare and health, railways, Post office and
some public utilities. The membership of all unions in one or more of
these branches has been classified in the public sector.

3. LABOUR FORCE STATISTICS

The time series of the dependent labour force before 1948 is based upon
interpolation for the years in between of the census years (1910, 1920,
1930, 1946, and 1950), and can be found in various sources: Bain &
Price, 1980: 158-159; Galenson, 1949: 9-14; and Flora, Kraus &
Pfenning, 1987: 608. The 1948-1970 series of wage and salary earners,

including the unemployed, is taken from the Historiskk Statistikk (Oslo, 1978: 80, table 43, and 84, table 48) of the Norwegian Bureau of Statistics. The series is based on insurance and registration data, and was revised in 1972 on the basis of (micro-)census data. The 1972-1985 series is more inclusive and not consistent with the series up and until 1970 (see also Bain & Price, 1980: 157). The 1972-1985 series for employed wage and salary earners and for unemployment are annually published in the Statistical Yearbook.

The data on the dependent labour force by sex, industry and status are based upon the 1920, 1930, 1950, 1960 and 1970 population censuses (Flora, Kraus & Pfenning, 1987: 575-581). Note that the census--definition of the dependent labour force is wider that the one on which the labour force series before 1970 was based; however it fits better the 1972-revision. The figures relating to 1980 and 1985 are added on the basis of the ILO Yearbook of labour Statistics, which provided also for a broad manual/non-manual distinction in 1960, 1970 and 1980.

Employment in the public sector was estimated on the basis of man-year data presented in the National Accounts Statistics 1954-1970 and the Arbeitsmarkedstatistikk 1974, 1975 and 1976, published by the Norwegian Bureau of Statistics, on the basis of which I have estimated public employment in persons for 1960, 1970 and 1980. It includes the same categories and services as specified above. See also Flora (1983: 228) for some of the public services included.

4. TABLES

table: NO 1/1	Membership by Confederation							NORWAY
year	LO	EL	AF	FSO	ST	YH	other	total
	1	2	3	4	5	6		
1913	63,8						.	63,8
1914	67,6						.	67,6
1915	78,0						.	78,0
1916	80,6						.	80,6
1917	93,9	.					.	93,9
1918	107,5	.					.	107,5
1919	143,9	.					.	143,9
1920	142,6	.					.	142,6
1921	96,0	.					.	96,0
1922	83,6	.					.	83,6
1923	85,7	.		.			.	85,7
1924	92,8	.		.			.	92,8
1925	95,9	.		.			.	95,9
1926	93,1	.		.			.	93,1
1927	94,2	.		.			.	94,2
1928	106,2	.		.			.	106,2
1929	127,0	.		.			.	127,0
1930	139,6	.		.			.	139,6
1931	144,6	.		.			.	144,6
1932	153,4	.		.			.	153,4
1933	157,5	.		.			.	157,5
1934	172,5	.		.			.	172,5
1935	214,6	.		.			.	214,6
1936	268,3	.		.			.	268,3
1937	316,0	.		.			.	316,0
1938	340,0	.		.			.	340,0
1939	352,5	.		.			.	352,5
1940	306,3	.		.			.	306,3
1941	293,8	.		.			.	293,8
1942	299,7	.		.			.	299,7
1943	280,5	.		.			.	280,5
1944	.	.		.			.	.
1945	339,9	.		.			.	339,9
1946	407,0	.		.			.	407,0
1947	442,4	.		.			.	442,4
1948	456,3	.		.			.	456,3
1949	473,6	.		.			.	473,6

table: NO 1/2	Membership by Confederation							NORWAY
year	LO	EL	AF	FSO	ST	YH	other	total
	1	2	3	4	5	6		
1950	488,4	.			.		.	488,4
1951	503,4	.		.	.		.	503,4
1952	515,6	.		.	.		.	515,6
1953	526,0	.		.	.		.	526,0
1954	538,6	.		.	.		.	538,6
1955	542,1	.		.	.		.	542,1
1956	545,4	8,8		35,8	10,5		49,8	650,3
1957	540,9	7,7		36,0	10,6		64,5	659,7
1958	543,5	8,7		37,9	10,3		69,3	669,7
1959	541,4	11,3		37,7	10,4		69,2	670,0
1960	541,6	11,7		32,5	10,9		78,6	675,3
1961	562,0	11,8		33,7	11,0		75,0	693,5
1962	565,1	12,7		24,1	11,5		89,8	703,2
1963	568,6	13,4		25,4	14,0		89,2	710,6
1964	571,0	14,0		26,5	14,2	10,6	89,4	725,7
1965	574,3	15,5			14,9	10,2	111,1	726,0
1966	574,0	15,5			15,4	9,3	114,0	728,2
1967	570,2	15,6			15,6	9,9	124,6	735,9
1968	574,1	15,8			16,8	10,3	132,4	749,4
1969	582,3	16,5			17,2	10,6	134,6	761,2
1970	594,4	17,7			17,8	11,0	140,9	781,8
1971	601,9	19,9			18,8	11,8	148,3	800,7
1972	603,7	20,2			19,3	12,2	155,4	810,8
1973	613,8	20,6 ─┐			21,4	13,2	163,7	832,7
1974	635,8		41,0		23,1	14,8	153,2	867,9
1975	655,0		65,1		22,2	12,6	148,2	903,1
					└ YS (7) ┘			
1976	673,7		78,6		73,1		107,8	933,2
1977	692,2		83,8		77,9		111,5	965,4
1978	712,7		89,2		81,7		117,1	1,000,7
1979	721,0		95,5		86,3		138,6	1,041,4
1980	748,0		100,7		96,3		146,6	1,091,6
1981	755,0		110,7		104,7		152,1	1,122,5
1982	751,4		113,8		113,6		157,2	1,136,0
1983	745,1		117,0		116,9		160,3	1,139,3
1984	759,3		122,7		120,3		165,3	1,167,6
1985	769,6		131,1		126,2		170,0	1,196,9

table: NO 2	Confederal Membership Shares in per centage of total members				NORWAY
year	LO	AF	FSO	YS	total
	%	%	%	%	

1950	100.0				100.0
1956	85.3		5.5		100.0
1960	81.7		4.8		100.0
1965	80.8				100.0
1970	77.8				100.0
1975	74.7	4.6			100.0
1980	70.8	6.2		9.1	100.0
1985	66.6	7.7		10.9	100.0

172

table: NO 3 Retired and selfemployed workers in membership NORWAY					
year	LO		AF		other
	abs	%	abs	%	abs
1955	.		.		.
1956	.		.		10,6
1957	.		.		11,1
1958	.		.		11,1
1959	.		.		12,5
1960	.		.		12,5
1961	.		.		12,6
1962	.		.		13,7
1963	.		.		14,1
1964	.		.		13,4
1965	.		.		15,0
1966	.		.		15,6
1967	.		.		15,9
1968	.		.		16,8
1969	.		.		16,7
1970	.		.		17,8
1971	.		.		19,0
1972	.		.		20,0
1973	.		.		20,8
1974	.		18,8	45.9	2,0
1975	.		24,8	38.1	1,6
1976	.		29,6	37.7	0
1977	.		30,3	36.2	0
1978	104,0	14.6	30,9	34.6	0
1979	103,0	14.3	33,6	35.2	0
1980	117,0	15.6	34,7	34.5	0
1981	125,0	16.6	34,9	31.5	0
1982	128,0	17.0	36,8	32.3	0
1983	127,0	17.0	38,0	32.5	0
1984	129,0	17.0	39,5	32.2	0
1985	131,0	17.0	41,9	32.0	0

table: NO 4/1		density rates					NORWAY
year	membership		dep.labour force		density rates		
	total	less pens.	total	employed only	gross	employed only	net
	1	2	3	4	1:3	1:4	2:3
1913	63,8	.	.	.	.	.	.
1914	67,6	.	.	.	.	.	.
1915	78,0	.	.	.	.	.	.
1916	80,6	.	.	.	.	.	.
1917	93,9	.	.	.	.	.	.
1918	107,5	.	.	.	.	.	.
1919	143,9	.	.	.	.	.	.
1920	142,6	.	701	.	20.3	.	.
1921	96,0	.	703	.	13.7	.	.
1922	83,6	.	705	.	11.9	.	.
1923	85,7	.	707	.	12.1	.	.
1924	92,8	.	709	.	13.1	.	.
1925	95,9	.	710	.	13.5	.	.
1926	93,1	.	712	.	13.1	.	.
1927	94,2	.	716	.	13.2	.	.
1928	106,2	.	721	.	14.7	.	.
1929	127,0	.	729	.	17.4	.	.
1930	139,6	.	736	.	19.0	.	.
1931	144,6	.	744	.	19.4	.	.
1932	153,4	.	752	.	20.4	.	.
1933	157,5	.	760	.	20.7	.	.
1934	172,5	.	763	.	22.6	.	.
1935	214,6	.	776	.	27.7	.	.
1936	268,3	.	783	.	34.3	.	.
1937	316,0	.	795	.	39.7	.	.
1938	340,0	.	807	.	42.1	.	.
1939	352,5	.	821	.	42.9	.	.
1940	306,3	.	834	.	36.7	.	.
1941	293,8	.	848	.	34.7	.	.
1942	299,7	.	861	.	34.8	.	.
1943	280,5	.	876	.	32.0	.	.
1944	.	.	893	.	.	.	.
1945	339,9	.	911	.	37.3	.	.
1946	407,0	.	930	.	43.8	.	.
1947	442,4	.	935	.	47.3	.	.
1948	456,3	.	940	931	48.5	49.0	.
1949	473,6	.	959	951	49.4	49.8	.

year	membership		dep.labour force		density rates		
	total	less pens.	total	employed only	gross	employed only	net
	1	2	3	4	1:3	1:4	2:3
1950	488,4	.	974	965	50.2	50.6	.
1951	503,4	.	984	973	51.1	51.7	.
1952	515,6	.	987	975	52.3	52.9	.
1953	526,0	.	1,000	986	52.6	53.4	.
1954	538,6	.	1,016	1,003	53.0	53.7	.
1955	542,1	.	1,029	1,016	52.7	53.4	.
1956	639,7	.	1,034	1,020	61.9	62.7	.
1957	648,6	.	1,042	1,027	62.3	63.2	.
1958	658,6	.	1,042	1,019	63.2	64.7	.
1959	657,5	.	1,046	1,024	62.8	64.2	.
1960	662,8	.	1,056	1,039	62.8	63.8	.
1961	680,9	.	1,071	1,058	63.6	64.4	.
1962	689,5	.	1,086	1,071	63.5	64.4	.
1963	696,5	.	1,096	1,078	63.6	64.6	.
1964	712,3	.	1,107	1,091	64.4	65.3	.
1965	711,0	.	1,118	1,105	63.6	64.4	.
1966	712,6	.	1,130	1,118	63.1	63.7	.
1967	720,0	.	1,145	1,134	62.9	63.5	.
1968	732,6	.	1,163	1,147	63.0	63.9	.
1969	744,5	.	1,183	1,168	62.9	63.8	.
1970	764,0	.	1,215	1,203	62.9	63.5	.
1971	781,7	.	.	.	.	.	.
1972	790,8	.	1,363	1,335	58.0	59.2	.
1973	811,9	.	1,403	1,377	57.9	59.0	.
1974	847,1	.	1,425	1,400	59.4	60.5	.
1975	876,7	.	1,491	1,451	58.8	60.4	.
1976	903,6	.	1,557	1,525	58.0	59.3	.
1977	935,1	.	1,593	1,566	58.7	59.7	.
1978	969,8	834,9	1,627	1,593	59.6	60.9	51.3
1979	1,007,8	871,2	1,657	1,619	60.8	62.2	52.6
1980	1,056,9	905,2	1,685	1,652	62.7	64.0	53.7
1981	1,087,6	927,7	1,702	1,662	63.9	65.4	54.5
1982	1,099,2	934,4	1,736	1,684	63.3	65.3	53.8
1983	1,101,3	936,3	1,772	1,705	62.2	64.6	52.8
1984	1,128,1	959,6	1,784	1,723	63.2	65.5	53.8
1985	1,155,0	982,1	1,832	1,781	63.0	64.9	53.6

table: NO 4/2   density rates   NORWAY

Table NO 5/1 Union Membership by Sex, Industry and Status — NORWAY

isic	conf.	total all	total female	market b-c	market w-c	market total	public b-c	public w-c	public total	status b-c	status w-c
1	LO	2	.	2		2				2	
		2	*.*	*2*		*2*				*2*	
2-4	LO	97	.	97		97				97	
		97	*.*	*97*		*97*				*97*	
5	LO	10	.	10		10				10	
		10	*.*	*10*		*10*				*10*	
7	LO	27	.	15		15	12	1	13	26	1
		27	*.*	*15*		*15*	*12*	*1*	*13*	*26*	*1*
9	LO	6	.			1	4	1	5	5	1
		6	*.*			*1*	*4*	*1*	*5*	*5*	*1*
	LO	143	.	124	1	125	16	2	18	140	3
		143	*.*	*124*	*1*	*125*	*16*	*2*	*18*	*140*	*3*

Table NO 5/2 Union Membership by Sex, Industry and Status — NORWAY

isic	conf.	total all	total female	market b-c	market w-c	market total	public b-c	public w-c	public total	status b-c	status w-c
1	LO	17	.	17		17				17	
		17	*.*	*17*		*17*				*17*	
2-4	LO	79	.	79		79				79	
		79	*.*	*79*		*79*				*79*	
5	LO	13	.	13		13				13	
		13	*.*	*13*		*13*				*13*	
7	LO	21	.	11		11	8	2	10	18	2
		21	*.*	*11*		*11*	*8*	*2*	*10*	*18*	*2*
9	LO	10	.				8	2	10	8	2
		10	*.*				*8*	*2*	*10*	*8*	*2*
	LO	140	.	119		119	16	4	20	135	4
		140	*.*	*119*		*119*	*16*	*4*	*20*	*135*	*4*

Table NO 5/3 Union Membership by Sex, Industry and Status											NORWAY
year:1939		total		market			public			status	
isic	conf.	all	female	b-c	w-c	total	b-c	w-c	total	b-c	w-c
1	LO	26	.	26		26				26	
		26	*.*	*26*		*26*				*26*	
2-4	LO	165	.	165		165				165	
		165	*.*	*165*		*165*				*165*	
5	LO	36	.	36		36				36	
		36	*.*	*36*		*36*				*36*	
6+8	LO	20	.		20	20					20
		20	*.*		*20*	*20*					*20*
7	LO	69	.	49		49	16	5	21	64	5
		69	*.*	*49*		*49*	*16*	*5*	*21*	*64*	*5*
9	LO	37	.	7	1	8	22	7	29	29	8
		37	*.*	*7*	*1*	*8*	*22*	*7*	*29*	*29*	*8*
	LO	352	.	282	21	303	37	12	50	320	33
		352	*.*	*282*	*21*	*303*	*37*	*12*	*50*	*320*	*33*

Table NO 5/4 Union Membership by Sex, Industry and Status											
year:1950		total		market			public			status	
isic	conf.	all	female	b-c	w-c	total	b-c	w-c	total	b-c	w-c
1	LO	24	.	24		24				24	
		24	.	24		24				24	
2-4	LO	215	.	215		215				215	
		215	.	215		215				215	
5	LO	57	.	57		57				57	
		57	.	57		57				57	
6+8	LO	29	.		29	29					29
		29	.		29	29					29
7	LO	101	.	62	6	68	24	10	33	85	16
		101	.	62	6	68	24	10	33	85	16
9	LO	62	.	6	2	8	32	22	54	38	23
		62	.	6	2	8	32	22	54	38	23
	LO	488	84	364	37	401	56	32	87	420	69
		488	84	364	37	401	56	32	87	420	69

Table NO 5/5 Union Membership by Sex, Industry and Status										NORWAY
year:1960		total		market			public			status
isic	conf.	all	female	b-c	w-c	total	b-c	w-c	total	b-c	w-c
1	LO	24	.	24		24				24	
		24	*.*	*24*		*24*				*24*	
2-4	LO	238	.	233	5	237				233	5
2-4	Other	16	.	1	15	16				1	15
		253	*.*	*234*	*19*	*253*				*234*	*19*
5	LO	56	.	56		56				56	
		56	*.*	*56*		*56*				*56*	
6+8	LO	33	.		33	33					33
6+8	FSO	10	.		10	10					10
6+8	Other	5	.		5	5					5
		47	*.*		*47*	*47*					*47*
7	LO	112	.	72		72	23	18	40	94	18
7	SF	4	.					4	4		4
7	FSO	8	.		8	8					8
7	Other	8	.		8	8					8
		132	*.*	*72*	*16*	*88*	*23*	*22*	*45*	*94*	*38*
9	LO	80	.	7	2	9	33	37	71	41	39
9	EL	12	.					12	12		12
9	SF	7	.					7	7		7
9	FSO	15	.					15	15		15
9	Other	38	.		1	1		37	37		37
		152	*.*	*7*	*3*	*10*	*33*	*108*	*141*	*41*	*110*
	LO	542	98	391	40	431	56	55	111	447	95
	EL	12	.					12	12		12
	SF	11	.					11	11		11
	FSO	33	.		18	18		15	15		33
	Other	66	.	1	28	29		37	37	1	65
		663	*98*	*392*	*85*	*477*	*56*	*130*	*186*	*448*	*215*

Table NO 5/6 Union Membership by Sex, Industry and Status										NORWAY	
year:1970		total		market			public			status	
isic	conf.	all	female	b-c	w-c	total	b-c	w-c	total	b-c	w-c
1	LO	15	.	15		15				15	
1	Other	1	.		1	1					1
		16	*.*	*15*	*1*	*16*				*15*	*1*
2-4	LO	269	.	260	9	269				260	9
2-4	Other	22	.	1	21	22				1	21
		291	*.*	*261*	*30*	*291*				*261*	*30*
5	LO	53	.	53		53				53	
		53	*.*	*53*		*53*				*53*	
6+8	LO	41	.		41	41					41
6+8	Other	22	.		22	22					22
		63	*.*		*63*	*63*					*63*
7	LO	91	.	49		49	19	23	42	68	24
7	SF	4	.					4	4		4
7	Other	17	.		15	15	3		3	3	15
		113	*.*	*49*	*15*	*64*	*22*	*28*	*49*	*70*	*43*
9	LO	125	.	11	1	12	39	74	113	49	76
9	EL	18	.					18	18		18
9	SF	14	.					14	14		14
9	YH	11	.					11	11		11
9	Other	61	.		1	1		60	60		61
		229	*.*	*11*	*3*	*13*	*39*	*177*	*216*	*49*	*179*
	LO	594	138	388	52	440	57	98	155	445	150
	EL	18	.					18	18		18
	SF	18	.					18	18		18
	YH	11	.					11	11		11
	Other	123	.	1	59	60	3	60	63	4	119
		764	*138*	*389*	*111*	*500*	*60*	*204*	*264*	*449*	*315*

year:1980		total		market			public			status	
isic	conf.	all	female	b-c	w-c	total	b-c	w-c	total	b-c	w-c
1	LO	10	.	10		10				10	
1	Other	1	.		1	1					1
		11	*.*	*10*	*1*	*11*				*10*	*1*
2-4	LO	313	.	299	15	313				299	15
2-4	AF	20	.		20	20					20
2-4	YS	2	.	2		2				2	
2-4	Other	17	.	1	16	17				1	16
		352	*.*	*302*	*51*	*352*				*302*	*51*
5	LO	56	.	56		56				56	
		56	*.*	*56*		*56*				*56*	
6+8	LO	59	.		59	59					59
6+8	YS	29	.		29	29					29
6+8	Other	8	.		8	8					8
		96	*.*		*96*	*96*					*96*
7	LO	101	.	40		40	24	37	61	64	37
7	YS	10	.				4	6	10	4	6
7	Other	15	.		15	15					15
		126	*.*	*40*	*15*	*55*	*28*	*43*	*71*	*68*	*58*
9	LO	209	.	15	2	17	57	135	193	72	137
9	AF	45	.		2	2		43	43		45
9	YS	56	.		4	4		51	51		56
9	Other	106	.					105	105		106
		416	*.*	*15*	*8*	*23*	*57*	*335*	*393*	*72*	*344*
	LO	748	243	419	75	494	82	172	254	501	247
	AF	66	.		23	23		43	43		66
	YS	96	.	2	33	35	4	58	62	6	90
	Other	147	.	1	40	41		105	105	1	146
		1,057	*243*	*422*	*171*	*593*	*86*	*378*	*464*	*508*	*549*

Table NO 5/7 Union Membership by Sex, Industry and Status — NORWAY

Table NO 5/8 Union Membership by Sex, Industry and Status										NORWAY
year:1985		total		market			public			status	
isic	conf.	all	female	b-c	w-c	total	b-c	w-c	total	b-c	w-c
1	LO	8	.	8		8				8	
		8	*.*	*8*		*8*				*8*	
2-4	LO	303	.	288	15	303				288	15
2-4	AF	28	.		28	28					28
2-4	Other	18	.	1	17	18				1	17
		349	*.*	*289*	*60*	*349*				*289*	*60*
5	LO	58	.	58		58				58	
		58	*.*	*58*		*58*				*58*	
6+8	LO	58	.		58	58					58
6+8	AF	1	.		1	1					1
6+8	YS	36	.		36	36					36
6+8	Other	10	.		10	10					10
		104	*.*		*104*	*104*					*104*
7	LO	102	.	35		35	24	42	67	59	42
7	YS	13	.				5	8	12	5	8
7	Other	15	.		15	15					15
		130	*.*	*35*	*15*	*50*	*29*	*50*	*79*	*64*	*66*
9	LO	240	.	14	2	16	55	167	223	70	169
9	AF	61	.		3	3		58	58		61
9	YS	77	.		7	7		70	70		77
9	Other	127	.					127	127		127
		505	*.*	*14*	*13*	*27*	*55*	*422*	*477*	*70*	*434*
	LO	770	269	404	75	479	80	210	289	483	285
	AF	89	.		31	31		58	58		89
	YS	126	.		44	44	5	78	82	5	122
	Other	170	.	1	42	43		127	127	1	169
		1,155	*269*	*405*	*193*	*597*	*84*	*472*	*556*	*489*	*665*

Table NO 6/1 Dependent Labour Force by Sex, Industry and Status   NORWAY

1920	total		market			public			status	
isic	all	female	b-c	w-c	total	b-c	w-c	total	b-c	w-c
1	209	.	.	.	.	.	.	.	205	4
2-4	198	.	.	.	.	.	.	.	197	1
5	43	.	.	.	.	.	.	.	43	.
6+8	47	.	.	.	.	.	.	.	15	33
7	79	.	.	.	.	.	.	.	57	22
9	155	.	.	.	.	.	.	.	128	27
0	61	.	.	.	.	.	.	.	4	57
	793	*263*	.	.	.	.	.	.	*648*	*144*

Table NO 6/2 Dependent Labour Force by Sex, Industry and Status   NORWAY

1930	total		market			public			status	
isic	all	female	b-c	w-c	total	b-c	w-c	total	b-c	w-c
1	199	.	.	.	.	.	.	.	194	5
2-4	216	.	.	.	.	.	.	.	201	16
5	41	.	.	.	.	.	.	.	39	2
6+8	85	.	.	.	.	.	.	.	22	64
7	99	.	.	.	.	.	.	.	71	28
9	200	.	.	.	.	.	.	.	155	45
0	4	.	.	.	.	.	.	.	3	1
	844	*274*	.	.	.	.	.	.	*685*	*160*

Table NO 6/3 Dependent Labour Force by Sex, Industry and Status   NORWAY

1950	total		market			public			status	
isic	all	female	b-c	w-c	total	b-c	w-c	total	b-c	w-c
1	147	.	138	9	.	.	.	.	138	9
2-4	335	.	292	44	.	.	.	.	292	44
5	106	.	100	5	.	.	.	.	100	5
6+8	117	.	22	94	.	.	.	.	22	94
7	126	.	.	.	83	.	.	43	81	45
9	207	.	.	.	.	.	.	.	129	78
0	7	.	.	.	.	.	.	.	7	1
	1,045	*287*	.	.	.	.	.	.	*769*	*275*

1960	total		market			public			status	
isic	all	female	b-c	w-c	total	b-c	w-c	total	b-c	w-c
1	112	.	.	.	112	.	.	.	.	.
2-4	354	.	.	.	354	.	.	.	.	.
5	113	.	.	.	113	.	.	.	.	.
6+8	152	.	.	.	152	.	.	.	.	.
7	154	.	.	.	109	.	.	45	.	.
9	243	.	.	.	60	.	.	184	.	.
0	5	.	.	.	5	.	.	.	.	.
	1,133	*906*	.	.	*905*	.	.	*229*	*744*	*389*

1970	total		market			public			status	
isic	all	female	b-c	w-c	total	b-c	w-c	total	b-c	w-c
1	38	.	.	.	38	.	.	.	.	.
2-4	397	.	.	.	397	.	.	.	.	.
5	105	.	.	.	105	.	.	.	.	.
6+8	197	.	.	.	197	.	.	.	.	.
7	141	.	.	.	93	.	.	48	.	.
9	336	.	.	.	80	.	.	256	.	.
0	49	.	.	.	49	.	.	.	.	.
	1,264	*390*	.	.	*960*	.	.	*304*	*733*	*531*

Table NO 6/6 Dependent Labour Force by Sex, Industry and Status   NORWAY

1980	total		market			public			status	
isic	all	female	b-c	w-c	total	b-c	w-c	total	b-c	w-c
1	37	.	.	.	.	.	.	.	.	.
2-4	408	.	.	.	.	.	.	.	.	.
5	118	.	.	.	.	.	.	.	.	.
6+8	305	.	.	.	.	.	.	.	.	.
7	154	.	.	.	.	.	.	.	.	.
9	628	.	.	.	.	.	.	.	.	.
0	35	.	.	.	.	.	.	.	.	.
	1,685	724	.	.	1,198	.	.	487	812	873

Table NO 6/7 Dependent Labour Force by Sex, Industry and Status   NORWAY

1985	total		market			public			status	
isic	all	female	b-c	w-c	total	b-c	w-c	total	b-c	w-c
1	38	.	.	.	.	.	.	.	.	.
2-4	398	.	.	.	.	.	.	.	.	.
5	124	.	.	.	.	.	.	.	.	.
6+8	332	.	.	.	.	.	.	.	.	.
7	158	.	.	.	.	.	.	.	.	.
9	731	.	.	.	.	.	.	.	.	.
0	55	.	.	.	.	.	.	.	.	.
	1,836	831	.	.	.	.	.	.	799	1,037

LIST OF UNION CONFEDERATIONS: name, abbreviation and foundation year

1 *Landsorganisationen i Sverige* (LO): 1898-
Swedish Confederation of Trade Unions

2 *Sveriges Arbetares Centralorganisation* (SAC): 1909-
Central Organization of Swedish Workers

3 *De Anställdas Centralorganisationen* (DACO): 1931-1943
Employees Central Organization (merged with 4 to TCO)

4 *Tjänstemännens Centralorganisation* ("Gamla"TCO): 1937-1943
Central Organization of Government Employees
(merged with 3 to TCO)

5 *Tjänstemännens Centralorganisation* (TCO): 1944-
Central Organization of Salaried and Government Employees

6 *Statstjänstemännens Riksförbund* (SR): 1917-1973
National Federation of Civil Servants (merged with 5 to SACO-SR)

7 *Sveriges Akademikers Centralorganisation* (SACO): 1947-1973
The Swedish Confederation of Professional Associations
(merged with 6 to SACO-SR)

8 *Sveriges Akademikers Centralorganisation* (SACO-SR): 1974-
The Swedish Confederation of Professional Associations and
Civil Servants

1.   AGGREGATE MEMBERSHIP STATISTICS

1.1   General Series

Since 1948 the Statistisk Årsbok för Sverige (Swedish Statistical
Yearbook) has reported the membership of LO- and TCO-affiliates. From
1953 the membership of SACO and SR was reported as well, and after 1960
the SAC was added. Before 1948 the Yearbook reported only the LO-
-membership (see: Bain & Price, 1980: 138-139).
      For the years before 1948 I have taken the LO-membership from
Karlbom (1955: 247-248, table 2). Unlike the series published in Bain &
Price (1980: 142, table 7.1) or Kjellberg (1983: 269, table 1, and 272,
table 4) my membership figures refer to LO-affiliates only and do not
include the membership of independent unions which reported their

membership to the LO (see below). The membership of DACO-affiliates is reported in Bergstrand (1960: 143, table 6) for the years 1931-1937, and in the reports of the DACO-secretariat for the years 1938-1943 (DACO Sekretariats och revisorernas for År ...., Stockholm 1939-1945). The membership of "Gamla"-TCO is estimated by Sandberg (1969) for its foundation year. Kjellberg reports the membership for 1940-1943, and presents interpolated figures for 1938 and 1939 (Kjellberg, 1983: 272, table 4). The 'active' TCO-membership over the full period 1944-1985 is reported in TCO (Annual Report, 1986: 159) and, from 1948, in the Statistisk Årsbok. With respect to membership of SACO before 1953, I have relied upon Bain & Price (1980: 142-3, table 7.1) and Kjellberg (1983: 276, table 8). Kjellberg refers to 'active' members only and excludes self-employed professionals. The SR-membership before its reorganization in 1946 combines the membership of Sveriges Stats-tjänstemannanämnd (founded in 1917) and the Trafiktjänstemännens Riks-förbund (founded in 1920). Membership figures of the two organisations, both recruiting public employees, are presented in Samuelson (1963: 99-101) for every fifth year between 1920 and 1945. The membership in intermediate years has been interpolated (see also: Kjellberg, 1983: 272, table 4, with respect to 1935-1941 and 1944-1945). For later years the membership of SACO, SR and SACO-SR is taken from the Statistical Yearbook. The aggregate membership of SAC since 1910 has been published in its Activities Report for 1982 (Stockholm 1983: 60), and is since 1960 reported in the Swedish Statistical Yearbook as well.

Regarding the membership of non-affiliated unions - or the unions which later joined one or the other central organization mentioned above - a number of sources have been consulted. Firstly, with respect to independent unions which mainly though not only recruited manual workers the task is relatively easy, given the fact that these unions, although not affiliated, submitted annual membership figures to the LO. As was mentioned before, both Bain & Price and Kjellberg included their membership in that of the LO. I have preferred to give the two series separately. It appears that after 1940 all these unions had either ceased to exist, merged to LO-unions or become affiliates. The figures thus obtained square with those presented, for some years only, by Åmark (1986: 205-209, table 1A; 213-218, table 3A) and Karlbom (1955: 349-350, table 3). Åmark author also presents some figures for unions which did not report to the LO (Åmark, 1986: 210-212, table 2A; 219--221, table 4A). Their combined membership declined from some 15,000 in 1920 to 11,000 in 1930 and 7-8,000 in 1939 and has, according to the author, dwindled to less than 3,000 since. I have not included these numbers in the aggregate membership series.

As to the unions which later came to found or join the DACO or "Gamla"TCO, our task is more difficult. On the basis of Bergstrand (1960: 121 and 143), Samuelson (1963: 81) and Sandberg (1969: 52-53 and 64-65) it was possible to arrive at five-yearly estimates for 1920, 1925, 1930 and, in the case of the "Gamla"TCO, for 1935. The DACO--reports (op cit.) also reported the membership of unions in the year before affiliation. Kjellberg (1983: 274, table 6) gives the membership of some of these white-collar employee unions before affiliation; additionally, membership figures of unions in banking, insurance, commercial offices, life insurance, and data controllers could be obtained for the period 1923-1945. With linear interpolations for intermediate years, it was thus possible to produce a relatively in-clusive series of white-collar and public employee union membership before or during the formative years of the TCO. The estimated member-ship of professional associations which had been founded earlier but later joined the SACO, is not included in the series as it proved to be impossible to gauge the 'wage earner' component in these associations. After 1947 this category in the SACO's membership is specified sepa-rately in addition to 'self-employed' and 'student' members as well as 'those outside the labour market'. From 1967 to 1969 and from 1979 to 1984 the membership in the rubric 'other unions' refers to the member-ship of *Sveriges Arbetsledareförbund* (SALF), the Swedish Union of Foremen and Supervisors, which during these years had disaffiliated from the TCO. In 1985 the SALF rejoined the TCO. For 1967-1969 and 1979-1981 is 'active' membership is reported by Kjellberg (1983: 276, note 3), for 1985 in the 1986 Annual report of the TCO. The figures for 1982-84 have been interpolated by the author.

All annual figures represent union membership as of 31 December each year.

1.2   Retired Members

Union membership figures in Sweden include a large proportion of retired members or members which have no 'active' status (either as job holders or as job seekers) in the labour market. Bain & Price admitted that 'from the 1950s onwards aggregate union density is overstated in comparison with that in other countries in this study by between 3 and 8 percentage points' (Bain & Price, 1980;139), but did not attempt to adjust their aggregate series so as to exclude retired members. Kjellberg (1983: 278, table 9) on the other hand did present adjusted figures. On the basis of the number of pensioners included in the LO-unions of manual workers (according to Kjellberg all but two small ones), which was known for some years, he estimated the number of pensioners included in the LO-statistics for the years 1965 to 1981. Using linear interpolation techniques I have estimated the number of pensioners between 1950 and 1965, and from 1981 to 1985, assuming that before 1950 the problem had a negligible impact on LO-membership or density. Unlike the LO, the TCO, SACO and SACO-SR report both their 'active' and 'non-active' membership. Until 1969 the TCO reported in fact only its 'active' membership. The SACO, and later the SACO-SR, report separate figures on the number of pensioners and students among its membership, and also specify the number of self-employed profes-sionals among the 'active' membership. For earlier years I have relied upon Kjellberg's figures, who also has provided the author with figures (for 1960, 1970, 1974 and 1984) about the very large proportion of 'non-active' members included in the SAC membership figures (letter to author, 1-3-1985). It was thus possible to present an 'adjusted' series (excluding retired members, students, self-employed professionals etc.) of trade union membership in Sweden for the full 1950-1985 period.

1.3   Female Membership

Female membership has been reported by the LO and the TCO and, in later years, also by the other organizations. Using Kjellberg's figures with respect to SACO and SR for 1960 and 1970 (Kjellberg, 1983: 277), I have

189

estimated female membership in these organizations by linear backward extrapolation. Note that the figures given for male and female membership do include pensioners in the case of the LO. On the assumption that, at least until recent years, females are less likely to have retain membership ties while being retired from the labour force, it should cause less distortion in the case of female density rates than in the unionization rates for males.

2. CLASSIFICATION BY INDUSTRY AND STATUS

2.1 Classification by Industry

The classification of union members by economic sector follows the one presented by Bain & Price (1980). The full list of unions and classifications can be found at pages 146 147 of their book. The SAC membership has not been classified. White-collar employee organizations, not included in Bain & Price's series, have been classified on a similar basis. The major difference between my series and theirs (Bain % Price, 1980: 145-146, table 7.2) is that I have as much as possible excluded the retired members included in the reported LO membership. Relying upon data for the 1960s and early 1970s provided by Kjellberg to the author, the proportion of retired members per sector could be estimated, assuming an increase in the proportion of retired workers, especially in industry (see also the figures for the Metalworkers' Union referred to by Lash, 1985) and in the public sector. It appears that membership in manufacturing in Sweden is overstated and understated in transport because of incomplete demarcation.

2.2 Classification by Status

A number of authors have classified all of the LO's membership in the manual category, although admitting that some of the LO-affiliates organize also lower-grade white-collar employees (Kassalow, 1969; Nilstein, 1966; Wheeler, 1975). Bain & Price classify three LO unions, the *Försäkringsanställdasförbund* (insurance), the *Handelanställdas-förbund* (HK, commerce) and the *Musikerförbundet* (musicians) as non--manual, together with all the membership of TCO, SACO and SR. The remaining LO membership and that of the SAC is placed in the manual category, although many authors concede that some of the public employee unions of the LO may also recruit a small number of white--collar employees (Bain & Price, 1980: 148). Kjellberg appears to follow the Swedish usage to consider sales workers and lower-grade commercial employees as manual workers and places only the first and the last of the aforementioned unions in the non-manual category (Kjellberg, 1983: 278). Fortunately, the HK has published a break-down of its membership by industry and status for each tenth year, distinguishing between commercial employees (primarily in co-operatives) and workers in storage, transport and warehouses (HK 1962: 17, table 2). The figures for 1970 and 1980, showing that nearly all its membership is in non-manual occupations, are based on the HK's annual reports. In accordance with the classification used elsewhere union members in the Post Office and Telephone services were also placed in the non-manual category; within the *Statsanställdasförbund*, now the LO's third largest affiliate, over three-quarter of the membership is in lower-grade white-collar occupations. The membership of the largest LO affiliate, the *Kommunalarbetareförbund* (municipal employees or local government) was categorized as manual, although it recruits some white-collar workers as well.

The main difference from Bain & Price series on manual and non--manual union membership in Sweden (table 7.3 in their book) is due to the fact that they do not exclude retired members in the LO-unions, causing inflated membership figures on manual membership in particular. On the basis of the figures published by Kjellberg (1983: 278, table 9), my series excludes retired members. The white-collar confederations provide separate figures on 'active' and 'passive' membership.

2.3 Public Sector Unionism

In addition to the membership of the two aforementioned LO-unions (and their predecessors), a large part of the TCO's and SACO-SR's membership is in the (semi-)public sector. The Swedish Statistical Yearbook provides a three-fold categorization of their 'active membership': central government, local government and private economy. The proportion of retired members in the LO unions was estimated (see above), and the SAC's membership placed in the private sector. Note that the public sector does not include state enterprises or nationalized industries.

3. LABOUR FORCE STATISTICS

I have relied upon the aggregate series of potential membership published by Bain & Price (1980: 142-3, table 7.1). This series includes all economically active persons - excluding employers, self--employed persons and wives assisting their husbands in agriculture, fishery and forestry, but including the unemployed and members of the armed forces. Note that in most other countries - with the exception of the Netherlands - the armed forces have been excluded.

There is a major break in the series in 1963, following the introduction of quarterly and, later, monthly labour force sample surveys. The post-1963 series is considerably more extensive as it include a larger portion of the part-time (un)employed. Unlike Bain & Price I have used this new series, which is more in accordance with ILO--definitions used elsewhere, and not re-adjusted the new figures to the less comprehensive old series. The source of this new series is: Swedish Bureau of Statistics, Statistiska Meddelanden, series A: 'annual average number of employees in employment, excluding unpaid family workers but including the unemployed'. This series is given separately for males and females, and public and private sector employees.

The labour force figures by industry and status are based on the population census data as re-evaluated and published by Flora, Kraus & Pfenning (1987: 582-596). I have classified the population censuses of 1980 and 1985 in a similar way.

191

4. TABLES

table: SW 1/1		Membership by Confederation					SWEDEN
year	LO	SAC	Other	DACO	"GAMLA"	SR	SACO	Tota
	1	2		3	4	6	7	
1913	97,3	3,7	48,3					149,
1914	101,2	4,5	53,4					159,
1915	110,7	4,9	58,3					173,
1916	140,7	9,3	64,7					214,
1917	186,2	15,2	79,7			7,2		288,
1918	222,2	20,3	100,2			7,5		350,
1919	259,1	24,1	133,5			7,5		424,
1920	280,0	32,3	150,1			8,2		470,
1921	252,3	28,8	139,1			8,3		428,
1922	292,9	30,8	82,0			8,3		414,
1923	313,0	32,8	83,2			8,3		437,
1924	360,3	37,4	89,6			8,5		495,
1925	384,6	37,2	93,2			8,6		523,
1926	414,9	36,2	93,4			8,5		553,
1927	438,0	32,0	94,7			8,5		573,
1928	469,4	28,0	101,8			8,5		607,
1929	508,1	26,3	106,9			8,6		649,
1930	553,5	28,2	110,9			10,1		702,
1931	589,2	30,9	77,3	21,1		9,7		728,
1932	638,6	34,0	50,9	23,3		10,3		757,
1933	633,4	36,6	52,3	24,3		10,4		757,
1934	653,3	36,1	54,2	25,8		11,1		780,
1935	701,2	35,5	51,3	28,4		11,9		828,
1936	757,4	33,2	69,4	31,8		11,5		903,
1937	840,2	31,2	25,0	46,6	40,0	12,1		995,
1938	897,9	30,6	18,6	49,6	50,0	13,0		1,059,
1939	961,2	27,9	12,8	53,8	55,0	12,5		1,123,
1940	971,1	23,3	9,4	59,2	62,5	12,2		1,137,
1941	991,3	23,4		64,2	75,0	13,0		1,166,
1942	1,023,1	22,6		72,2	82,3	14,0		1,214,
1943	1,038,8	22,1		77,1	94,5	15,0		1,247,
				└─TCO─┘				
1944	1,069,3	21,9		180,4		16,0		1,287,
1945	1,106,9	22,1		204,7		17,0		1,350,
1946	1,147,0	22,2		222,1		17,6		1,408,
1947	1,194,2	21,4		238,1		18,1	15,0	1,486,
1948	1,238,6	20,5		254,1		17,2	19,0	1,549,
1949	1,255,9	20,0		259,5		18,1	22,0	1,575,

year	LO	SAC	Other	TCO	SR	SACO	Total
	1	2		5	6	7	
1950	1,278,4	19,9		271,8	20,6	23,1	1,613,8
1951	1,313,2	19,5		291,5	21,7	34,5	1,680,4
1952	1,338,8	19,6		308,0	21,5	37,1	1,725,0
1953	1,350,9	19,0		313,1	15,4	37,9	1,736,3
1954	1,354,6	17,2		323,2	15,6	39,2	1,749,8
1955	1,384,5	17,0		337,5	15,0	42,6	1,796,6
1956	1,404,3	16,6		345,0	14,8	44,0	1,824,7
1957	1,422,5	16,2		352,8	15,3	47,0	1,853,8
1958	1,447,2	16,7		365,3	16,7	49,2	1,895,1
1959	1,467,1	17,0		374,9	17,0	52,3	1,928,3
1960	1,485,7	17,6		393,5	17,2	57,1	1,971,1
1961	1,501,2	18,0		420,6	17,6	61,1	2,018,5
1962	1,522,7	18,7		446,8	18,0	66,0	2,072,2
1963	1,547,3	19,8		465,5	18,2	69,8	2,120,6
1964	1,563,3	20,5		489,4	18,2	73,6	2,165,0
1965	1,564,6	21,7		509,9	17,3	83,0	2,196,5
1966	1,587,6	22,8		543,0	17,8	90,4	2,261,6
1967	1,607,1	23,0	60,5	504,9	18,3	97,0	2,310,8
1968	1,625,1	23,9	61,9	555,9	19,0	103,4	2,389,2
1969	1,659,7	23,8	63,5	601,6	18,7	108,2	2,475,5
1970	1,680,1	23,5		719,5	19,3	115,0	2,557,4
1971	1,733,1	22,6		769,4	19,5	119,9	2,664,5
1972	1,771,5	21,7		805,0	19,9	122,4	2,740,5
1973	1,807,6	21,1		839,8	20,1	130,5	2,819,1
					└SACO-SR (8)┘		
1974	1,863,5	20,0		881,6	153,4		2,918,5
1975	1,918,1	19,0		951,4	165,0		3,053,5
1976	1,961,2	18,5		1,006,8	178,6		3,165,1
1977	2,017,8	18,1		1,059,4	191,8		3,287,1
1978	2,057,3	17,9		1,087,1	202,5		3,364,8
1979	2,089,4	18,0	90,0	1,012,8	214,0		3,424,2
1980	2,126,8	18,2	90,0	1,042,8	224,8		3,502,6
1981	2,140,8	17,6	88,5	1,062,4	233,6		3,542,9
1982	2,161,8	17,1	87,5	1,080,0	246,6		3,593,0
1983	2,195,8	18,0	86,0	1,101,7	257,9		3,659,4
1984	2,238,6	16,1	83,0	1,120,1	269,6		3,727,4
1985	2,262,9	15,5		1,203,4	280,5		3,762,3

table: SW 2		Confederal Membership Shares in percent of total membership					SWEDEN
year	LO	TCO	SR	SACO	SACO-SR	SAC	total
	1	5	6	7	8	2	
1915	63.7					2.8	100.0
1920	59.5		1.7			6.9	100.0
1925	73.5		1.6			7.1	100.0
1930	78.8		1.4			4.0	100.0
1935	84.7		1.4			4.3	100.0
1940	85.4		1.1			2.0	100.0
1945	82.0	15.2	1.3			1.6	100.0
1950	79.2	16.8	1.3	1.4		1.2	100.0
1955	77.1	18.8	0.8	2.4		0.9	100.0
1960	75.4	20.0	0.9	2.9		0.9	100.0
1965	71.2	23.2	0.8	3.8		1.0	100.0
1970	65.7	28.1	0.8	4.5		0.9	100.0
1975	62.8	31.2	└────────┴────		5.4	0.6	100.0
1980	60.7	29.8			6.4	0.5	100.0
1985	60.1	32.0			7.5	0.4	100.0

table: SW 3	Retired and selfemployed workers in Membership								SWEDEN	
year	LO		TCO		SACO		SAC		Other	total	
	abs	%	abs	%	abs	%	abs	%	abs	abs	%
1945	26,9	2.4	0				1.4	6.3		28,3	2.1
1946	29,0	2.5	0				1,5	6.8		30,5	2.2
1947	33,2	2.8	0		3,0	20.0	1,5	7.0		37,7	2.5
1948	36,6	3.0	0		4,0	21.1	1,5	7.3		42,1	2.7
1949	39,9	3.2	0		6,0	27.3	1,5	7.5		47,4	3.0
1950	43,4	3.4	0		7,1	30.7	1,6	8.0		52,1	3.2
1951	47,2	3.6	0		9,5	27.5	1,7	8.7		58,4	3.5
1952	49,8	3.7	0		9,1	24.5	1,7	8.7		60,6	3.5
1953	52,9	3.9	0		8,9	23.5	1,7	8.9		63,5	3.7
1954	55,6	4.1	0		9,2	23.5	1,6	9.3		66,4	3.8
1955	60,5	4.4	0		10,6	24.9	1,6	9.4		72,7	4.0
1956	63,3	4.5	0		11,0	25.0	1,6	9.6		75,9	4.2
1957	66,5	4.7	0		11,4	24.3	1,6	9.9		79,5	4.3
1958	71,2	4.9	0		12,2	24.8	1,7	10.2		85,1	4.5
1959	75,1	5.1	0		13,3	25.4	1,8	10.6		90,2	4.7
1960	78,7	5.3	0		15,1	26.4	1,9	10.8		95,7	4.9
1961	83,2	5.5	0		16,1	26.4	2,0	11.1		101,3	5.0
1962	86,7	5.7	0		18,0	27.3	2,2	11.8		106,9	5.2
1963	91,3	5.9	0		18,8	26.9	2,3	11.6		112,4	5.3
1964	95,3	6.1	0		20,6	28.0	2,5	12.2		118,4	5.5
1965	97,6	6.2	0		20,0	24.1	2,7	12.4		120,3	5.5
1966	106,6	6.7	0		23,4	25.9	2,9	12.7		132,9	5.9
1967	123,1	7.7	0		27,0	27.8	3,0	13.0	0	153,1	6.6
1968	133,1	8.2	26,1	4.7	30,4	29.4	3,2	13.4	0	192,8	8.1
1969	135,7	8.2	45,2	7.5	30,2	27.9	3,3	13.9	0	214,4	8.7
1970	138,1	8.2	61,8	8.6	34,0	29.6	3,3	14.0		237,2	9.3
1971	145,1	8.4	60,6	7.9	34,9	29.1	3,5	15.5		244,1	9.2
1972	152,5	8.6	62,6	7.8	35,4	28.9	4,2	19.4		253,7	9.3
1973	165,6	9.2	65,6	7.8	36,5	28.0	4,7	22.3		272,4	9.7
					SACO-SR						
1974	167,5	9.0	66,1	7.5	40,1	26.1	5,0	25.0		278,7	9.5
1975	178,1	9.3	70,8	7.4	43,0	26.1	5,3	27.9		297,2	9.7
1976	209,2	10.7	84,8	8.4	44,3	24.8	5,3	28.6		343,6	10.9
1977	216,8	10.7	91,2	8.6	46,4	24.2	5,4	29.8		359,8	10.9
1978	224,3	10.9	95,9	8.8	47,3	23.4	5,4	30.2		372,9	11.1
1979	232,4	11.1	77,1	7.6	49,5	23.1	5,6	31.1	16.4	381,0	11.1
1980	234,8	11.0	83,8	8.0	50,4	22.4	5,8	31.9	16.0	390,8	11.2
1981	247,8	11.6	86,9	8.2	50,8	21.7	5,6	31.8	15.2	406,3	11.5
1982	259,8	12.0	90,1	8.3	54,2	22.0	5,7	33.3	14.7	424,5	11.8
1983	271,8	12.4	99,5	9.0	57,3	22.2	6,1	33.9	13.7	448,4	12.3
1984	285,6	12.8	101,9	9.1	60,7	22.5	5,6	34.8	11.2	465,0	12.5
1985	299,9	13.3	94,9	7.9	61,0	21.7	5,5	35.5		461,3	12.3

year	membership		dep.labour force		density rates		
	total	less pens.	total	employed only	gross	net	employed only
	1	2	3	4	1:3	2:3	2:4
1913	149,3	149,3	1,592	.	9.4	9.4	.
1914	159,1	159,1	1,600	.	9.9	9.9	.
1915	173,9	173,9	1,634	.	10.6	10.6	.
1916	214,7	214,7	1,671	.	12.9	12.9	.
1917	288,3	288,3	1,676	.	17.2	17.2	.
1918	350,2	350,2	1,702	.	20.6	20.6	.
1919	424,2	424,2	1,737	.	24.4	24.4	.
1920	470,6	470,6	1,697	.	27.7	27.7	.
1921	428,5	428,5	1,722	.	24.9	24.9	.
1922	414,0	414,0	1,747	.	23.7	23.7	.
1923	437,3	437,3	1,772	.	24.7	24.7	.
1924	495,8	495,8	1,797	.	27.6	27.6	.
1925	523,6	523,6	1,822	.	28.7	28.7	.
1926	553,0	553,0	1,847	.	29.9	29.9	.
1927	573,2	573,2	1,972	.	29.1	29.1	.
1928	607,7	607,7	1,897	.	32.0	32.0	.
1929	649,9	649,9	1,922	.	33.8	33.8	.
1930	702,7	702,7	1,947	.	36.1	36.1	.
1931	728,2	728,2	1,963	.	37.1	37.1	.
1932	757,1	757,1	1,979	.	38.3	38.3	.
1933	756,9	756,9	1,995	.	37.9	37.9	.
1934	780,5	780,5	2,011	.	38.8	38.8	.
1935	828,3	828,3	2,026	.	40.9	40.9	.
1936	903,3	903,3	2,042	.	44.2	44.2	.
1937	995,1	995,1	2,058	.	48.3	48.3	.
1938	1,059,7	1,059,7	2,074	.	51.1	51.1	.
1939	1,123,2	1,123,2	2,090	.	53.7	53.7	.
1940	1,137,7	1,137,7	2,106	.	54.0	54.0	.
1941	1,166,9	1,166,9	2,134	.	54.7	54.7	.
1942	1,214,2	1,214,2	2,161	.	56.2	56.2	.
1943	1,247,5	1,247,5	2,189	.	57.0	57.0	.
1944	1,287,6	1,287,6	2,217	.	58.1	58.1	.
1945	1,350,7	1,322,4	2,244	.	60.2	58.9	.
1946	1,408,9	1,378,4	2,272	.	62.0	60.7	.
1947	1,486,8	1,449,1	2,300	.	64.6	63.0	.
1948	1,549,4	1,507,3	2,328	.	66.6	64.7	.
1949	1,575,5	1,528,1	2,356	.	66.9	64.9	.

table: SW 4/1   density rates   SWEDEN

table: SW 4/2			density rates				SWEDEN
year	membership		dep.labour force		density rates		
	total	less pens.	total	employed only	gross	net	employed only
	1	2	3	4	1:3	2:3	2:4
1950	1,613,8	1,561,7	2,384	.	67.7	65.5	.
1951	1,680,4	1,622,0	2,416	.	69.6	67.1	.
1952	1,725,0	1,664,4	2,447	.	70.5	68.0	.
1953	1,736,3	1,672,8	2,479	.	70.0	67.5	.
1954	1,749,8	1,683,4	2,511	.	69.7	67.0	.
1955	1,796,6	1,723,9	2,543	.	70.7	67.8	.
1956	1,824,7	1,748,8	2,575	.	70.9	67.9	.
1957	1,853,8	1,774,7	2,606	.	71.1	68.1	.
1958	1,895,1	1,810,0	2,638	.	71.8	68.6	.
1959	1,928,3	1,838,1	2,670	.	72.2	68.8	.
1960	1,971,1	1,875,4	2,702	.	73.0	69.4	.
1961	2,018,5	1,917,2	2,748	.	73.4	69.8	.
1962	2,072,2	1,965,3	2,795	.	74.1	70.3	.
1963	2,120,6	2,008,2	3,137	3,075	67.6	64.0	65.3
1964	2,165,0	2,046,6	3,169	3,111	68.3	64.6	65.8
1965	2,196,5	2,076,2	3,217	3,173	68.3	64.5	65.4
1966	2,261,6	2,128,7	3,298	3,239	68.6	64.5	65.7
1967	2,310,8	2,157,7	3,291	3,211	70.2	65.6	67.2
1968	2,389,2	2,196,4	3,331	3,246	71.7	65.9	67.7
1969	2,475,5	2,261,1	3,383	3,310	73.2	66.8	68.3
1970	2,557,4	2,320,2	3,492	3,433	73.2	66.4	67.6
1971	2,664,5	2,420,4	3,568	3,467	74.7	67.8	69.8
1972	2,740,5	2,485,8	3,600	3,493	76.1	69.0	71.2
1973	2,819,1	2,546,7	3,619	3,521	77.9	70.4	72.3
1974	2,918,5	2,659,8	3,689	3,609	79.1	72.1	73.7
1975	3,053,5	2,756,3	3,782	3,715	80.7	72.9	74.2
1976	3,165,1	2,821,5	3,818	3,752	82.9	73.9	75.2
1977	3,287,1	2,927,3	3,845	3,770	85.5	76.1	77.6
1978	3,364,8	2,991,9	3,877	3,783	86.8	77.2	79.1
1979	3,424,2	3,043,2	3,931	3,843	87.1	77.4	79.2
1980	3,502,6	3,111,8	3,981	3,896	88.0	78.2	79.9
1981	3,542,9	3,136,6	3,998	3,890	88.6	78.5	80.6
1982	3,593,0	3,168,5	4,013	3,876	89.5	79.0	81.8
1983	3,659,4	3,211,0	4,042	3,891	90.5	79.4	82.5
1984	3,727,4	3,262,4	4,067	3,931	91.6	80.2	83.0
1985	3,762,3	3,301,0	4,111	3,986	91.5	80.3	82.8

Table SW 5/1 Union Membership by Sex, Industry and Status										SWEDEN	
year:1920		total		market			public			status	
isic	conf.	all	female	b-c	w-c	total	b-c	w-c	total	b-c	w-c
1	LO	18	.	18		18				18	
		18	*.*	*18*		*18*				*18*	
2-4	LO	249	.	249		249				249	
2-4	Other	8	.		8	8					8
		257	*.*	*249*	*8*	*257*				*249*	*8*
5	LO	11	.	11		11				11	
5	Other	3	.		3	3					3
		14	*.*	*11*	*3*	*14*				*11*	*3*
6+8	LO	8	.	5	3	8				5	3
6+8	Other	6	.		6	6					6
		14	*.*	*5*	*9*	*14*				*5*	*9*
7	LO	77	.	23		23	51	4	54	73	4
7	SR	3	.					3	3		3
7	Other	1	.		1	1					1
		81	*.*	*23*	*1*	*24*	*51*	*7*	*57*	*73*	*8*
9	LO	34	.	4		4	18	13	30	22	13
9	SR	5	.					5	5		5
9	Other	15	.					15	15		15
		55	*.*	*4*		*4*	*18*	*33*	*51*	*22*	*33*
0	SAC	32	.	32		32				32	
		32	*.*	*32*		*32*				*32*	
	LO	397	33	310	3	313	68	16	85	378	19
	SR	8	.					8	8		8
	SAC	32	.	32		32				32	
	Other	33	.		18	18		15	15		33
		471	*.*	*342*	*21*	*363*	*68*	*40*	*108*	*410*	*60*

198

Table SW 5/2 Union Membership by Sex, Industry and Status									SWEDEN	
year:1930		total		market			public			status
isic	conf.	all	female	b-c	w-c	total	b-c	w-c	total	b-c	w-c
1	LO	21	.	21		21				21	
		21	.	21		21				21	
2-4	LO	381	.	381		381				381	
2-4	Other	7	.		7	7					7
		388	.	381	7	388				381	7
5	LO	50	.	50		50				50	
5	Other	3	.		3	3					3
		53	.	50	3	53				50	3
6+8	LO	19	.	10	8	19				10	8
6+8	Other	10	.		10	10					10
		28	.	10	18	28				10	18
7	LO	91	.	41		41	45	6	50	86	6
7	SR	3	.					3	3		3
7	Other	3	.		3	3					3
		97	.	41	3	44	45	9	54	86	11
9	LO	49	.	10		10	29	10	39	40	10
9	SR	7	.					7	7		7
9	Other	31	.		1	1		30	30		31
		87	.	10	1	11	29	47	76	40	48
0	SAC	28	.	28		28				28	
		28	.	28		28				28	
	LO	611	58	513	8	521	74	15	90	587	24
	SR	10	.					10	10		10
	SAC	28	.	28		28				28	
	Other	54	.		24	24		30	30		54
		703	.	541	32	573	74	56	130	615	88

isic	conf.	all	female	b-c (market)	w-c (market)	total (market)	b-c (public)	w-c (public)	total (public)	b-c (status)	w-c (status)
1	LO	78	.	78		78				78	
1	DACO	2	.		2	2					2
		80	.	*78*	*2*	*80*				*78*	*2*
2-4	LO	535	.	535		535				535	
2-4	DACO	23	.		23	23					23
2-4	Other	2	.		2	2					2
		560	.	*535*	*25*	*560*				*535*	*25*
5	LO	89	.	89		89				89	
5	DACO	5	.		5	5					5
		94	.	*89*	*5*	*94*				*89*	*5*
6+8	LO	44	.	18	26	44				18	26
6+8	DACO	19	.		19	19					19
		63	.	*18*	*45*	*63*				*18*	*45*
7	LO	105	.	44		44	49	11	61	94	11
7	DACO	4	.		4	4					4
7	SR	4	.					4	4		4
		112	.	*44*	*4*	*48*	*49*	*15*	*65*	*94*	*18*
9	LO	127	.	27	8	36	64	27	91	91	35
9	DACO	7	.		7	7					7
9	GAMLA	63	.					63	63		63
9	SR	9	.					9	9		9
9	Other	1	.		1	1					1
		206	.	*27*	*17*	*44*	*64*	*98*	*162*	*91*	*114*
0	SAC	23	.	23		23				23	
		23	.	*23*		*23*				*23*	
	LO	977	158	791	34	825	114	38	152	905	72
	DACO	59	.		59	59					59
	GAMLA	63	.					63	63		63
	SR	12	.					12	12		12
	SAC	23	.	23		23				23	
	Other	3	.		3	3					3
		1,136	.	*814*	*97*	*910*	*114*	*113*	*226*	*928*	*204*

ar:1950		total		market			public			status	
ic	conf.	all	female	b-c	w-c	total	b-c	w-c	total	b-c	w-c
	LO	78	.	78		78				78	
	TCO	2	.		2	2					2
	SACO	1	.		1	1					1
		80	.	*78*	*3*	*80*				*78*	*3*
	LO	594	.	594		594				594	
	TCO	74	.		74	74					74
	SACO	3	.		3	3					3
		671	.	*594*	*77*	*671*				*594*	*77*
	LO	181	.	181		181				181	
	TCO	10	.		10	10					10
		191	.	*181*	*10*	*191*				*181*	*10*
	LO	73	.	31	43	73				31	43
	TCO	28	.		28	28					28
		101	.	*31*	*70*	*101*				*31*	*70*
	LO	128	.	55		55	46	27	73	101	27
	TCO	13	.		4	4		9	9		13
	SR	6	.					6	6		6
		147	.	*55*	*4*	*60*	*46*	*42*	*88*	*101*	*46*
	LO	181	.	38	14	53	96	33	129	134	47
	TCO	146	.		24	24		122	122		146
	SACO	12	.					12	12		12
	SR	14	.					14	14		14
		353	.	*38*	*38*	*76*	*96*	*181*	*277*	*134*	*219*
	LO	1,235	240	977	57	1,034	141	60	201	1,118	117
	TCO	272	98		140	140		131	131		272
	SACO	16	7		4	4		12	12		16
	SR	21	2					21	21		21
	SAC	18	1	18		18				18	
		1,562	*348*	*996*	*201*	*1,197*	*141*	*224*	*365*	*1,137*	*425*

Table SW 5/5 Union Membership by Sex, Industry and Status

year:1960		total		market			public			status	
isic	conf.	all	female	b-c	w-c	total	b-c	w-c	total	b-c	w-c
1	LO	68	.	68		68				68	
1	TCO	1	.		1	1					1
1	SACO	2	.		2	2					2
		71	.	68	3	71				68	3
2-4	LO	671	.	671		671				671	
2-4	TCO	137	.		137	137					137
2-4	SACO	15	.		15	15					15
		823	.	671	152	823				671	152
5	LO	220	.	220		220				220	
5	TCO	12	.		12	12					12
		232	.	220	12	232				220	12
6+8	LO	106	.	31	75	106				31	75
6+8	TCO	51	.		51	51					51
		157	.	31	126	157				31	126
7	LO	124	.	50		50	45	29	74	95	29
7	TCO	14	.		5	5		9	9		14
7	SR	5	.					5	5		5
		143	.	50	5	55	45	44	88	95	48
9	LO	219	.	55	17	73	120	26	146	176	43
9	TCO	179	.		11	11		169	169		179
9	SACO	25	.					25	25		25
9	SR	12	.					12	12		12
		435	.	55	28	83	120	232	352	176	259
	LO	1,408	335	1,095	93	1,187	165	55	220	1,259	148
	TCO	394	153		216	216		178	178		394
	SACO	42	17		17	17		25	25		42
	SR	17	3					17	17		17
	SAC	16	1	16		16				16	
		1,875	509	1,110	325	1,436	165	275	440	1,275	601

year:1970		total		market			public			status	
isic	conf.	all	female	b-c	w-c	total	b-c	w-c	total	b-c	w-c
1	LO	42	.	42		42				42	
1	TCO	1	.		1	1					1
1	SACO	3	.		3	3					3
		46	.	*42*	*4*	*46*				*42*	*4*
2-4	LO	725	.	725		725				725	
2-4	TCO	245	.		245	245					245
2-4	SACO	16	.		16	16					16
		985	.	*725*	*261*	*985*				*725*	*261*
5	LO	239	.	239		239				239	
5	TCO	20	.		20	20					20
		259	.	*239*	*20*	*259*				*239*	*20*
6+8	LO	128	.	27	101	128				27	101
6+8	TCO	95	.		95	95					95
		224	.	*27*	*197*	*224*				*27*	*197*
7	LO	122	.	49		49	33	40	73	82	40
7	TCO	15	.		7	7		9	9		15
7	SR	6	.					6	6		6
		143	.	*49*	*7*	*55*	*33*	*54*	*88*	*82*	*61*
9	LO	287	.	45	11	56	185	46	231	230	57
9	TCO	280	.		15	15		265	265		280
9	SACO	63	.		2	2		61	61		63
9	SR	14	.					14	14		14
		644	.	*45*	*28*	*73*	*185*	*386*	*571*	*230*	*413*
	LO	1,542	481	1,126	112	1,238	218	86	304	1,344	198
	TCO	658	286		383	383		274	274		658
	SACO	81	34		20	20		61	61		81
	SR	19	5					19	19		19
	SAC	24	2	20		20				20	
		2,558	*807*	*1,146*	*515*	*1,661*	*218*	*440*	*658*	*1,364*	*955*

year:1980		total		market			public			status	
isic	conf.	all	female	b-c	w-c	total	b-c	w-c	total	b-c	w-c
1	LO	35	.	35		35				35	
1	TCO	2	.		2	2					2
1	SACOSR	4	.		4	4					4
		41	.	*35*	*5*	*41*				*35*	*6*
2-4	LO	800	.	800		800				800	
2-4	TCO	283	.		283	283					283
2-4	SACOSR	19	.		19	19					19
2-4	Other	45	.		45	45					45
		1,147	.	*800*	*347*	*1,147*				*800*	*347*
5	LO	221	.	221		221				221	
5	Other	29	.		29	29					29
		249	.	*221*	*29*	*249*				*221*	*29*
6+8	LO	172	.	35	137	172				35	137
6+8	TCO	157	.		157	157					157
		328	.	*35*	*293*	*328*				*35*	*294*
7	LO	131	.	53		53	27	51	78	80	51
7	TCO	18	.		5	5		13	13		18
7	SACOSR	3	.					3	3		3
		152	.	*53*	*5*	*57*	*27*	*67*	*95*	*80*	*72*
9	LO	534	.	66	11	77	394	63	457	460	74
9	TCO	500	.		10	10		490	490		500
9	SACOSR	149	.		17	17		132	132		148
		1,182	.	*66*	*37*	*103*	*394*	*685*	*1,079*	*460*	*722*
	LO	1,892	855	1,210	147	1,357	421	114	535	1,631	261
	TCO	959	550		456	456		504	504		959
	SACOSR	174	77		40	40		135	135		174
	SAC	12	2	12		12				12	
	Other	74	5		74	74					74
		3,112	*1,489*	*1,222*	*716*	*1,938*	*421*	*753*	*1,174*	*1,643*	*1,469*

Table SW 5/7 Union Membership by Sex, Industry and Status   SWEDEN

		total		market			public			status	
isic	conf.	all	female	b-c	w-c	total	b-c	w-c	total	b-c	w-c
1	LO	38	.	38		38				38	
1	TCO	2	.		2	2					2
1	SACOSR	5	.		5	5					5
		45	.	*38*	*6*	*45*				*38*	*6*
2-4	LO	786	.	786		786				786	
2-4	TCO	327	.		327	327					327
2-4	SACOSR	26	.		26	26					26
		1,138	.	*786*	*352*	*1,138*				*786*	*352*
5	LO	209	.	209		209				209	
5	TCO	29	.		29	29					29
		238	.	*209*	*29*	*238*				*209*	*29*
6+8	LO	177	.	17	161	177				17	161
6+8	TCO	176	.		176	176					176
		354	.	*17*	*337*	*353*				*17*	*337*
7	LO	137	.	58		58	26	53	78	84	53
7	TCO	20	.		3	3		17	17		20
7	SACOSR	4	.					4	4		4
		161	.	*58*	*3*	*61*	*26*	*73*	*99*	*84*	*77*
9	LO	616	.	79	9	89	460	67	527	540	76
9	TCO	542	.		7	7		549	549		555
9	SACOSR	185	.		21	21		164	164		185
		1,343	.	*79*	*37*	*117*	*460*	*780*	*1,240*	*540*	*817*
	LO	1,963	976	1,187	170	1,358	486	120	606	1,673	290
	TCO	1,109	632		543	543		566	566		1,109
	SACOSR	220	106		51	51		168	168		220
	SAC	10	3	10		10				10	
		3,301	*1,717*	*1,197*	*764*	*1,962*	*486*	*853*	*1,339*	*1,683*	*1,618*

Table SW 5/8 Union Membership by Sex, Industry and Status

year:1985

Table SW 6/1 Dependent Labour Force by Sex, Industry and Status   SWEDEN

1920	total		market			public			status	
isic	all	female	b-c	w-c	total	b-c	w-c	total	b-c	w-c
1	299	.	.	.	.	.	.	.	290	9
2-4	632	.	.	.	.	.	.	.	586	46
5	105	.	.	.	.	.	.	.	102	3
6+8	133	.	.	.	.	.	.	.	31	102
7	142	.	.	.	.	.	.	.	119	23
9	353	.	.	.	.	.	.	.	266	87
0	25	.	.	.	.	.	.	.	25	.
	1,689	*509*	.	.	.	.	.	.	*1,418*	*270*

Table SW 6/2 Dependent Labour Force by Sex, Industry and Status   SWEDEN

1930	total		market			public			status	
isic	all	female	b-c	w-c	total	b-c	w-c	total	b-c	w-c
1	323	.	.	.	.	.	.	.	314	9
2-4	653	.	.	.	.	.	.	.	599	54
5	136	.	.	.	.	.	.	.	131	5
6+8	184	.	.	.	.	.	.	.	52	133
7	176	.	.	.	.	.	.	.	147	30
9	431	.	.	.	.	.	.	.	324	106
0	21	.	.	.	.	.	.	.	21	.
	1,923	*615*	.	.	*1,615*	.	.	*308*	*1,586*	*337*

Table SW 6/3 Dependent Labour Force by Sex, Industry and Status   SWEDEN

1950	total		market			public			status	
isic	all	female	b-c	w-c	total	b-c	w-c	total	b-c	w-c
1	188	.	164	24	188	.	.	.	164	24
2-4	924	.	753	171	924	.	.	.	753	171
5	214	.	194	20	214	.	.	.	194	20
6+8	312	.	66	245	312	.	.	.	66	245
7	226	.	.	.	83	.	.	143	145	81
9	498	.	.	.	98	.	.	400	215	283
0	23	.	.	.	23	.	.	.	15	8
	2,384	*711*	.	.	*1,841*	.	.	*543*	*1,553*	*831*

Table SW 6/4 Dependent Labour Force by Sex, Industry and Status									SWEDEN	
1960	total		market			public			status	
isic	all	female	b-c	w-c	total	b-c	w-c	total	b-c	w-c
1	157	.	134	23	157	.	.	.	134	23
2-4	1,101	.	808	294	1101	.	.	.	808	294
5	260	.	223	37	260	.	.	.	223	37
6+8	344	.	61	283	344	.	.	.	61	283
7	217	.	.	.	91	.	.	127	115	102
9	613	.	.	.	91	.	.	522	237	376
0	10	.	.	.	10	.	.	.	8	2
	2,702	884	.	.	2,054	.	.	648	1,586	1,116

Table SW 6/5 Dependent Labour Force by Sex, Industry and Status									SWEDEN	
1970	total		market			public			status	
isic	all	female	b-c	w-c	total	b-c	w-c	total	b-c	w-c
1	113	.	.	.	113	.	.	.	.	.
2-4	1,074	.	.	.	1,074	.	.	.	.	.
5	334	.	.	.	334	.	.	.	.	.
6+8	525	.	.	.	525	.	.	.	.	.
7	240	.	.	.	115	.	.	126	.	.
9	1,147	.	.	.	329	.	.	818	.	.
0	59	.	.	.	59	.	.	.	59	.
	3,492	1,430	.	.	2,548	.	.	944	1,960	1,532

Table SW 6/6 Dependent Labour Force by Sex, Industry and Status   SWEDEN

1980	total		market			public			status	
isic	all	female	b-c	w-c	total	b-c	w-c	total	b-c	w-c
1	83	.	.	.	83	.	.	.	.	.
2-4	1,054	.	.	.	1,054	.	.	.	.	.
5	257	.	.	.	257	.	.	.	.	.
6+8	598	.	.	.	598	.	.	.	.	.
7	270	.	.	.	96	.	.	175	.	.
9	1,633	.	.	.	350	.	.	1,283	.	.
0	86	.	.	.	86	.	.	.	86	.
	3,080	*1,866.8*	.	.	*2,520*	.	.	*1,155*	*1,909*	*1,991*

Table SW 6/7 Dependent Labour Force by Sex, Industry and Status   SWEDEN

1985	total		market			public			status	
isic	all	female	b-c	w-c	total	b-c	w-c	total	b-c	w-c
1	80	.	.	.	80	.	.	.	.	.
2-4	1,002	.	.	.	1,002	.	.	.	.	.
5	232	.	.	.	232	.	.	.	.	.
6+8	613	.	.	.	613	.	.	.	.	.
7	279	.	.	.	105	.	.	174	.	.
9	1,779	.	.	.	407	.	.	1,372	.	.
0	125	.	.	.	125	.	.	.	125	.
	4,111	*1,987*	.	.	*2,565*	.	.	*1,546*	*1,831*	*2,280*

Chapter 9: SWITZERLAND

LIST OF UNION CONFEDERATIONS: name, abbreviation and foundation year

1 *Schweizerischer Gewerkschaftsbund* (SGB): 1880-
   Confederation of Swiss Trade Unions

2 *Christlich-Nationaler Gewerkschaftsbund* (CNG): 1907-
   Christian-National Confederation of Swiss Trade Union

3 *Schweizerischer Verband evangelischer Arbeitnehmer* (SVEA): 1920-82
   Swiss Federation of Protestant Workers (affiliated to CNG in 1982

4 *Landesverband freier Schweizer Arbeitnehmer* (LFSA): 1919-
   Liberal Federation of Swiss Workers

5 *Vereinigung Schweizerischer Angestelltenverbände* (VSA): 1918-
   Central Organization of Swiss White-Collar Employee Unions

---

1. AGGREGATE MEMBERSHIP STATISTICS

1.1 General Series

The Federal Statistical Bureau in Bern reports annually the membership in Swiss union confederations in the Statistisches Jahrbuch für die Schweiz (Swiss Statistical Yearbook). As a rule it reproduces the more detailed statistics - e.g., on individual affiliates of the peak organizations and a number of independent unions or federations - collected by the SGB and presented in an annual overview ('Die Gewerkschaftsverbände der Schweiz im Jahre ...') in its monthly revue, the Gewerkschaftliche Rundschau für die Schweiz, SGB, Bern. These SGB-statistics cover the whole period. Additionally and with regard to the membership of unions before they affiliated with the SGB or amalgamated with SGB affiliates I have consulted the Geschäftsberichte (Annual Reports) of SGB, Bern. Particularly rich are the Annual Reports published between 1945 and 1948 (see also Hardmeier, 1980; Meister, 1930 and SGB, 1942 for the formative years of the SGB). Considering that with respect to its political and ideological rivals (CNG, SVEA and LFSA) the SGB statistics were perhaps less reliable (but see in defence of the SGB statistics: Bernasconi, 1951), I have consulted a number of other sources in order to ascertain the membership in these confederations: Mangold, 1931: 1456; Egli, 1969 and SVEA, 1970. The series for the Central Organization of Swiss White-Collar Employee Unions, the VSA, deviates in some minor points from the later published statistics by the Federal Statistical Bureau. The reason is that disaffiliations are not always taken account of in the retrospective series. The most important disaffiliations concern the *Verband Schweizerischer Angestelltenvereine der Maschinen- und Elektroindustrie und verwandter Industrien* (VSAM), a federation of staff associations which disaffiliate in 1936 and rejoined the VSA in 1958, and the *Schweizerischer Bankpersonalverband* (SBV) which left the VSA in 1943 without rejoining. In 1985 the *Angestelltenverein des Schweizer Buchhandels* ceased its affiliation with the SVA.

Three groups of independent unions exist. The first group regards those of manual workers - mostly occupational unions - which never affiliated with one of the centres or broke away because of disagreements over domains and policies. A group of these independent unions joined the short-lived *Schweizerischer Verband Neutraler Gewerkschaften* (1930-1933). The printsetters left the SGB in 1925-1926; the butchers joined the SGB only in 1939 but left again in 1943; the bakers and workers in horticulture left the SGB in 1920 and remained independent as did the machinists and the craft unions of tailors and cobblers. The CNG's largest affiliate - the union of building and wood workers - cut its ties with the confederation between 1945 and 1950. Until 1950 it was possible to obtain membership figures for these independent unions from the SGB's annual overview (as published in the Rundschau). After 1950 no such data are available. The omission has no serious implications for the aggregate membership series given the very small size of these independent craft bodies.

Under independent unions of white-collar workers in the private sector I have grouped the *Schweizerischer Kaufmännischer Verband* (SKV) and the *Werkmeisterverband* before the foundation of the VSA in 1918. Other independent union and federations of white-collar employees are the *Fédération Romande des Employés* (FRE), an independent regional federation (included from 1938), the *Versicherungspersonalverband* (from 1929), and the three aforementioned unions which left for some years the VSA. I have excluded the *Schweizer Techniker Verband* (STV) on the ground that as a 'mixed employer-employee' organization it does not qualify as a union. In 1976 10% of its members were employers and over 40% directors, but more important is the fact that it is governed on a 'paritary' basis which precludes the STV to act as independent representative of employee interests (see Höpflinger, 1980: 86-88). The STV was affiliated with the VSA until 1921. I have therefore subtracted its membership from the VSA membership figures in these years. The 1918--1920 membership of the VSAM is reported in Enz, 1957: 98 and Höpflinger, 1980: 103. The VSA membership for the period 1919-1950 is also reproduced in König et.al., 1985: 600-601, table 12 (less STV--membership: 620-621: table 35) The white-collar membership before the foundation of the VSA combines the membership of the *Schweizerischer Kaufmännischer Verband* and the *Werkmeisterverband* (König et.al., 1985: 600, table 12; 605, table 15). The pre-1928 membership of independent white-collar unions is reconstructed with the help of the same sources (in particular: Enz, 1957: 98, 103, 111; and Mangold, 1931.

Under independent white-collar unions in the public sector I have grouped the *Verband Schweizerischer Polizeibeamter* (included from 1948), the *Schweizerischer Lehrerverein* (from 1929), the *Zentralverband des Staats- und Gemeindepersonal*, a centre of civil servant unions (included from 1929), the *Personalverband der SUVA* (social insurance, included from 1929), and a number of unions in the Post Office before their affiliation with the SGB in 1928. A further three unions, the

Personalverband der allgemeinen Bundesverwaltung, the *Schweizerischer Posthalterverband* and the *Verband Schweizerischer Zollbeamter*, although independent, co-operate with the SGB-unions in the public sector through a cartel: the *Föderativverband des Personals öffentlicher Verwaltungen und Betriebe*, which was founded way back in 1903. The membership of all these independent unions could be obtained from the Federal Statistical Bureau and the Annual Reports of the *Föderativverband*.

All membership figures refer to 31 december of each year. The membership of the *Föderativverband*, which is reported at 1 January until 1948, has been redefined to 31 December of the previous year.

1.2 Retired Members

The reported membership of the SGB includes pensioners after 1948. Their number in the public employee unions, in particular railways, the Post Office and in public administration, is known from the Annual Reports of the *Föderativverband*. I have no information regarding the other SGB affiliates. Some VSA unions and all public sector unions exclude pensioners, but it is impossible to tell whether and to what extent they inflate the figures of the CNG, LSFA, SVEA and the independent white-collar unions.

1.3 Female Members

The SGB is the only confederation which reports membership statistics by gender. Membership of females and males in the CNG is only known for the pre-war period. Enz (1957) presents some figures on female membership in the VSA and some other white-collar organizations in the private sector in the early 1950s.

2. CLASSIFICATION BY INDUSTRY AND STATUS

2.1 Classification by Industry

1 Agriculture, Forestry & Fishing: *Berufsgärtnerverband; Christl. Landarbeiterverband; Christl. Landangestelltenverband*

2-5 Mining, Manufacturing, Construction and Utilities: *Bäckerei- und Konditoreipersonalverband; Baukader-Verband; Buchbinder- und Kartonager-Verband; Buchdruckerverband; Christl. Chemie-, Textil-, Bekleidungs- und Papierpersonalverband; Christl. Holz- und Bauarbeiterverband; Christl. Metallarbeiterverband; Gew. Bau- und Holz; Gew. Druck und Papier; Gew. Textil-Chemie-Paper; Graphische Gewerkschaft; Heizer- und Machinistenverband; Hutmacher; Laborpersonal-Verband; Lithographenverband; Metall- und Uhrenarbeitnehmer Verband; Metzgerpersonalverband; Stickereipersonalverband; Textil-Fabrikarbeiter; Textil-Heimarbeiter; Typographenbund; Verband Bekleidungs- und Lederarbeiter; Verband Bekleidungs-Leder- und Ausrüstungsarbeitnehmer; Verband christl. Buchbinder; Verband Kalkulatoren und Betriebsfachleute; Verband Seidenbeutel-*

*weberei; VSAM; Verband Schweizerischer Vermessungstechniker;
Verband Technischer Betriebskader; Verband Schweizericher
Vermessungstechniker; Werkmeisterverband; Zahntechnikerverband*

6+8   Commerce, Banking & Insurance: *Angestelltenverein des Schweizer
Buchhandels; Droga Helvetia; Fédération Romande des Employés;
Hermes; Kaufmännischer Verband; Verband christl. Angestellten der
Schweiz.; Bankpersonalverband; Bankangestellenverband Zürich;
Verband der Versicherings-Inspektoren und -Agenten; Versicherungs-
personalverband*

7   Transport & Communication: *Arbeiter-Union Scheizerischer
Transportanstalten; Christl. Transport-, Handels- und
Lebensmittelpersonalverband; Eisenbahnerverband; Gew. christl.
Verkehrspersonal; Posthalterverband; PTT-Union; Telefon- und
Telegrafenarbeiterverband; Union Schweizer PTT-beamter; Gewerk-
schaft Verkauf-Handel-Transport und Lebensmittel; Verband christl.
PTT-Personals; Verband Schweiz. Postbeamter; Verband Schweiz.
Posthalter; Verband Schweiz. Telephon- und Telegraphenbeamter*

9   Other Services: *Chor- und Ballettverband; Lehrerverein; Musiker-
und Theaterunion; Musikerverband; Personalverband der allgemeinen
Bundesverwaltung; Personalverband der SUVA; Syndikat Schweiz.
Medienschaffender; Union Helvetia; Verband des christl. Staats-
und Gemeindepersonals; Verband des Personals Öffentliche Dienste;
Verband Schweiz. Polizeibeamter; Verband Schweiz. Zollbeamter;
Zentralverband des Staats- und Gemeindepersonals; Verband des
Schweiz. Zollpersonals*

With respect to the industrial classification of the VSA's membership, we need to further disaggregate the membership of its largest
affiliate, the *Schweizerischer Kaufmännischer Verband* (SKV). A similar
problem arises with respect to the independent *Fédération Romande des
Employés* (FRE). On the basis of König et.al., 1981 for the early years
and surveys for 1970 and 1976 reported by Höpflinger (1980:137), I have
allocated 40% of the SKV's and FRE's membership to industry, 35% to
commerce and 25% to banking, insurance and business services. Half of
the membership of the SGB- and CNG-transport unions has been allocated
to industry (food manufacturing), and one-fifth to commerce (retail).

Not classifiable is the membership of two small unions in the CNG
(the *Tschechoslowakischer Verband christlicher Arbeitnehmer der Schweiz*
and the *Verband der Ungarischen christlicher Arbeitnehmer der Schweiz*);
nor have I been able to disaggregate the membership of protestant SVEA
and the liberal LFSA.

2.2   Classification by Status

Generally, the SGB - except for the early 1920s when musicians and bank
employees in Zürich belonged to this general confederation - and also
the CNG unions in the private sector represent almost exclusively
manual workers (König, 1981: 186-187; Enz, 1957: 146-163; Höpflinger,
1980: 41-43). Few lower-grade clerical and sales workers are included
in the SGB- and CNG-unions in food, commerce and transport. There is
also a small union of Angestellten in the CNG, founded in 1935 and

212

refounded in 1964. Its membership is mainly in commerce.

The VSA-membership has been classified as non-manual, although its affiliate in hotels and restaurants organizes workers who however seem to enjoy the status of employees. The independent unions could easily be divided according to status (see under 1.1), and the membership of the SVEA and the LFSA has been deemed manual.

2.3 Public Sector Unionism

Swiss unions neatly divide between private and public services, except, perhaps, in the case of public utilities and military production (included in industry unions). It was not possible to disaggregate the membership of SVEA and LFSA, although it has been suggested that these confederations mainly cater for members among manual workers in the private sector (Mangold, 1931a; Enz, 1957: 166; Egli, 1969; SVEA 1970; Höpflinger, 1974 and 1980; Meynaud, 1963; NZZ, 1977).

3. LABOUR FORCE STATISTICS

A time-series of the Swiss dependent labour force does not exist. Annual data referring to September each year of the employed work force in factories (Fabrikpersonal) in manufacturing, is available from 1924 and based on reports of the factory inspectorate (EVWD, 1973). But this series does not include wage and salary earners in small firms, and is only useful as an employment indicator of business cycles. For later years there exists a somewhat more inclusive Industriestatistik based on a representative survey among enterprises. Annual data on employment in services is only available as from 1961 (Kull, 1979; BIGA, 1980).

Interpolation of census-data (1920, 1930, 1941, 1950, 1960, 1970, 1980) is therefore the only possibility. From the series on the 'labour force without family workers' (Flora, Kraus & Pfenning, 1987: 608), I have subtracted the employers and self-employed on the basis of the outcomes of the decennial censuses. The series refers to the resident dependent labour force and includes apprentices and the unemployed. The omission of non-resident foreign workers causes a understatement of the actual Swiss dependent labour force. For the years between 1970 and 1985 the series has been extended on the basis of the Statistik der Erwerbstätigen nach Wirtschaftsklassen (old series, less owners and self-employed - estimated on the basis of the Population Censuses) published by the Federal Statistical Bureau in Bern. Although the series was adjusted in 1982 so as to include seasonal and part-time employment, I have continued to use the old series. The unemployed have been added on the basis of the figures published by the Federal Statistical Bureau. These data refer to the full-time unemployed (Ganzarbeitslose) only.

On the basis of census-data (Flora, Kraus & Pfenning, 1987: 601-607) it is possible to arrive at a disaggregation by industry, status and sex. Apprentices are included and added to the manual labour force if employed in agriculture, mining, manufacturing, construction, public utilities and transport. The figures for 1980 and 1985 relate to the Population Census of 1980 and the Enterprise Statistic of 1985 ('Beschäftigte in den Arbeitsstatten des sekundären und tertiären Sektors nach Heimat, Geschlecht, ausgewahlten Personenkategorien und

Wirtschaftsklassen 1985'). I have added the number of employed persons in agriculture and in the non-enterprise services has been added. Employers and self-employed people are subtracted on the basis of the proportions found in the 1980 Census.

Figures on employment in public railways, the Post Office and public administration at Federal levels are published annually by the Federal Statistical Bureau since 1950. From 1960 employment in cantonal and municipal administration, in education and research as well as social insurance is reported in the 'Statistik der Erwerbstätigen nach Wirtschaftsklassen', published by the Federal Statistical Bureau. I have estimated the figure for 1950 figure on the basis of the 1955 and 1965 enterprise censuses (see also: De Seitlitz, 1977).

4. TABLES

table: SZ 1/2		Membership by Confederation					SWITZERLAND
year	SGB	CNG	SVEA	LSFA	VSA	Other	total
	1	2	3	4	5		
1913	89.4					33.0	122.4
1914	65.2	1.6				34.5	101.3
1915	65.0	1.7				35.2	101.9
1916	88.6	2.7				36.6	127.9
1917	148.9	4.6				38.9	192.4
1918	177.1	8.2			38.6	16.4	240.3
1919	223.6	16.7		2.0	50.6	16.9	309.8
1920	223.6	16.7	2.2	2.3	52.5	16.1	313.4
1921	179.4	14.8	2.7	2.7	50.9	16.6	267.1
1922	154.7	12.5	2.8	2.8	49.0	16.4	238.2
1923	151.4	11.0	3.7	2.8	45.9	18.2	233.0
1924	151.5	10.2	4.0	2.9	45.3	17.2	231.1
1925	150.0	9.8	4.1	2.9	46.2	17.6	230.6
1926	153.8	14.0	5.3	3.2	46.9	17.9	241.1
1927	165.5	18.1	6.2	3.4	48.9	16.9	259.0
1928	176.4	18.8	6.3	3.3	49.6	16.9	271.3
1929	186.7	21.3	6.3	3.3	51.6	32.0	301.2
1930	194.0	23.5	6.5	3.4	54.1	38.2	319.7
1931	206.9	33.6	8.8	4.5	57.8	36.7	348.3
1932	224.2	38.6	10.7	7.1	61.9	37.1	379.6
1933	229.8	40.5	11.6	7.5	62.3	30.6	382.3
1934	223.4	41.3	12.0	8.1	61.2	30.2	376.2
1935	221.4	40.5	12.7	8.5	60.8	30.7	374.6
1936	218.4	39.9	13.0	8.5	59.6	33.5	372.9
1937	222.4	40.3	12.6	8.5	61.3	34.3	379.4
1938	225.5	40.3	12.8	8.5	60.1	40.4	387.6
1939	223.1	39.7	12.5	8.5	60.5	40.3	384.6
1940	212.6	36.8	11.5	8.5	60.6	41.7	371.7
1941	217.3	36.1	11.6	8.5	63.2	43.8	380.5
1942	231.3	38.2	12.0	8.5	67.8	45.7	403.5
1943	250.2	42.3	10.6	10.0	63.3	55.2	431.6
1944	267.6	42.5	10.5	10.2	66.1	56.9	453.8
1945	312.9	46.7	11.2	12.7	67.6	71.0	522.1
1946	367.1	44.7	13.4	15.5	68.9	73.9	583.5
1947	381.6	47.2	13.8	15.3	71.1	78.9	607.9
1948	393.5	48.2	15.1	15.2	73.2	88.3	633.5
1949	380.9	48.1	15.5	15.3	74.3	89.8	623.9

table: SZ 1/2		Membership by Confederation				SWITZERLAND	
year	SGB	CNG	SVEA	LSFA	VSA	Other	total
	1	2	3	4	5		
1950	377.3	49.6	16.6	15.6	75.2	92.5	626.8
1951	382.8	50.1	16.9	15.8	76.2	79.1	620.9
1952	389.2	64.3	16.4	16.0	77.6	73.4	636.9
1953	393.1	64.2	16.2	16.0	79.0	75.9	644.4
1954	400.9	70.5	16.3	17.1	80.0	78.7	663.5
1955	404.0	73.2	15.6	17.2	81.4	81.5	672.9
1956	414.3	75.2	15.4	17.3	83.3	85.9	691.4
1957	426.5	78.0	15.1	17.8	85.6	90.2	713.2
1958	430.2	79.7	15.1	18.2	87.4	94.2	724.8
1959	431.4	78.0	14.6	18.3	101.0	84.9	728.2
1960	437.0	79.7	14.7	18.2	102.5	87.7	739.8
1961	445.4	84.0	15.0	18.9	104.5	90.4	758.2
1962	451.0	89.9	14.9	18.5	107.0	93.3	774.6
1963	451.1	93.4	13.8	18.7	110.5	95.1	782.6
1964	450.7	92.6	15.0	18.4	116.3	98.0	791.0
1965	449.6	92.5	14.8	18.7	120.3	100.9	796.8
1966	444.2	92.7	14.6	18.2	122.4	102.8	794.9
1967	441.2	91.6	14.2	18.2	124.8	104.9	794.9
1968	436.5	90.5	14.1	18.5	126.0	106.5	792.1
1969	434.8	92.9	13.9	18.1	123.6	107.0	790.3
1970	436.7	93.7	13.9	18.2	123.4	110.1	796.0
1971	437.9	94.8	13.8	18.2	124.4	112.2	801.3
1972	441.4	97.8	13.8	18.4	126.4	115.3	813.1
1973	446.4	98.9	13.9	19.9	126.7	120.6	826.4
1974	455.2	99.8	13.8	20.1	127.6	123.4	839.9
1975	471.6	106.1	13.8	21.5	139.0	135.5	887.5
1976	474.7	107.0	14.8	21.7	148.7	139.4	906.3
1977	468.5	101.3	15.1	22.3	149.8	141.5	898.5
1978	463.1	101.3	15.0	22.5	146.8	142.3	891.0
1979	459.0	101.4	14.9	22.7	146.0	141.7	885.7
1980	459.9	103.3	14.7	22.3	144.4	144.6	889.2
1981	459.2	105.4	10.1	22.5	144.9	145.6	887.7
1982	458.9	111.4 ⏌		22.9	152.1	141.9	887.2
1983	456.2	109.6		22.9	152.0	140.3	881.0
1984	451.2	107.6		22.5	149.8	143.3	874.4
1985	443.6	106.9		22.3	148.8	144.9	866.5

216

table: SZ 2	Confederal Membership Shares in per centage of total members					SWITZERLAND
year	SGB	CNG	SVEA	LSFA	VSA	total
	1	2	3	4	5	
1915	63.8	1.7				100.0
1920	71.3	5.3	0.7	0.7	16.8	100.0
1925	65.0	4.2	1.8	1.3	20.0	100.0
1930	60.7	7.4	2.0	1.1	16.9	100.0
1935	59.1	10.8	3.4	2.3	16.2	100.0
1940	57.2	9.9	3.1	2.3	16.3	100.0
1945	59.9	8.9	1.3	1.4	12.9	100.0
1950	60.2	7.9	2.6	2.5	12.0	100.0
1955	60.0	10.9	2.3	2.6	12.1	100.0
1960	59.1	10.8	2.0	2.5	13.9	100.0
1965	56.4	11.6	1.9	2.3	15.1	100.0
1970	54.9	11.8	1.7	2.3	15.5	100.0
1975	53.1	12.0	1.6	2.4	15.7	100.0
1980	51.7	11.6	1.7	2.5	16.2	100.0
1985	51.2	12.3		2.6	17.2	100.0

table: SZ 3		Retired Workers among membership			SWITZERLAND	
year	SGB		Other Unions		total	
	abs	%	abs	%	abs	%
1945	0		0		0	
1946	0		0		0	
1947	0		0		0	
1948	17.0	4.3	0		17.0	2.7
1949	23.0	6.0	0		23.0	3.7
1950	21.1	5.6	0		21.1	3.4
1951	22.5	5.9	0		22.5	3.6
1952	22.2	5.7	0		22.2	3.5
1953	22.6	5.7	0		22.6	3.5
1954	24.5	6.1	0		24.5	3.7
1955	25.2	6.2	0		25.2	3.7
1956	24.8	6.0	1.0	1.2	25.8	3.7
1957	25.4	6.0	1.1	1.2	26.5	3.7
1958	25.4	5.9	1.2	1.2	26.6	3.7
1959	27.7	6.4	1.3	1.5	29.0	4.0
1960	28.2	6.5	1.7	1.9	29.9	4.0
1961	29.2	6.6	1.5	1.7	30.7	4.0
1962	28.9	6.4	1.6	1.7	30.5	3.9
1963	27.9	6.2	1.7	1.8	29.6	3.8
1964	28.3	6.3	1.8	1.8	30.1	3.8
1965	28.3	6.3	1.9	1.9	30.2	3.8
1966	28.0	6.3	2.0	1.9	30.0	3.8
1967	28.2	6.4	2.1	2.0	30.3	3.8
1968	28.3	6.5	2.1	2.0	30.4	3.8
1969	28.2	6.5	2.2	2.1	30.4	3.8
1970	28.1	6.4	2.3	2.1	30.4	3.8
1971	28.4	6.5	2.5	2.2	30.9	3.9
1972	29.1	6.6	2.7	2.3	31.8	3.9
1973	28.8	6.5	2.8	2.3	31.6	3.8
1974	28.6	6.3	3.0	2.4	31.6	3.8
1975	29.1	6.2	3.2	2.4	32.3	3.6
1976	28.9	6.1	3.4	2.4	32.3	3.6
1977	30.0	6.4	3.6	2.5	33.6	3.7
1978	30.4	6.6	3.7	2.6	34.1	3.8
1979	30.7	6.7	4.0	2.8	34.7	3.9
1980	30.6	6.7	4.1	2.8	34.7	3.9
1981	30.6	6.7	4.4	3.0	35.0	3.9
1982	31.0	6.8	4.4	3.1	35.4	4.0
1983	31.4	6.9	4.5	3.2	35.9	4.1
1984	31.9	7.1	4.5	3.1	36.4	4.2
1985	32.7	7.4	4.6	3.2	37.3	4.3

table: SZ 4/1		density rates			SWITZERLAND		
year	membership		dep.labour force		density rates		
	total	less pens.	total	employed only	gross	net	employed only
	1	2	3	4	1:3	2:3	2:4
1913	122,4	122,4	.	.	.	.	.
1914	101,3	101,3	.	.	.	.	.
1915	101,9	101,9	.	.	.	.	.
1916	127,9	127,9	.	.	.	.	.
1917	192,4	192,4	.	.	.	.	.
1918	240,3	240,3	.	.	.	.	.
1919	309,8	309,8	.	.	.	.	.
1920	313,4	313,4	1,193	.	26.3	26.3	.
1921	267,1	267,1	1,200	.	22.3	22.3	.
1922	238,2	238,2	1,208	.	19.7	19.7	.
1923	233,0	233,0	1,214	.	19.2	19.2	.
1924	231,1	231,1	1,219	.	19.0	19.0	.
1925	230,6	230,6	1,233	.	18.7	18.7	.
1926	241,1	241,1	1,250	.	19.3	19.3	.
1927	259,0	259,0	1,269	.	20.4	20.4	.
1928	271,3	271,3	1,290	.	21.0	21.0	.
1929	301,2	301,2	1,334	.	22.6	22.6	.
1930	319,7	319,7	1,355	.	23.6	23.6	.
1931	348,3	348,3	1,364	.	25.5	25.5	.
1932	379,6	379,6	1,372	.	27.7	27.7	.
1933	382,3	382,3	1,378	.	27.7	27.7	.
1934	376,2	376,2	1,384	.	27.2	27.2	.
1935	374,6	374,6	1,389	.	27.0	27.0	.
1936	372,9	372,9	1,393	.	26.8	26.8	.
1937	379,4	379,4	1,397	.	27.2	27.2	.
1938	387,6	387,6	1,401	.	27.7	27.7	.
1939	384,6	384,6	1,406	.	27.4	27.4	.
1940	371,7	371,7	1,412	.	26.3	26.3	.
1941	380,5	380,5	1,421	.	26.8	26.8	.
1942	403,5	403,5	1,434	.	28.1	28.1	.
1943	431,6	431,6	1,448	.	29.8	29.8	.
1944	453,8	453,8	1,465	.	31.0	31.0	.
1945	522,1	522,1	1,487	.	35.1	35.1	.
1946	583,5	583,5	1,512	.	38.6	38.6	.
1947	607,9	607,9	1,538	.	39.5	39.5	.
1948	633,5	616,5	1,564	.	40.5	39.4	.
1949	623,9	600,9	1,590	.	39.2	37.8	.

table: SZ 4/2		density rates			SWITZERLAND		
year	membership		dep.labour force		density rates		
	total	less pens.	total	employed only	gross	net	employe only
	1	2	3	4	1:3	2:3	2:4
1950	626,8	605,7	1,616	.	38.8	37.5	.
1951	620,9	598,4	1,653	.	37.6	36.2	.
1952	636,9	614,7	1,695	.	37.6	36.3	.
1953	644,4	621,8	1,736	.	37.1	35.8	.
1954	663,5	639,0	1,773	.	37.4	36.0	.
1955	672,9	647,7	1,811	.	37.2	35.8	.
1956	691,4	665,6	1,854	.	37.3	35.9	.
1957	713,2	686,7	1,904	.	37.5	36.1	.
1958	724,8	698,2	1,923	.	37.7	36.3	.
1959	728,2	699,2	1,995	.	36.5	35.0	.
1960	739,8	709,9	2,030	.	36.4	35.0	.
1961	758,2	727,5	2,130	.	35.6	34.2	.
1962	774,6	744,1	2,218	.	34.9	33.5	.
1963	782,6	753,0	2,286	.	34.2	32.9	.
1964	791,0	760,9	2,337	.	33.8	32.6	.
1965	796,8	766,6	2,370	.	33.6	32.3	.
1966	794,9	764,9	2,393	.	33.2	32.0	.
1967	794,9	764,6	2,469	.	32.2	31.0	.
1968	792,1	761,7	2,512	.	31.5	30.3	.
1969	790,3	759,9	2,546	.	31.0	29.8	.
1970	796,0	765,6	2,626	2,626	30.3	29.2	29.2
1971	801,3	770,4	2,629	2,629	30.5	29.3	29.3
1972	813,1	781,3	2,695	2,695	30.2	29.0	29.0
1973	826,4	794,8	2,754	2,754	30.0	28.9	28.9
1974	839,9	808,3	2,772	2,772	30.3	29.2	29.2
1975	887,5	855,2	2,652	2,642	33.5	32.2	32.4
1976	906,3	874,0	2,593	2,572	35.0	33.7	34.0
1977	898,5	864,9	2,614	2,602	34.4	33.1	33.2
1978	891,0	856,9	2,635	2,624	33.8	32.5	32.7
1979	885,7	851,0	2,670	2,660	33.2	31.9	32.0
1980	889,2	854,5	2,728	2,722	32.6	31.3	31.4
1981	887,7	852,7	2,784	2,778	31.9	30.6	30.7
1982	887,2	851,8	2,788	2,775	31.8	30.6	30.7
1983	881,0	845,1	2,783	2,757	31.7	30.4	30.7
1984	874,4	838,0	2,798	2,766	31.3	29.9	30.3
1985	866,5	829,2	2,833	2,806	30.6	29.3	29.6

year:1920		total		market			public			status	
isic	conf.	all	female	b-c	w-c	total	b-c	w-c	total	b-c	w-c
2-5	SGB	162	.	158		159				158	
2-5	CNG	15	.	15		15				15	
2-5	VSA	25	.		25	25					25
2-5	Other	1	.	1		1				1	
		203	.	174	26	200				174	26
6+8	SGB	6	.	3	3	6				3	3
6+8	VSA	21	.		21	21					21
6+8	Other	1	.		1	1					1
		28	.	3	25	28				3	25
7	SGB	45	.	5		5	40		40	45	
7	CNG	1	.				1		1	1	
7	Other	10	.				1	9	10	1	9
		56	.	5		5	42	9	51	47	9
9	SGB	10	.				10		10	10	
9	VSA	7	.		7	7					7
9	Other	4	.					4	4		4
		22	.		7	7	11	4	15	11	11
0	SVEA/LFSA	5	.	5		5				5	
		5	.	5		5				5	
	SGB	224	42	169	4	173	51		51	220	4
	CNG	17	6	16		16	1		1	17	
	VSA	53	.		53	53					53
	SVEA/LFSA	5	.	5		5				5	
	Other	16	.	1	1	2	1	13	14	1	14
		313	.	191	57	248	52	13	66	243	71

Table SZ 5/2 Union Membership by Sex, Industry and Status										SWITZERLAND
year:1930		total		market			public			status
isic	conf.	all	female	b-c	w-c	total	b-c	w-c	total	b-c	w-c
2-5	SGB	124	.	124		124				124	
2-5	CNG	20	.	20		20				20	
2-5	VSA	26	.		26	26					26
2-5	Other	9	.	9		9				9	
		179	.	*153*	*26*	*179*				*153*	*26*
6+8	SGB	4	.	2	2	4				2	2
6+8	CNG	1	.	1	1	1				1	1
6+8	VSA	21	.		21	21					21
6+8	Other	1	.		1	1					1
		27	.	*3*	*25*	*27*				*3*	*25*
7	SGB	50	.	4		4	37	9	46	41	9
7	CNG	2	.	1		1	1		1	2	
7	Other	9	.					9	9		9
		60	.	*5*		*5*	*38*	*17*	*56*	*43*	*17*
9	SGB	16	.				16		16	16	
9	VSA	7	.		7	7					7
9	Other	19	.					19	19		19
		42	.		*7*	*7*	*16*	*19*	*35*	*16*	*26*
0	SVEA/LFSA	10	.	10		10				10	
		10	.	*10*		*10*				*10*	
	SGB	194	19	130	2	132	53	9	62	183	11
	CNG	24	6	21	1	22	2		2	23	1
	VSA	54	.		54	54					5
	SVEA/LFSA	10	.	10		10				10	
	Other	38	.	10	1	11		27	27	10	28
		320	.	*171*	*58*	*229*	*55*	*36*	*91*	*226*	*9*

| year:1941 | | total | | market | | | public | | | status | |
isic	conf.	all	female	b-c	w-c	total	b-c	w-c	total	b-c	w-c
2-5	SGB	141	.	141		141				141	
2-5	CNG	31	.	31		31				31	
2-5	VSA	24	.		24	24					24
2-5	Other	10	.	8	2	10				8	2
		207	.	*180*	*26*	*206*				*180*	*26*
6+8	SGB	6	.	3	3	6				3	3
6+8	CNG	1	.	1	1	1				1	1
6+8	VSA	33	.		33	33					33
6+8	Other	4	.		4	4					4
		44	.	*3*	*41*	*44*				*3*	*41*
7	SGB	52	.	6		6	32	14	46	38	14
7	CNG	4	.	1		1	3		3	4	
7	Other	3	.					3	3		3
		58	.	*7*		*7*	*35*	*17*	*52*	*42*	*17*
9	SGB	18	.				16	3	18	16	3
9	VSA	6	.		6	6					6
9	Other	27	.					27	27		27
		52	.		*6*	*6*	*16*	*30*	*46*	*16*	*36*
0	SVEA/LFSA	20	.	20		20				20	
		20	.	*20*		*20*				*20*	
	SGB	217	22	150	3	153	48	17	64	198	19
	CNG	36	9	32	1	33	3		3	36	1
	VSA	63	.		63	63					63
	SVEA/LFSA	20	.	20		20				20	
	Other	44	.	8	6	14		30	30	8	36
		380	.	*210*	*73*	*283*	*51*	*46*	*97*	*262*	*119*

year:1950		total		market			public			status	
isic	conf.	all	female	b-c	w-c	total	b-c	w-c	total	b-c	w-c
2-5	SGB	243	.	243		243				243	
2-5	CNG	39	.	39		39				39	
2-5	VSA	32	.		32	32					32
2-5	Other	32	.	23	9	32				23	9
		346	.	304	41	346				304	41
6+8	SGB	10	.	5	5	10				5	5
6+8	CNG	2	.	1	1	2				1	1
6+8	VSA	33	.		33	33					33
0,0	Other	17	.		17	17					17
		62	.	5	56	62				5	56
7	SGB	74	.	10		10	43	21	64	53	21
7	CNG	8	.	1		1	5	2	7	6	2
7	Other	4	.					4	4		4
		85	.	11		11	48	26	74	59	26
9	SGB	30	.				20	10	30	20	10
9	CNG	1	.				1		1	1	
9	VSA	10	.		10	10					10
9	Other	40	.					40	40		40
		81	.		10	10	21	50	71	21	60
0	SVEA/LFSA	32	.	32		32				32	
		32	.	32		32				32	
	SGB	356	44	258	5	262	64	30	94	321	35
	CNG	50	.	40	1	41	6	2	8	46	3
	VSA	75	21		75	75					75
	SVEA/LFSA	32	.	32		32				32	
	Other	93	.	23	27	50		43	43	23	70
		606	.	353	108	460	70	76	145	422	184

year:1960	total		market			public			status	
isic conf.	all	female	b-c	w-c	total	b-c	w-c	total	b-c	w-c
2-5 SGB	286	.	286		286				286	
2-5 CNG	64	.	64		64				64	
2-5 VSA	52	.		52	52					52
2-5 Other	6	.		6	6					6
	408	.	*350*	*58*	*408*				*350*	*58*
6+8 SGB	10	.	5	5	10				5	5
6+8 CNG	2	.	1	2	2				1	2
6+8 VSA	38	.		38	38					38
6+8 Other	23	.		23	23					23
	73	.	*6*	*67*	*73*				*6*	*67*
7 SGB	77	.	11		11	44	23	67	55	23
7 CNG	12	.	1		1	6	5	11	7	5
7 Other	3	.					3	3		3
	92	.	*12*		*12*	*50*	*31*	*81*	*61*	*31*
9 SGB	35	.				23	13	35	23	13
9 CNG	2	.				2		2	2	
9 VSA	13	.		13	13					13
9 Other	54	.					54	54		54
	104	.		*13*	*13*	*24*	*67*	*91*	*24*	*80*
0 SVEA/LFSA	33	.	33		33				33	
	33	.	*33*		*33*				*33*	
SGB	409	43	302	5	307	67	35	102	368	40
CNG	80	.	66	2	67	7	5	12	73	7
VSA	103	.		103	103					103
SVEA/LFSA	33	.	33		33				33	
Other	86	.		29	29		57	57		86
	710	.	*401*	*138*	*539*	*74*	*97*	*171*	*474*	*236*

Table SZ 5/5 Union Membership by Sex, Industry and Status   SWITZERLAND

Table SZ 5/6 Union Membership by Sex, Industry and Status									SWITZERLAND	
year:1970		total		market			public			status	
isic	conf.	all	female	b-c	w-c	total	b-c	w-c	total	b-c	w-c
1	CNG	1	.	1		1				1	
		1	*.*	*1*		*1*				*1*	
2-5	SGB	286	.	286		286				286	
2-5	CNG	71	.	71		71				71	
2-5	VSA	65	.		65	65					65
2-5	Other	8	.		8	8					8
		430	*.*	*357*	*73*	*430*				*357*	*73*
6+8	SGB	8	.	4	4	8				4	4
6+8	CNG	4	.		3	4					3
6+8	VSA	42	.		42	42					42
6+8	Other	30	.		30	30					30
		84	*.*	*4*	*79*	*84*				*4*	*79*
7	SGB	79	.	8		8	42	28	70	50	28
7	CNG	14	.	1		1	7	7	13	7	7
7	Other	3	.					3	3		3
		95	*.*	*9*		*9*	*49*	*38*	*86*	*57*	*38*
9	SGB	35	.				21	14	35	21	14
9	CNG	4	.				4		4	4	
9	VSA	17	.		17	17					17
9	Other	67	.					67	67		67
		123	*.*		*17*	*17*	*25*	*82*	*106*	*25*	*99*
0	CNG	1	.	1		1				1	
0	SVEA/LFSA	32	.	32		32				32	
		33	*.*	*33*		*33*				*33*	
	SGB	409	37	299	4	303	63	43	106	362	47
	CNG	94	.	74	3	77	10	7	17	84	10
	VSA	123	.		123	123					123
	SVEA/LFSA	32	.	32		32				32	
	Other	108	.		38	38		70	70		108
		766	*.*	*405*	*169*	*573*	*73*	*119*	*193*	*478*	*288*

226

| Table SZ 5/7 Union Membership by Sex, Industry and Status SWITZERLAND |

year:1980		total		market			public			status	
isic	conf.	all	female	b-c	w-c	total	b-c	w-c	total	b-c	w-c
1	CNG	1	.	1		1				1	
		1	*.*	*1*		*1*				*1*	
2-5	SGB	305	.	305		305				305	
2-5	CNG	76	.	76		76				76	
2-5	VSA	79	.		79	79					79
2-5	Other	10	.		10	10					10
		470	*.*	*381*	*89*	*470*				*381*	*89*
6+8	SGB	7	.	4	4	7				4	4
6+8	CNG	3	.		3	3					3
6+8	VSA	46	.		46	46					46
6+8	Other	43	.		43	43					43
		99	*.*	*4*	*95*	*99*				*4*	*95*
7	SGB	79	.	8		8	40	32	71	47	32
7	CNG	16	.	1		1	7	8	15	8	8
7	Other	3	.					3	3		3
		97	*.*	*8*		*9*	*46*	*43*	*89*	*55*	*43*
9	SGB	39	.		2	2	21	17	37	21	18
9	CNG	6	.				6		6	6	
9	VSA	20	.		20	20					20
9	Other	85	.					85	85		85
		150	*.*		*22*	*22*	*26*	*102*	*128*	*26*	*124*
0	CNG	2	.	2		2				2	
0	SVEA/LFSA	37	.	37		37				37	
		39	*.*	*39*		*39*				*39*	
	SGB	429	55	316	5	321	60	48	108	376	53
	CNG	103	.	80	3	83	12	8	21	92	11
	VSA	144	.		144	144					144
	SVEA/LFSA	37	.	37		37				37	
	Other	141	.		53	53		88	88		141
		855	*.*	*433*	*205*	*638*	*73*	*144*	*217*	*505*	*349*

227

Table SZ 5/8 Union Membership by Sex, Industry and Status   SWITZERLAND

year:1985		total		market			public			status	
isic	conf.	all	female	b-c	w-c	total	b-c	w-c	total	b-c	w-c
1	CNG	1	.	1		1				1	
		1	*.*	*1*		*1*				*1*	
2-5	SGB	287	.	287		287				287	
2-5	CNG	74	.	74		74				74	
2-5	VSA	79	.		79	79					79
2-5	Other	8	.		8	8					8
		448	*.*	*361*	*87*	*448*				*361*	*87*
6+8	SGB	7	.	4	4	7				4	4
6+8	CNG	3	.		2	3					2
6+8	VSA	48	.		48	48					48
6+8	Other	39	.		39	39					39
		97	*.*	*4*	*93*	*97*				*4*	*93*
7	SGB	80	.	7		7	38	34	73	46	34
7	CNG	18	.	1		1	6	11	17	7	11
7	Other	3	.						3	3		3
		100	*.*	*8*		*8*	*44*	*48*	*92*	*52*	*48*
9	SGB	37	.		2	2	19	17	36	19	19
9	CNG	6	.				6		6	6	
9	VSA	22	.		22	22					22
9	Other	90	.					90	90		90
		155	*.*		*24*	*24*	*25*	*107*	*132*	*25*	*131*
0	CNG	6	.	6		6				6	
0	LFSA	22	.	22		22				22	
		28	*.*	*28*		*28*				*28*	
	SGB	411	54	298	5	303	57	51	108	355	56
	CNG	107	.	82	2	84	11	11	22	94	13
	VSA	149	.		149	149					149
	LFSA	22	.	22		22				22	
	Other	140	.		47	47		93	93		140
		829	*.*	*402*	*203*	*606*	*68*	*155*	*223*	*471*	*358*

Table SZ 6/1 Dep. Labour Force by Sex, Industry and Status SWITZERLAND

1920	total		market			public			status	
isic	all	female	b-c	w-c	total	b-c	w-c	total	b-c	w-c
1	114	.	.	.	.	.	.	.	111	3
2-4	536	.	.	.	.	.	.	.	470	67
5	82	.	.	.	.	.	.	.	75	7
6+8	90	.	.	.	.	.	.	.	23	67
7	87	.	.	.	.	.	.	.	60	27
9	271	.	.	.	.	.	.	.	177	94
0	14	.	.	.	.	.	.	.	11	3
	1,193	421	.	.	.	.	.	.	926	267

Table SZ 6/2 Dep. Labour Force by Sex, Industry and Status SWITZERLAND

1930	total		market			public			status	
isic	all	female	b-c	w-c	total	b-c	w-c	total	b-c	w-c
1	102	.	.	.	.	.	.	.	99	3
2-4	588	.	.	.	.	.	.	.	506	81
5	118	.	.	.	.	.	.	.	109	10
6+8	127	.	.	.	.	.	.	.	23	104
7	80	.	.	.	.	.	.	.	49	31
9	325	.	.	.	.	.	.	.	229	97
0	14	.	.	.	.	.	.	.	14	1
	1,355	473	.	.	.	.	.	.	1,030	326

Table SZ 6/3 Dep. Labour Force by Sex, Industry and Status SWITZERLAND

1950	total		market			public			status	
isic	all	female	b-c	w-c	total	b-c	w-c	total	b-c	w-c
1	84	.	81	3	84	.	.	.	81	3
2-4	718	.	583	135	718	.	.	.	583	135
5	144	.	126	18	144	.	.	.	126	18
6+8	181	.	39	142	181	.	.	.	39	142
7	93	.	.	.	28	.	.	66	52	42
9	378	.	.	.	257	.	.	120	241	137
0	17	.	.	.	17	.	.	.	12	5
	1,616	539	.	.	1,420	.	.	195	1,134	482

Table SZ 6/4   Dep. Labour Force by Sex, Industry and Status   SWITZERLAND

1960	total		market			public			status	
isic	all	female	b-c	w-c	total	b-c	w-c	total	b-c	w-c
1	65	.	62	3	65	.	.	.	62	3
2-4	929	.	726	204	929	.	.	.	726	204
5	213	.	181	32	213	.	.	.	181	32
6+8	255	.	60	195	255	.	.	.	60	195
7	128	.	.	.	54	.	.	74	75	53
9	431	.	.	.	278	.	.	153	248	183
0	9	.	.	.	9	.	.	.	7	2
	2,030	659	.	.	1,803	.	.	227	1,358	672

Table SZ 6/5   Dep. Labour Force by Sex, Industry and Status   SWITZERLAND

1970	total		market			public			status	
isic	all	female	b-c	w-c	total	b-c	w-c	total	b-c	w-c
1	48	.	43	5	48	.	.	.	43	5
2-4	1,072	.	751	320	1,072	.	.	.	751	320
5	256	.	189	67	256	.	.	.	189	67
6+8	427	.	97	329	427	.	.	.	97	329
7	161	.	.	.	73	.	.	88	82	79
9	573	.	.	.	379	.	.	194	272	301
0	9	.	.	.	9	.	.	.	7	2
	2,546	891	.	.	2,264	.	.	282	1,442	1,104

Table SZ 6/6 Dep. Labour Force by Sex, Industry and Status   SWITZERLAND

1980	total		market			public			status	
isic	all	female	b-c	w-c	total	b-c	w-c	total	b-c	w-c
1	38	.	.	.	38	.	.	.	.	.
2-4	952	.	.	.	952	.	.	.	.	.
5	203	.	.	.	203	.	.	.	.	.
6+8	653	.	.	.	653	.	.	.	.	.
7	176	.	.	.	86	.	.	90	.	.
9	676	.	.	.	417	.	.	259	.	.
0	28	.	.	.	28	.	.	.	.	.
	2,724	1,009	.	.	2,376	.	.	349	1,251	1,473

Table SZ 6/7 Dep. Labour Force by Sex, Industry and Status   SWITZERLAND

1985	total		market			public			status	
isic	all	female	b-c	w-c	total	b-c	w-c	total	b-c	w-c
1	36	.	.	.	36	.	.	.	.	.
2-4	937	.	.	.	937	.	.	.	.	.
5	207	.	.	.	207	.	.	.	.	.
6+8	695	.	.	.	695	.	.	.	.	.
7	192	.	.	.	98	.	.	94	.	.
9	741	.	.	.	473	.	.	268	.	.
0	25	.	.	.	25	.	.	.	.	.
	2,833	.	.	.	2,470	.	.	363	.	.

Chapter 10: UNITED KINGDOM

LIST OF UNION CONFEDERATIONS: name, abbreviation and foundation year
1   *Trade Union Congress* (TUC): 1868-

1.   AGGREGATE MEMBERSHIP STATISTICS

1.1   General Series

The TUC reports its membership annually at the time of its congress as
of 31 December of the previous year. The series presented here is taken
from the TUC 1984 Annual Report (London 1985: 699-700: 'Details of Past
Congresses'). The same series until 1974 can be found in Pelling,
1976:302-305. The series on total membership in the United Kingdom
(England, Wales, Scotland and Northern Ireland) is based on the statistics of the Department of Employment and its predecessors. Bain & Price
(1980: 37-38, table 2.1) have published the series until 1977. Updates
till 1981 are equally published by Bain & Price (1983: 5, table 1.1).
Their series is based on the annual publication of the Department of
Employment ('The Membership of Trade Unions in 19..'), in the Employment Gazette, London, Monthly. I have used the same source for updating
the series until 1984, taking the latest available (and slightly
revised) figures published by the department (Employment Gazette,
January 1981, February 1982, January 1983, January 1984, January 1985
and January 1986).

As Bain & Price (1980: 13-15) observe, the Department of Employment's series has decisive advantages over the second official source
of British aggregate union statistics, the Registrars and their succes-
sor the Certification Office, especially since the first source applies
a broader definition of unions and lends itself better to a comparison
with other countries. The difference relates in particular to non-
-affiliated unions and professional associations. Like in other many
other countries, the series has become more inclusive with the passing
of time. Conversely, membership is sometimes reported of unions that
have ceased to operate. Perhaps the latter tendency is somewhat more
pronounced in Britain but it affects only small numbers as such organizations are generally very small craft or local bodies (they inflate
the number of unions in Britain, however). A more serious distortion
arises from the fact that the series refers to the membership of all
trade unions with their head office in the United Kingdom and, therefore, includes the membership in the Irish Republic and overseas of
unions based in the United Kingdom. A second distortion, which also
adds to an exaggerated aggregate density rate, arises from the inclusion of pensioners in the reported membership.

1.2   Retired and Overseas Membership:

Both problems are largely overcome in the adjusted series which Bain &
Price (1980: 39-40, table 2.2; updated until 1979 in Price & Bain,
1983:49, table 3) have compiled. This series excludes the membership in
Eire and overseas, excludes the retired membership in unions (such as
the National Union of Mineworkers) where they make up a large proportion of the overall membership, and includes the membership of such
organizations as the British Medical Association or the Royal College
of Nursing on a more continuous basis. Bain & Price thought that
retired members in other unions would not exceed 5%; in other words,
the overstatement of membership and density figures relating to Great
Britain can only be slight. I have used this adjusted series for my
statistics on membership and density by sex, industry and status (see
below).
      However, since I had no access to (a few hundred) individual union
files it was impossible to update this adjusted series for Great
Britain beyond 1979; nor is there a separate statistic for the British
membership of the TUC. Hence, the use of the unadjusted UK-series in
order to allow for an account of the post-1979 years, and a comparison
between TUC- and overall union membership.

1.3   Female Membership

The figures on female and male membership are based on the adjusted
series for Great Britain (Bain & Price, 1980:39-40, table 2.2; and for
1975-1979: Price & Bain, 1983:49, table 5). As was noted before, it is
not easy to update this series. Bain & Price have also published a
breakdown between male and female membership for the unadjusted series
for the United Kingdom (Bain & Price, 1980:37-38, table 37-38) which
covers the period until 1977. It is possible to update this series
until 1981 on the basis of the annual publication in the Employment
Gazette. After 1981 the Department of Employment stopped publishing
separate figures on male and female membership as fewer unions were
able to report such data. A similar problem was encountered with
respect to the TUC-membership: fewer unions reported separate figures
on male and female members in 1983 than in 1979. Nevertheless, it does
not seem impossible to estimate male and female membership, adjusted
for the number of unions which reported (see table at page 235).

2.   MEMBERSHIP BY INDUSTRY AND STATUS

Given the presence of large general and multi-industrial (in some cases
ex-craft) unions, the disaggregation of union membership by industry
presents numerous problems. For many such unions one must have access
to the membership files and the disaggregation of membership by section
of individual unions. The (adjusted) series on membership by status and
industry in Great Britain which Bain & Price have constructed on the
basis of such individual files is the only available source.

234

Male and Female Membership in the U.K.: TUC and Total, recent years						
	1971	1975	1979	1981	1983	1984
TUC female	.	.	3,466	.	2,996	
TUC male	.	.	8,707	.	7,087	
% female	.	.	28.5%	.	29.7%	
Total female	2,753	3,464	3,902	3,776	.	3,437
Total male	8,382	8,729	9,544	8,406	.	7,649
% female	24.6%	28.4%	29.0%	31.0%	.	31.0%

source: TUC-Annual Reports and Employment-Gazette.

Membership Changes in TUC-union between December 1979 and December 1983				
Type of unions:	Membership in:		Changes 1979-1984	
	1979	1983	absolute	in %
Mainly manual	*6,956,6*	*5,178,3*	*-1,778,3*	*-25.6%*
- general unions	3,325,0	2,422,6	-902,4	-27.1%
- metal & steel	1,587,8	1,152,3	-435,5	-27.4%
- other manufacturing	1,329,8	1,052,8	-277,1	-20.8%
- mining	289,4	240,7	- 48,7	-16.8%
- construction	350,5	262,3	- 88,2	-25.2%
- sea & road transport	74,1	47,6	- 26,4	-35.7%
Mainly non-manual	*1,695,5*	*1,521,0*	*-174,5*	*-10.3%*
- general unions	151,2	100,2	- 51,0	-33.7%
- industry	772,5	679,2	- 93,3	-12.1%
- commerce & retail	492,5	425,5	- 67,1	-13.6%
- banking & finance	151,8	176,0	24,1	15.9%
- miscell. services	127,4	140,3	12,1	10.1%
Public Sector	*3,520,4*	*3,383,9*	*-136,6*	*- 3,9%*
- railways	277,1	220,3	- 56,7	-20.5%
- other transport	39,5	28,1	- 11,4	-28.8%
- post & communication	386,0	371,3	- 14,7	- 3.8%
- nat&local government	2,117,4	2,087,5	- 29,9	- 1.4%
- education	466,6	436,1	- 30,5	- 6.5%
- health services	233,9	240,6	6,7	2.9%
Total TUC	*12,172,5*	*10,083,1*	*-2,090,4*	*-17.2%*

source: TUC-Annual Reports

2.1 Membership by Industry

From the tables on membership by industry presented by Bain & Price (1980: 43-78, tables 2.5-2.39 for 1921-1931; and Price & Bain 1983: 54-55, table 6 for 1948-1979), I have calculated my figures by re--aggregating theirs into the categories used elsewhere.

1   Agriculture: *agriculture; horticulture and forestry; fishing*

2-4 Mining, Industry & Gas, Water & Electricity: *coal mining; other mining and quarrying; manufacturing of food & drink; tobacco; chemicals and allied industries; metals & engineering; cotton, flax & man-made fibres; other textiles; leather, leather goods & fur; clothing; footwear; bricks & building materials; pottery; glass; timber & furniture; paper & board; printing & publishing; other manufacturing; gas, electricity & water*

5   Construction: *building & construction*

6+8 Commerce, Banking & Insurance: *retail & distribution; insurance; banking & finance*

7   Transport & Communication: *railways; road transport; sea transport; port & inland water transport; air transport; post & communications*

9   Other Services: *entertainment; local government & education; health services; national government; miscellaneous services (including business services; religious organizations; hotel & restaurants; sport and other recreation; repair & personal services; domestic services*

The most important adjustment made refers to the category 'miscellaneous services' which Bain & Price did only include for the post-war period but which I estimated (as a residual) for the pre-war period as well for reasons of comparability over time and between countries.

2.2 Membership by Status

For manual and non-manual union-membership: Bain & Price 1980: 41-42, table 2.3; and for 1974-1979: Price & Bain 1983: 51, table 2.4; for 1948, 1968, 1973 and 1979 the last mentioned source gives also manual and non-manual membership in manufacturing industries only.

2.3 Public Sector Unionism

The calculation of trade union membership in the public sector is also based on the statistics published by Bain & Price (ibid.). For reasons of comparability with other countries I have however operated on a somewhat less inclusive definition of public sector membership than they did and excluded gas, water & electricity as well as (nationalized) coal mining. Like them I have also excluded the nationalized iron and steel industry (see Price & Bain 1983: 52, table 5 and note c.).

Thus, the public sector membership comprises: national and local government, education & health, post office and telecommunications, railways, air, port & inland water transport. Note that, in Britain, union membership does not include the armed forces or the police.

2.4   Developments After 1979

As was mentioned earlier, the Bain & Price series on membership by status, industry and employment sector cannot easily be extended to the period after 1979. The figures published by the Department of Employment do not allow for a disaggregation similar to theirs, since the Department does not give a breakdown of the membership in the large general unions. This problem is compounded by the change, in 1982, of the classification of union membership, apportioning an even larger section of membership to the category 'covering various industries'. In its overview of union membership in the U.K. in 1984 the Department writes: 'Between 1979 and 1984 both employees in employment and membership of trade union have declined, but it is not possible to follow the industrial pattern of union membership over this period accurately because there has been a movement towards large multi-industrial unions' (Employment-Gazette, January 1986: 17).
    Regarding the membership in unions affiliated to the TUC we encounter the same problem. Indeed, in recent years the TUC has ceased to report its membership by 'industry group' which in itself was quite inaccurate. However, by classifying the same unions into the same category and taking into account mergers and 'transferred engagements', that is, grouping the membership of the merging union together with the 1979-membership of the target union, it is possible to depict the broad pattern of membership changes between 1979 and 1983 in the TUC. The calculation of the figures in the table at page 235 are based on the reported membership by affiliates published in the Annual Reports of the TUC relevant to these years. I have used the now defunct classification of the TUC itself.

3.   LABOUR FORCE STATISTICS

The data on the dependent labour force are also taken from Bain & Price (ibid.), who did rely on British Labour Statistics: Historical Abstracts 1886-1968, London 1971; and the reference statistics on employees in employment and unemployment (in the United Kingdom and in great Britain) published by the Department of Employment in the Employment Gazette. For updating purposes I have used the same source. The figures for the total dependent labour force exclude employers, the self-employed, and members of the armed forces, but include the unemployed of mid-june. Due to the many revisions, in particular with respect to the unemployment statistics, there are a number of small breaks after 1981.
    With respect to the disaggregated labour force I have similarly relied on the data published by Bain & Price. They did use the old classification, which is fortunately highly comparable with the 1958 ISIC industry classification which is used elsewhere.

4. TABLES

table: UK 1/1	Membership by Confederations			UNITED KINGDOM
year	TUC		non-affiliated	total
	abs	%	abs	abs
1913	2,232,4		1,902,6	4,135
1914	2,682,4		1,462,6	4,145
1915	2,850,5	65.4	1,508,5	4,359
1916	3,082,4		1,561,6	4,644
1917	4,532,1		966,9	5,499
1910	5,203,7		1,229,3	6,523
1919	6,505,5		1,420,5	7,926
1920	6,417,9	76.9	1,930,1	8,348
1921	5,128,6		1,504,4	6,633
1922	4,369,3		1,255,7	5,625
1923	4,328,3		1,100,7	5,429
1924	4,351,0		1,193,0	5,544
1925	4,365,6	79.3	1,140,4	5,506
1926	4,164,0		1,055,0	5,219
1927	3,874,8		1,044,2	4,919
1928	3,673,1		1,132,9	4,806
1929	3,744,3		1,113,7	4,858
1930	3,719,4	76.8	1,122,6	4,842
1931	3,613,3		1,010,7	4,624
1932	3,367,9		1,076,1	4,444
1933	3,294,6		1,097,4	4,392
1934	3,388,8		1,201,2	4,590
1935	3,614,6	74.3	1,252,4	4,867
1936	4,008,6		1,286,4	5,295
1937	4,660,6		1,181,4	5,842
1938	4,669,2		1,383,8	6,053
1939	4,866,7		1,431,3	6,298
1940	5,079,1	76.8	1,533,9	6,613
1941	5,432,6		1,732,4	7,165
1942	6,024,4		1,841,6	7,866
1943	6,642,3		1,531,7	8,174
1944	6,575,7		1,511,3	8,087
1945	6,671,1	84.7	1,203,9	7,875
1946	7,540,4		1,262,6	8,803
1947	7,791,5		1,353,5	9,145
1948	7,937,1		1,425,9	9,363
1949	7,883,4		1,434,6	9,318

table: UK 1/2 Membership by Confederations				UNITED KINGDOM
year	TUC		non-affiliated	total
	abs	%	abs	abs
1950	7,827,9	84.3	1,461,1	9,289
1951	8,020,1		1,509,9	9,530
1952	8,088,5		1,499,5	9,588
1953	8,093,8		1,433,2	9,527
1954	8,107,0		1,459,0	9,566
1955	8,263,7	84.8	1,477,3	9,741
1956	8,304,7		1,473,3	9,778
1957	8,337,3		1,491,7	9,829
1958	8,176,3		1,462,7	9,639
1959	8,128,3		1,494,7	9,623
1960	8,299,4	84.4	1,535,6	9,835
1961	8,312,9		1,603,1	9,916
1962	8,315,3		1,698,7	10,014
1963	8,325,8		1,741,2	10,067
1964	8,771,0		1,447,0	10,218
1965	8,867,5	85.9	1,457,5	10,325
1966	8,787,3		1,471,7	10,259
1967	8,725,6		1,468,4	10,194
1968	8,875,4		1,324,6	10,200
1969	9,402,2		1,076,8	10,479
1970	10,002,2	89.4	1,184,8	11,187
1971	9,894,9		1,240,1	11,135
1972	10,001,4		1,357,6	11,359
1973	10,002,2		1,453,8	11,456
1974	10,363,7		1,400,3	11,764
1975	11,036,3	91.8	989,7	12,026
1976	11,515,9		870,1	12,386
1977	11,865,4		980,6	12,846
1978	12,128,1		983,9	13,112
1979	12,172,5		1,116,5	13,289
1980	11,601,4	89.6	1,345,6	12,947
1981	11,006,0		1,100,0	12,106
1982	10,510,2		1,082,8	11,593
1983	10,082,1		1,254,9	11,337
1984	9,851,2	88.9	1,234,8	11,086

table: UK 4/1			density rates		UNITED KINGDOM		
year	membership		dep.labour force		density rates		
	total	less pens.	total	employed only	gross	employed only	net
	1	2	3	4	1:3	1:4	2:3
1913	4,135	.	17,920	.	23.1	.	.
1914	4,145	.	17,998	.	23.0	.	.
1915	4,359	.	18,077	.	24.1	.	.
1916	4,644	.	18,155	.	25.6	.	.
1917	5,499		18,234	.	30.2		
1918	6,523	.	18,312	.	35.6	.	.
1919	7,926	.	18,391	.	43.1	.	.
1920	8,348	.	18,469	.	45.2	.	.
1921	6,633	.	18,548	.	35.8	.	.
1922	5,625	.	17,804	.	31.6	.	.
1923	5,429	.	17,965	.	30.2	.	.
1924	5,544	.	18,125	.	30.6	.	.
1925	5,506	.	18,286	.	30.1	.	.
1926	5,219	.	18,446	.	28.3	.	.
1927	4,919	.	18,609	.	26.4	.	.
1928	4,806	.	18,771	.	25.6	.	.
1929	4,858	.	18,934	.	25.7	.	.
1930	4,842	.	19,096	.	25.4	.	.
1931	4,624	.	19,259	.	24.0	.	.
1932	4,444	.	19,340	.	23.0	.	.
1933	4,392	.	19,422	.	22.6	.	.
1934	4,590	.	19,503	.	23.5	.	.
1935	4,867	.	19,585	.	24.9	.	.
1936	5,295	.	19,666	.	26.9	.	.
1937	5,842	.	19,748	.	29.6	.	.
1938	6,053	.	19,829	.	30.5	.	.
1939	6,298	.	19,911	.	31.6	.	.
1940	6,613	.	19,992	.	33.1	.	.
1941	7,165	.	20,074	.	35.7	.	.
1942	7,866	.	20,155	.	39.0	.	.
1943	8,174	.	20,237	.	40.4	.	.
1944	8,087	.	20,318	.	39.8	.	.
1945	7,875	.	20,400	.	38.6	.	.
1946	8,803	.	20,481	.	43.0	.	.
1947	9,145	.	20,563	.	44.5	.	.
1948	9,363	.	20,732	.	45.2	.	.
1949	9,318	.	20,782	.	44.8	.	.

table: UK 4/2	density rates				UNITED KINGDOM		
year	membership		dep.labour force		density rates		
	total	less pens.	total	employed only	gross	employed only	net
	1	2	3	4	1:3	1:4	2:3
1950	9,289	.	21,055	.	44.1	.	.
1951	9,530	.	21,177	.	45.0	.	.
1952	9,588	.	21,252	.	45.1	.	.
1953	9,527	.	21,352	.	44.6	.	.
1954	9,566	.	21,658	.	44.2	.	.
1955	9,741	.	21,913	.	44.5	.	.
1956	9,778	.	22,180	.	44.1	.	.
1957	9,829	.	22,334	.	44.0	.	.
1958	9,639	.	22,290	.	43.2	.	.
1959	9,623	.	21,866	.	44.0	.	.
1960	9,835	.	22,229	.	44.2	.	.
1961	9,916	.	22,527	.	44.0	.	.
1962	10,014	.	22,879	.	43.8	.	.
1963	10,067	.	23,021	.	43.7	.	.
1964	10,218	.	23,166	.	44.1	.	.
1965	10,325	.	23,385	.	44.2	.	.
1966	10,259	.	23,545	.	43.6	.	.
1967	10,194	.	23,347	.	43.7	.	.
1968	10,200	.	23,203	.	44.0	.	.
1969	10,479	.	23,153	.	45.3	.	.
1970	11,187	.	23,050	.	48.5	.	.
1971	11,135	.	22,884	.	48.7	.	.
1972	11,359	.	22,961	.	49.5	.	.
1973	11,456	.	23,244	22,687	49.3	50.5	.
1974	11,764	.	23,339	22,811	50.4	51.6	.
1975	12,026	.	23,587	22,749	51.0	52.9	.
1976	12,386	.	23,871	22,605	51.9	54.8	.
1977	12,846	.	24,069	22,710	53.4	56.6	.
1978	13,112	.	24,203	22,860	54.2	57.4	.
1979	13,289	.	24,392	23,157	54.5	57.4	.
1980	12,947	.	24,485	22,972	52.9	56.4	.
1981	12,106	.	24,265	21,870	49.9	55.4	.
1982	11,593	.	24,170	21,400	48.0	54.2	.
1983	11,337	.	24,032	21,048	47.2	53.9	.
1984	11,086	.	24,192	21,162	45.8	52.4	.
1985	.	.	24,478	21,299	.	.	.

Table GB 5/1 Union Membership by Sex, Industry and Status GREAT BRITAIN

| year:1921 | | total | | market | | | public | | | status | |
isic	conf.	all	female	b-c	w-c	total	b-c	w-c	total	b-c	w-c
1	Total	217	.	.	.	217				.	.
2-4	Total	3,867	.	.	.	3,786	.	.	81	.	.
5	Total	493	.	.	.	493				.	.
6+8	Total	246	.	.	.	246				.	.
7	Total	1,044	.	.	.	333	.	.	711	.	.
9	Total	616	.	.	.	43	.	.	574	.	.
0	Total	28	.	.	.	28				.	.
		6,512	986			5,146			1,366	5,519	99?

Table GB 5/2 Union Membership by Sex, Industry and Status GREAT BRITAIN

| year:1931 | | total | | market | | | public | | | status | |
isic	conf.	all	female	b-c	w-c	total	b-c	w-c	total	b-c	w-c
1	Total	47	.	.	.	47				.	.
2-4	Total	2,408	.	.	.	2,354	.	.	54	.	.
5	Total	322	.	.	.	322				.	.
6+8	Total	233	.	.	.	233				.	.
7	Total	871	.	.	.	281	.	.	590	.	.
9	Total	668	.	.	.	22	.	.	646	.	.
0	Total	19	.	.	.	19				.	.
		4,569	749			3,280			1,290	3,544	1,025

Table GB 5/3 Union Membership by Sex, Industry and Status GREAT BRITAIN

| year:1948 | | total | | market | | | public | | | status | |
isic	conf.	all	female	b-c	w-c	total	b-c	w-c	total	b-c	w-c
1	Total	224	.	.	.	224				.	.
2-4	Total	4,630	.	4,439	191	4,412	.	.	219	.	.
5	Total	611	.	.	.	611				.	.
6+8	Total	463	.	.	.	463				.	.
7	Total	1,504	.	.	.	620	.	.	885	.	.
9	Total	1,671	.	.	.	187	.	.	1,484	.	.
0	Total	15	.	.	.	15				.	.
		9,118	1,650	.	.	6,531	.	.	2,588	7,056	2,062

Table GB 5/4 Union Membership by Sex, Industry and Status   GREAT BRITAIN

year:1968		total		market			public			status	
isic	conf.	all	female	b-c	w-c	total	b-c	w-c	total	b-c	w-c
1	Total	131	.	.	.	131				.	.
2-4	Total	4,843	.	4,456	386	4,537	.	.	306	4,456*	387*
5	Total	472	.	.	.	472				.	.
6+8	Total	545	.	.	.	545				.	.
7	Total	1,286	.	.	.	589	.	.	697	.	.
9	Total	2,416	.	.	.	186	.	.	2,230	.	.
		9,693	2,265			6,461			3,232	3,232	3,056

* only manufacturing

Table GB 5/5 Union Membership by Sex, Industry and Status   GREAT BRITAIN

year:1979		total		market			public			status	
isic	conf.	all	female	b-c	w-c	total	b-c	w-c	total	b-c	w-c
1	Total	86	.	.	.	86				.	.
2-4	Total	5,790	.	4,754	1,036	5,455	.	.	335	4,754*	1,036*
5	Total	520	.	.	.	520				.	.
6+8	Total	824	.	.	.	824				.	.
7	Total	1,305	.	.	.	535	.	.	770	.	.
9	Total	4,178	.	.	.	391	.	.	3,787	.	.
		12,702	3,837			7,809			4,892	7,578	5,125

* only manufacturing

Table GB 6/1 Dep. Labour Force by Sex, Industry and Status   GREAT BRITAIN

1921	total		market			public			status	
isic	all	female	b-c	w-c	total	b-c	w-c	total	b-c	w-c
1	918	.	.	.	918	.	.	.	.	.
2-4	7,756	.	.	.	7,578	.	.	178	.	.
5	731	.	.	.	731	.	.	.	.	.
6+8	2,128	.	.	.	2,128	.	.	.	.	.
7	1,631	.	.	.	518	.	.	1,113	.	.
9	3,146	.	.	.	2,094	.	.	1,052	.	.
0	884	.	.	.	884	.	.	.	884	.
	17,193	5,252	.	.	14,849	.	.	2,344	13,329	3,864

Table GB 6/2 Dep. Labour Force by Sex, Industry and Status   GREAT BRITAIN

1931	total		market			public			status	
isic	all	female	b-c	w-c	total	b-c	w-c	total	b-c	w-c
1	878	.	.	.	878	.	.	.	.	.
2-4	7,914	.	.	.	7,669	.	.	245	.	.
5	1,214	.	.	.	1,214	.	.	.	.	.
6+8	2,566	.	.	.	2,566	.	.	.	.	.
7	1,550	.	.	.	552	.	.	998	.	.
9	4,122	.	.	.	2,863	.	.	1,259	.	.
0	553	.	.	.	553	.	.	.	553	.
	18,796	5,835	.	.	16,294	.	.	2,502	14,157	4,639

Table GB 6/3 Dep. Labour Force by Sex, Industry and Status   GREAT BRITAIN

1948	total		market			public			status	
isic	all	female	b-c	w-c	total	b-c	w-c	total	b-c	w-c
1	989	.	.	.	989	.	.	.	.	.
2-4	8,415	.	.	.	8,091	.	.	324	.	.
5	1,326	.	.	.	1,326	.	.	.	.	.
6+8	2,441	.	.	.	2,441	.	.	.	.	.
7	1,712	.	.	.	671	.	.	1,041	.	.
9	4,609	.	.	.	2,137	.	.	2,472	.	.
0	778	.	.	.	778	.	.	.	778	.
	20,270	6,785	.	.	16,433	.	.	3,837	14,027	6,243

Table GB 6/4 Dep. Labour Force by Sex, Industry and Status   GREAT BRITAIN

1968	total		market			public			status	
isic	all	female	b-c	w-c	total	b-c	w-c	total	b-c	w-c
1	517	.	.	.	517	.	.	.	.	.
2-4	9,104	.	.	.	8,685	.	.	419	.	.
5	1,571	.	.	.	1,571	.	.	.	.	.
6+8	2,154	.	.	.	2,154	.	.	.	.	.
7	1496	.	.	.	622	.	.	874	.	.
9	6496	.	.	.	2,696	.	.	3,800	.	.
0	173	.	.	.	173	.	.	.	173	.
	22,703	8,251	.	.	17,610	.	.	5,093	13,322	9,381

Table GB 6/5 Dep. Labour Force by Sex, Industry and Status   GREAT BRITAIN

1979	total		market			public			status	
isic	all	female	b-c	w-c	total	b-c	w-c	total	b-c	w-c
1	378	.	.	.	378	.	.	.	.	.
2-4	8,044	.	.	.	7,692	.	.	352	.	.
5	1,415	.	.	.	1,415	.	.	.	.	.
6+8	3,593	.	.	.	3,593	.	.	.	.	.
7	1,338	.	.	.	537	.	.	801	.	.
9	8,528	.	.	.	3,691	.	.	4,837	.	.
0	390	.	.	.	390	.	.	.	390	.
	23,687	9,708	.	.	17,696	.	.	5,991	12,035	11,687

Table GB 6/6 Dep. Labour Force by Sex, Industry and Status   GREAT BRITAIN

1979 isic	total all	female	market b-c	w-c	total	public b-c	w-c	total	status b-c	w-c
1	359	.	.	.	359	.	.	.	.	.
2-4	7,825	.	.	.	7,487	.	.	338	.	.
5	1,216	.	.	.	1,216	.	.	.	.	.
6+8	3,693	.	.	.	3,693	.	.	.	.	.
7	1,452	.	.	.	678	.	.	774	.	.
9	8,094	.	.	.	3,379	.	.	4,715	.	.
0	1,175	328	.	.	1,175	.	.	.	.	.
	23,814	9,781	.	.	17,987	.	.	5,827	.	.

Table GB 6/7 Dep. Labour Force by Sex, Industry and Status   GREAT BRITAIN

1983 isic	total all	female	market b-c	w-c	total	public b-c	w-c	total	status b-c	w-c
1	339	.	.	.	339	.	.	.	.	.
2-4	6,152	.	.	.	5,831	.	.	321	.	.
5	987	.	.	.	987	.	.	.	.	.
6+8	3,657	.	.	.	3,657	.	.	.	.	.
7	1,306	.	.	.	585	.	.	721	.	.
9	8,140	.	.	.	3,225	.	.	4,915	.	.
0	2,871	809	.	.	2,871	.	.	.	.	.
	23,456	9,705	.	.	17,499	.	.	5,957	.	.

REFERENCES

ADAM, G. (1964) *La CFTC*, Paris
ADAM, G. (1965) *La CGT-FO*, Paris
ADAM, G. (1983) *Le Pouvoir Syndical*, Paris
AMORETTI, A. (1974) 'Risultati e problemi del tesseramento e del finanziamento del sindacato', *Quaderni di Rassegna Sindacale*, CGIL, Rome, no. 50
ARMINGEON, K. (1987) 'Gewerkschaften in der Bundesrepublik Deutschland 1950-1985: Mitglieder, Organisation und Aussenbeziehungen', *Politische Vierteljahresschrift*, Vol. 28
ÅMARK, K. (1986) *Facklig makt och facklight medlemskap*, Lund
BAGLIONI, G. (ed) (1980) *Analisi della CISL*, Rome, Vol. 1 + 2
BALDISSERA, A. (1988) *La svolta dei quarantamila. Dai quadri FIAT ai COBAS*, Milan
BAMBER, G. (1985) 'Unionism Among Managerial and Professional Employees', *Labour and Society*, Geneva, Vol. 10, no.1
BAIN, G.S. (1970) *The Growth of White-Collar Unionism*, Oxford
BAIN, G.S. & F.ELSHEIKH (1976) *Union Growth and the Business Cycle: An Econometric Analysis*, Oxford
BAIN, G.S & R.PRICE (1980) *Profiles of Union Growth. A Comparative Statistical Portrait of Eight Countries*, Oxford
BAIN, G.S. & R.PRICE (1983) 'Union Growth: Dimensions, Determinants, and Destiny', G.S.Bain (ed) *Industrial Relations in Britain*, Oxford
BARJONET, A. (1968) *La CGT. Histoire, structure et doctrine*, Paris
BAYER, H. (1980) *Zur gewerkschaftlichen Organisation der Angestellten im privaten Dienstleistungsgewerbe*, Frankfort
BAYER, H., W.STREECK & E.TREU (1981) *Die Westdeutsche Gewerkschaftsbewegi in Zahlen*, Königstein/Ts
BERGOUNIOUX, A. (1979) *Force Ouvrière*, Paris
BERGSTRAND, F. (1960) *DACO. Fackligt samarbete mellan de privatanställda tjänstemännen 1931-1937*, Lund
BERNASCONI, G. (1951) 'Zu einem Angriff auf die Gewerkschaftsstatistik', *Gewerkschaftliche Rundschau für die Schweiz*, Vol. 43
BIAGIONI, E. (1978) 'Due anni a confronto 1977-1978', *Rassegna Sindacale*, CGIL, Rome, no. 38
BIAGIONI, E., S.PALMIERI & T.PIPAN (1980) *Indagine sul sindacato. Profilo organizzativo della CGIL*, Rome
BIGA (1980) 'Die Grundlagen der schweizerischen Sozialstatistik', *Die Volkswirtschaft*, Bundesamt für Industrie, Gewerbe und Arbeit, Bern, Vol. 53
BIRIEN, J.-L. (1978) *Le fait syndical en France*, Paris
BLANPAIN, R. (ed) (1978) *Comparative Labour law and Industrial Relations*, 2th. revised ed. 1985, Deventer
BLUM, A.A. & A. PONAK (1970) 'White Collar Unions in Denmark', *Industrial Relations*, Vol. 10

BOTZ, G. (1981) 'Angestellte zwischen Ständegesellschaft, Revolution und Faschismus', in: J.Kocka (ed) *Angestellte im europäischen Vergleich*, Göttingen

BUKSTI, J.A. (1982) 'Tredie stand eller løndmodtagerfront', *Politica*, Vol. 14

BUKSTI, J.A. (1982) 'Samspli mellem organisationer og omgivelser -tilpasning eler kontrol?' in: B.Öhngren (ed) *Organisationerna och samhällsutvecklingen*, Stockholm, TCO

BUKSTI, J.A. & L.N. JOHANSEN (1977) *Danske organisationer. Hwem, hvae hvor?*, Copenhagen

BüCHII, W. (1969) *Die Arbeitslosigkeit in Italien 1951 bis 1965. Erscheinungsformen und Ursachen*, Winterthur

BüLOW, F. von (1931) 'Dänemark', in: L. Heyde (ed) *Internationales Handwörterbuch des Gewerkschaftswesen*, Berlin, Vol. 1

CAIRE., G. (1971) *Les syndicats ouvriers*, Paris

CAPDEVILLE, J. & MOURIAUX, R. (1970) *Les syndicats ouvriers français*, Paris

CARLSON, B. (1969) *Trade Unions in Sweden*, Stockholm

CBS (1967) *Arbeidsvolume en geregistreerde arbeidsreserve 1947-1966*, Centraal Bureau van de Statistiek, The Hague

CBS (1909-1942) *Overzicht van den omvang der vakbeweging in Nederland*, Centraal Bureau van de Statistiek, The Hague, annual

CBS (1946-1964) *Omvang der vakbeweging in nederland op 1 Januari 19..*, Centraal Bureau van de Statistiek, The Hague, annual

CBS (1967-1985) *Statistiek van de Vakbeweging*, Centraal Bureau van de Statistiek, The Hague, biennial

CESOS (1982) *Le relazioni sindacali in Italia. Rapporto 1981*, Rome 1982

CESOS (1984) *Le relazioni sindacali in Italia. Rapporto 1982/83*, Rome 1984

CESOS (1985) *Le relazioni sindacali in Italia. Rapporto 1983/84*, Rome 1985

CESOS (1986) *Le relazioni sindacali in Italia. Rapporto 1984/85*, Rome 1986

CESOS (1987) *Le relazioni sindacali in Italia. Rapporto 1985/86*, Rome 1987

CHéRAMY, R. (1974) *La FEN: 25 ans d'unité syndicale*, Paris

CHIESI, A. (1983) 'Impiegati e sindacato in Italia', in: A.Baldissera et.al, *Le ricerche sui lavoratori non-manuali e il sindacato in Italia*, Milan

COI, S. (1979) 'Sindacati in Italia: iscritti, apparato, finanziamento', *Il Mulino*, Vol. 28, no. 262

CóRDOVA, E. (1985) 'Strikes in the Public Sector: Some Determinants and Trends', *International Labour Review*, Geneva, vol. 24, no. 2

CROZIER, M. (1966) 'White-collar unions: the case of France', in: A. Sturmthal (ed), *White Collar Trade Unions. Contemporary Developments in Industrialized Societies*, Urbana

DAVIS, H.R. (1941) 'The Theory of Union Growth', *Quarterly Journal of Economics*, Vol. 55; reprint in: W.J.E.McCarthey (ed), *Trade Unions*, London 1972

DESCOSTES, M. & ROBERT, J.-L. (eds) (1984) *Clefs pour une histoire du syndicalisme cadre*, Paris

DHV (1960) *1950-1960. Zehn Jahre Wiederaufbau*, Hamburg

DIEST, B. van (1987) *De Vakcentrale MHP. Van kategoraal naar algemeen*, Amsterdam, SORU

DITTRICH, M. (1939) *Die Entstehung der Angestelltenschaft in Deutschland*, Stuttgart/Berlin

DORFMAN, H. (1966) *Labor Relations in Norway*, Oslo 1966

DUNLOP, J.T. (1949) 'The Development of Labor Organization: A Theoretical Framework', in: R.A.Lester & J.Shister (eds), *Insights into Labor Issues*, New York

EATON, J.K. (1976) *Union Growth in Canada in the Sixties*, Ottawa

EATON, J.K. & K. ASHAGRIE (1970) *Union Growth in Canada, 1921-1967*, Ottawa Canada Department of labour

EBBINGHAUS, B.O. (1986) 'The Collar-Divide. Associations of White-Collar Employees in Germany before 1933', DUES-research paper, Mannheim

EBBINGHAUS, B.O. (1988) *The Unionization of White-Collar Employees*, Mannheim, DUES Project

EGLI, G. (1969) *Fünfzig Jahre Landesverband Freier Schweizer Arbeiter*, Zürich

ENZ, M. (1957) *Die Zusammenschlüsse der weiblichen Handels- und Büroangestellten in der Schweiz*, Zürich

ESTIVILL, J. (1984) 'Spagna - Crisi e transizione. Verso la bipolarizzazione politica e sindacale? in: G.Baglioni & E.Santi (eds), *L'Europa sindacale nel 1982*, Bologna

ESTIVILL, J. & J.M. de la HOZ (1989) 'Spain' in: G.Baglioni (ed) *Industrial Relations in Europe in the 1980s*, London/Beverly Hills 1989

ETUI (1982) *The Unionization of Professional and Managerial Staff in Western Europe*, Brussels, European Trade Union Institute

EVWD (1973) *Handbuch der Scheizerischen Sozialstatistik*, special issue, no. 85, *Die Volkswirtschaft*, Eidgenossische Volkswirtschaftsdepartement, Bern

FAKIOLAS, R. (1978) *The Greek Trade Unions*, Athens (in Greek)

FERRI, P. (1971) *La disoccupazione in un processo di sviluppo economico. Alcuni aspetti dell'esperienza italiana 1951-1968*, Milan

FIORITO,J. & C.GREER (1982) 'Determinants of U.S.Unionism: Past Research and Future Needs', *Industrial Relations*, Vol. 21

FIVELSDAL, E. (1965) 'White-Collar Unions and the Norwegian Labor Movement' *Industrial Relations*, Vol. 5

FLORA. P. (1981) 'Stein Rokkans Makro-Modell der politischen Entwicklung Europas. Ein Rekonstruktionsversuch', *Kölner Zeitschrift für Soziologie und Sozialpsychologie*, Vol. 33

FLORA, P. (1983) *State, Economy, and Society in Western Europe. A Data Handbook*, Vol. 1: 'The Growth of Mass Democracies and Welfare States', Frankfurt-London-Chicago

FLORA, P., F.KRAUS & W.PFENNING (1987) *State, Economy, and Society i Western Europe 1815-1975. A Date Handbook*, Vol. 2: 'The growth of Industrial Societies and Capitalist Economies', Frankfurt /London/Chicago

FLORYAN, J.J. & S.LINDBHOLM (1980) 'Akademikernes organisering -udvikling, struktur og problemen', in: J.A. Buksti (ed) *Organisationer under forandring*, Aarhus 1980

GALENSON, W. (1949) *Labor in Norway*, Cambridge (Mass.)

GALENSON, W. (1952) *The Danish System of Labor Relations*, Cambirdge (Mass)

GANSER, W & W.HERBERZ (1985) *Die Bundesrepublik Deutschland. Staatshandbuch*, Teilausgabe 'Verbände, Vereinigungen, wissenschaftliche Einrichtungen, juristische Personen des öffentlichen Rechts', Cologne/Berlin/Bonn/ Munich

GARBANI, Ph. & .SCHMID (1980) *Le syndicalisme suisse. Histoire politique de l'Union syndicale, 1880-1980*, Laussanne

GOLDTHORPE, J.H. (1980, 1986) *Social Mobility and Class Structure in Modern Britain*, Oxford (2th.ed)

GRAIS, B. (1982) *Lay-offs and Short-time Working in Selected OECD Countries*, Paris

GROUX, G. (1983) *Les cadres*, Paris

GRUNBERG, G. & MOURIAUX, R. (1979) *L'univers politique e syndical des cadres*, Paris

GUéRIN, J.C. (1973) *La FEN: un syndicat?*, Paris
GüLICK, Ch.A. (1948) *Österreich von Habsburg bis Hitler*, Vienna, Vol. 1
HAGELSTANGE, Th. (1979) *Der Einflusz der ökonomischen Konjunktur auf di Streiktätigkeit und die Mitgliederstärke der Gewerkschaften in der BRD von 1950 bis 1975*, Stuttgart
HAMON, H. & ROTMAN, P. (1982) *La deuxième gauche. Histoire intellectuelle e politique de la CFDT*, Paris
HARDMEIER, B. (1980) 'Einige Daten und Hinweise zur Gewerkschafts geschichte', *Gewerkschaftliche Rundschau für die Schweiz*, Vol. 72
HARMEL, C. (1967) 'Les effectifs de la CGT', *Les études sociales et syndicales*, no. 8
HARMEL, C. (1970) 'A propos des effectifs de la CGT', *Les études sociales et syndicales*, no. 4
HARMEL, C. (1972) 'Les effectifs de la CGT-FO', *Les études sociales et syndicales*, no. 3
HARMEL, C. (1982) *La CGT, 1947-1981*, Paris
HARMSEN, G. & B.REINALDA (1975) *Voor de bevrijding van de arbeid. beknop geschiedenis van de Nederlandse vakbeweging*, Nijmegen
HARTFIEL, G. (1966) 'Germany', in: A.Sturmthal (ed) *White-Collar Trade Unions*, Urbana
HEIDAR, K. (1983) 'Norwegen', in: S.Mielke (ed) *Internationales Gewerkschaftshandbuch*, Opladen
HK (1962) *Organisationsformer och effektivitet*, Malmö, Handelsanställdes Förbund
HUBER, A. (1987) *Staatskunde Lexikon*, Luzern
HÖPFLINGER, F. (1974) *Gewerkschaften und Konfliktregulierung in der Schweiz*, Zürich
HÖPFLINGER, F. (1980) *Die andere Gewerkschaften. Angestellte unc Angestelltenverbände in der Schweiz*, Zürich
ILO (1978) *Collective bargaining in Industrialised Market Economies*, Geneva
JACOBS, H. (1984) *Using Published Data. Errors and remedies*, Beverly Hills, 1984
JIL (1983) *Labor Unions and Labor-Managment Relations*, Tokyo, Japanese Institute of Labor, Industrial Relations series, no. 2.
JüHE, R., H.-U. NIEDENHOFF & W.PEGE (1982) *Gewerkschaften in der B* Cologne, Institut der deutschen Wirtschaft
KARLBOM, T. (1955) *Den svenska fackföreningsrörelsen*, Stockholm
KARLSEN, J.E. (1976) *Hva skjer i fagbevegelsen*, Oslo
KASSALOW, E. (1969) 'Professional Unionism in Sweden', *Industrial Relations*, Vol. 8
KATSANEVAS, Th. (1984) *Trade Unionism in Greece*, Athens (in Greek)
KELLER, B. (1983) *Arbeitsbeziehungen im öffentlichen Dienst. Tarifpolitik der Gewerkschaften und Interessenpolitik der Beamtenverbände*, Frankfort
KJELLBERG, A. (1983) *Facklig organisering i tolv länder*, Lund
KLENNER, F. (1951, 1953, 1979) *Die Österreichische Gewerkschaftsbund*, Vienna, Vol. 1, 2 + 3
KLOOSTERMAN, R. (1985) *Werkloosheid in Nederland. 1920-1939*, Utrecht
KOCKA, J. (1980) *White Collar Workers in America 1890-1940. A Social-Political History in International Perspective*, London/Beverly Hills
KRIEGEL, A. (1966) *La Croîssance de la C.G.T. 1918-1921*, Paris-The Hague
KULL, W. (1979) 'Die Entwicklung der Sozialstatistik in der Schweiz', *Die Volkwirtschaft*, Bern, Vol. 52

KÖNIG, F. et.al. (1981) 'Zür Sozialgeschichte der Angestellten in der Schweiz', in J.Kocka (ed) *Angestelte im europaischen Vergleich*, Göttingen 1981

KÖNIG, F. et.al. (1985) *Warten und Aufrücken. Die Angestellten in der Schweiz*, Zürich

LABI, M. (1964) *La grande division des travailleurs. Première scission de la CGT, 1914-1921*, Paris

LAKENBACHER, E. (1967) *Die Österreichische Angestelltengewerkschaften. Geschichte und Gegenwart*, Vienna 1967

LANDIER, H. (1975) *La CFTC pourquoi?*, Paris

LANDIER, H. (1980) *Les organisations syndicales en France*, Paris

LANDIER, H. (1981) *Demain, quel syndicats?*, Paris

LASH, S. (1985) 'The End of Neo-Corporatism? The Breakdown of Centralized Bargaining in Sweden' in: *British Journal of Industrial Relations*, Vol. 23

LEFRANC, G. (1969) *Le mouvement syndical de la Liberation aux événements de Mai-Juin 1968*, Paris

LIPSET, S.M. (1961) 'Trade Unions and Social Structure', *Industrial Relations*, Vol. 1

LO (1955) *The Trade Union Movement in Norway*, Oslo, 2th ed

LORWIN, V.R. (1954) *The French Labor Movement*, Cambridge (Mass.)

LUDEVID, M. (1987) 'Labour Movement and Social Change in Spain (1975-1985), in: G.Spyropoulos (ed) *Trade Unions Today and Tomorrow*, Maastricht, Vol. 1

LUND, R. (1981) 'Scandinavia', in: A.A.Blum (ed) *International Handbook of Industrial relations*, London

LUND, R. (1983) 'Denmark', in: S.Mielke (ed) *Internationales Gewerkschafts Handbuch*, Opladen

LÆGREID, A.P. (1982) 'Tjenestemannsorganisasjoner op personaldemokrati i offentlig sector i Norge', in: B.Öhngren (ed) *Organisationerna och samhällsutvecklingen*, Stockholm, TCO

MANGOLD, F. (1931) 'Schweiz', in: L.Heyde (ed) *Internationales Handwörterbuch des Gewerkschaftswesen*, Berlin 1931

MARTENS, A. (1985) 'Vakbondsgroei en vakbondsmacht in Belgie', *Tijdschrift voor Arbeidsvraagstukken*, Vol. 1, no. 2

MARSH, A. & V. RYAN (1980) *Historical Directory of Trade Unions, Vol. 1: Non-manual Unions*, Westmead

MARSH, A. (1983) *Trade Union Handbook*, 3th ed, Aldershot

MARUANI, M. (1979) *Les Syndicats à l'épreuve du féminisme*, Paris

MEISTER, M. (1930) *Fünfzig jahre Gewerkschaftsbewegung in der Schweiz*, Amsterdam, ICTU

MEYNAUD, J. (1963) *Les Organisations professionelles en Suisse*, Lausanne

MOREN, J. (1976) *Norske Organisasjoner*, Oslo

MOSES, J.A. (1979) *Trade Unionism In Germany From Bismarck To Hitler 1869-1933*, Vol. 1 + 2, Ottowa N.J.

MOURIAUX, R. (1982) *La CGT*, Paris

MOURIAUX, R. (1983) *Les syndicats dans la société française*, Paris

MOURIAUX, R. (1986) *Le syndicalisme face à la crise*, Paris

NIEDENHOFF, H.-U, & W. PEGE (1987) *Gewerkschaftshandbuch 1987*, Cologne Institut der deutschen Wirtschaft

NIESS, F.(1979) *Geschichte der Arbeitslosigkeit*, Cologne

NILSSON, T. (1985) *Fran kamratforeninger till facklig rörelse. De svenska tjanstemannens organisationsutveckling 1900-1980*, Lund

NILSTEIN, A.H. (1966) 'White-Collar Unionism in Sweden', in: A.Sturmthal (ed) *White-Collar Trade Unions*, Urbana

NZZ (1977) *Organigram der schweizerischen Wirtschaft*, Zürich, Neue Zürcher Zeitung, Schriften zur Zeit

OOMENS, C.A. & J.E.M. van der KOLK (1949) 'De ontwikkeling van beroepsbevolking van Nederland van 1921 to 1963', *Statistische en Econometrische Onderzoekingen*, Centraal Bureau van de Statistiek (CBS), The Hague, niewe reeks, Vol. 4

ÖTV (1977) *Argumente und Materialien zur DAG*, Stuttgart, Vol. 1

PALLA, E. (1931) 'Österreich', in: L.Heyde (ed) *Internationales Handwörterbuch des Gewerkschaftswesen*, Berlin

PEDERSEN, P.J. (1977) 'Arbejdsstyrke og beskæftigelse 1911-70, *Socialt Tidsskrift*

PEDERSEN, P.J. (1979) *Aspekter af fagbevægelsens vækst i Danmark 1911-197(* Aarhus, Institute of Economics

PEDERSEN, P.J. (1982) 'Union Growth in Denmark: 1911-1939', *Scandinaviar Journal of Economics*, Vol. 84

PELLING, H. (1976) *A Hisory of British Trade Unionism*, London/Basingstoke

PINTO, M. (1989) 'Portugal', in: G.Baglioni (ed) *Industrial Relations in Europe in the 1980s*, London/Beverly Hills 1989

PLOVSING, J. (1971) *Die nye middelklassers organisationsproblematik i Danmark*, Copenhagen

PLOVSING, J. (1973) *Funktionær: organiseret eller unorganiset?*, Copenhagen

PRICE, R. & G.S.BAIN (1976) 'Union Growth Revisited: 1948-1974 in Perspective', *British Journal of Industrial Relations*, Vol. 16

PRICE, R. & G.S.BAIN (1983) 'Union Growth in Britain: Retrospect and Prospect', *British journal of Industrial Relations*, Vol. 21

PROST, A. (1964) *La CGT a l'époque du Front populaire 1934-1939*, Paris

RAWSON, D.W. (1977) *A Handbook of Australian Trade Unions and Employ Associations*, Camberra, 3th ed.

REGAGLIA, I. (1980) 'Il ruolo delle politiche di reclutamento', in: U.Romagnoli et.al., *La sindacalizzazzione tra ideologia e pratica. Il caso italiano 1950-1977*, Rome, Vol. 1

REGAGLIA, I. (1987) 'Participare al sindacato. Forme, modelli, ipotesi di lavoro', *Quaderni di Sociologia*, Vol. 23, no. 9

REINALDA, B. (1981) *Bedienden georganiseerd. Ontstaan en ontwikkeling van de vakbeweging van handels- en kantoorbedienden in Nederland van het begin tot in de Tweede Wereldoorlog*, Nijmegen

REINALDA, B. (1985) *De Dienstenbonden. Klein maar strijdbaar*, Baarn

REYNAUD, J.-D. (1975) *Les syndicats en France*, Vol. 1 + 2, Paris, 2th ed

REYNAUD, J.-D. (1983) 'Francia, dopo la continuità' in: G.Baglioni & P.Santi (eds) *L'Europa sindacale agli inizi degli anni '80*, Bologna

REYNAUD, J.-D. (1984) 'Un cambiamento più politico-istituzionale che sindacale', in G.Baglioni & E.Santi (eds) *L'Europa sindacale nel 1981*, Bologna

RIBEILL, G. (1986) 'Le syndicalisme cheminot', unpubl. paper presented at Journée d'étude du CRHMSS, Université de Paris I, 20 March 1986

ROCHE, W.K. & J.LARRAGY (1987) 'The Trend of Unionization in the Republi in: *Industrial Relations in Ireland. Contemporary Issues and Developments*, Department of Industrial Relations, University College Dublin

ROMAGNOLI, G. et.al. (1980) *La sindacalizzazione tra ideologia e pratica. Il caso italiano 1950/1977*, Rome, Vol. 1 + 2

ROMAGNOLI, G. & G. della ROCCA (1982) 'Il sindacato', in: G.Prima Cella T.Treu (eds) *Relazioni industriali. Manuale per l'analisi della esperienza italiana*, Bologna

ROMAGNOLI, G. & T.TREU (1977) *I sindacati in Italia dal '45 ad oggi. Storia di una strategia*, Bologna
ROKKAN, S (1970) *Citizens, Elections, Parties*, Oslo
ROKKAN, S. & S.M. LIPSET (1969) 'Cleavage Structures, Party Systems, and Voter Alignments: An Introduction', in: S.M.Lipset & S.Rokkan (eds.) *Party Systems and Voter Alignments. Cross-National Perspectives*, New York
ROTHSCHILD, K.W. (1977) *Arbeitslosigkeit in Österreich 1955-1975*, Vienna 1977
SAMUELSON, K.-W. (1963) *Fackliga organisationssträvanden bland statstjänstemännen före 1945*, Stockholm
SANDBERG, P. (1969) *Tjänstemänna Rörelsen. Uppkomst och utveckling*, Stockholm
SAPOSS, D.J. (1931) *The Labor Movement in post-war France*, New York
SCHARPF, F.W. (1986) 'Strukturen der post-industrielen Gesellschaft, oder: Verschwindet die Massenarbeitslosigkeit in der Dienstleistungs- und Informations-Ökonomie?', *Soziale Welt*, Vol.37. no.1
SCHEUER, S. (1986) *Arbejdsløsheden og den faglige organisering*, Copenhagen, Institute for Organisation og Arbejdssociologi
SCHEUER, S. (1987) *Fagforeninger mellem kollektiv og profession*, Copenhagen
SCHÖNHOVEN, K. (1987) *Die Deutsche Gewerkschaften*, Frankfort
SCHÖSSLER, D.'Militär und Gewerkschaften. Berufsproblematik und Interessenartikulation der westdeutschen Berufssoldaten', Kölner Zeitschrift für Soziologie und Sozialpsychologie, Sonderheft 12
SEITLITZ, H. de (1977) 'Das Wirtschaftliche Gewicht des Staats in der Schweiz', *Neue Zürcher Zeitung*, 10 May 1977
SGB (1942) 'Zechzig Jahre Mitgliederstatistik des Schweizerischen Gewerkschaftsbundes', *Gewerkschaftliche Rundschau für die Schweiz*, Vol. 34
SHORTER, E. & TILLY, Ch. (1974) *Strikes in France 1830-1968*, Cambridge
SIEGELMAN (1978) *From Agriculture to Services. The Transformation of Industrial Employment*, London
SIMONCINI, F. (1986) *Dall'interno della Uil. 1950-1985*, Milan
SMID, G. (1979) 'De Franse vakbeweging', in: G.Smid, W.Sprenger & J.Visser (eds) *Vakbondswerk moet je leren. Vakbonden en kaderleden in Frankrijk, Engeland, Westduitsland en Nederland*, Amsterdam
SPINEUX, A. (1981) *Forces et Politiques syndical en Begique*, Louvain, Institut des Sciences politiques et sociales
SPINEUX, A. (1984) 'Belgio: il declino della concertazione e della guida sindacale nelle relazioni industriali', in: G.Baglioni & E.Santi (eds) *L'Europa sindacale nel 1982*, Bologna
SPITAELS, G. (1967) *Le mouvement syndical en Belgique. Etudes d'économie sociale*, Brussels
STEFANELLI, R. (ed) (1981) *I sindacati autonomi. Particularismo e strategie confederali negli anni Settanta*, Bari
STIEFEL, D. (1979) *Arbeitslosigkeit. Soziale, politische und wirtschaftliche Auswirkungen - Am Beispiel Österreichs 1918-1938*, Berlin 1979
STREECK, W. (1981) *Gewerkschaftliche Organisationsprobleme in der sozialstaatlichen Demokratie*, Königstein
SUTCLIFFE, J.T. (1967) *A History of Trade Unionism in Australia*, Melbourne
SVEA (1970) *Fünfzig Jahr SVEA. Rückblick und Ausblick*, Bale
TCO (1986) *TCOs yttranden m m under 1985*, Stockholm
TERRAIN, L. (1985) 'La politique syndicale CGC: Cadres ou Encadrement?', *Les études sociales et syndicales*, no. 3

TRAXLER, F. (1982) *Evolution gewerkschaftlicher Interessenvertretung*, Vienna

TROY, L. (1965) *The Growth of American Trade Unions, 1880-1923*, New Yo National Bureau of Economic Research

TROY, L. (1986) 'The Rise and Fall of American Trade Unions: The Labc Movement from FDR to RR', in S.M.Lipset (ed) *Unions in Transition. Entering the Second Century*, San Fransisco

TROY, L. & SHEFLIN, N. (1985) *Union Sourcebook: Membership, Structur Finance, Directory*, IRDIS, West Orange.

VELTMAN, J. & J. VISSER (1986) 'Ontwikkeling ledental en organisatiegraad van de Nederlandse vakbeweging', onderzoekspaper, Sociologisch Instituut, UvA

VISSER, J. (1986) 'De crisis van een verouderend verzorgingsarrangement', *Namens, Tijdschrift voor vertegenwoordiging en bestuur*, Deventer, no. 3

VISSER, J. (1989) 'New Working Time Arrangements in the Netherlands', in: A. Gladstone et.al. (eds) *Current Issures in Labour Relations - An International Perspective*, Berlin/New York

VISSER, J. (1989) *In Search of Inclusive Unionism*, Deventer, special issue of Bulletin of Comparative Industrial Relations, no. 18

VIVIER, B. (1985) 'La FEN: un discours unitaire en six tendances', *Les études sociales et syndicales*, no. 3

WHEELER, C. (1975) *White-Collar Power. Changing Patterns of Interest Grou Behaviour in Sweden*, Urbana

WOLMAN, L. (1936) *Ebb and Flow in Trade Unions*, New York